Great Moments in Sports

Great Moments in Sports

Edited by Mark Mulvoy

The Rutledge Press
New York, New York

Photo Credits

All photos United Press International except:
Brown Brothers 9 left, 18 right, 64, 65
Culver Pictures, Inc. 8, 9 right, 10, 11, 12, 16, 19 left, 29, 60-61
World Wide Photos 22, 23

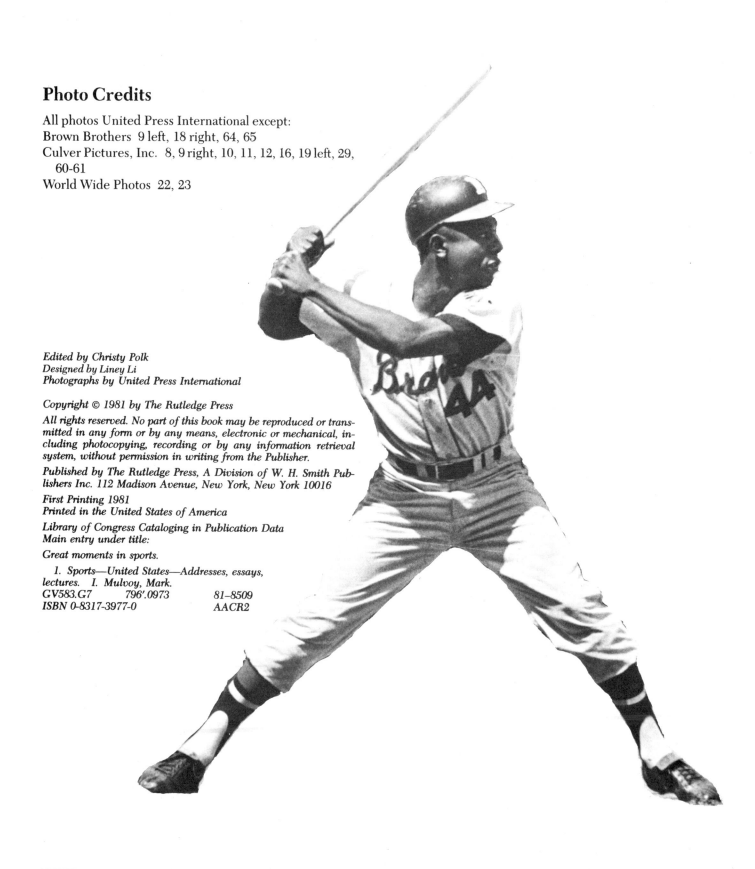

Edited by Christy Polk
Designed by Liney Li
Photographs by United Press International

Copyright © 1981 by The Rutledge Press

All rights reserved. No part of this book may be reproduced or transmitted in any form or by any means, electronic or mechanical, including photocopying, recording or by any information retrieval system, without permission in writing from the Publisher.

Published by The Rutledge Press, A Division of W. H. Smith Publishers Inc. 112 Madison Avenue, New York, New York 10016

First Printing 1981
Printed in the United States of America

Library of Congress Cataloging in Publication Data
Main entry under title:

Great moments in sports.

*   1. Sports—United States—Addresses, essays, lectures. I. Mulvoy, Mark.*
GV583.G7   796'.0973   81–8509
ISBN 0-8317-3977-0   AACR2

Contents

Baseball

1912: A VERY GOOD YEAR

The era belonged to Walter Johnson, but the year belonged to Smokey Joe Wood

For baseball fans, young or old, there is nothing better than a good old-fashioned rhubarb. So, now let's play a little game of "Who's better?"—and let's not get mad. I say Sandy Koufax; you say Juan Marichal. I say Willie Mays; you say Mickey Mantle. I say Ted Williams; you say Joltin' Joe DiMaggio. I say Joe McCarthy; you say John McGraw. I say Cy Young; you say Christy Mathewson. I say the Dodgers; you say the Yankees. I say the White Sox; you say the Cubs. I say Stan Musial; you say Bill Terry. I say Luke Appling; you say Marty Marion. I say the National League; you say the American League. I say Walter Johnson; you say Smokey Joe Wood.

Now wait a minute. Except for one season, 1912, there's no way that you can mention Smokey Joe Wood in the same breath with Walter Johnson. What are you, crazy or something? Johnson is in the Hall of Fame. Johnson won 416 games in his career, more than anyone other than Cy Young, who won 511. C'mon, now, get serious.

"What about 1912?" you say. Okay, I'll give you 1912.

The year 1912 was a very good year for (1) Smokey Joe Wood, (2) the Boston Red Sox, and (3) baseball. And, yes, also for Walter Johnson. Starting in early summer, Johnson went on an absolute pitching tear, reeling off 16 straight victories before his streak was broken. But Johnson pitched all that time in the shadow of a 22-year-old phenom named Joe Wood, who played for the Boston Red Sox. A right-hander, Wood hurled a baseball with such velocity that he was given the name "Smokey."

One day someone asked Johnson if he could throw harder and faster than Smokey Joe. The Washington pitcher shook his head and smiled. "Listen, my friend," he said, "there's no man alive who can throw harder than Smokey Joe."

While Johnson was completing his 16-game win streak, Wood was on a streak of his own, and by the first week of September he had won 13 games in a row. The Senators came to Boston for a weekend series, and on Friday, September 6, Johnson was listed as the Washington starter. Wood was not scheduled to pitch until the following afternoon, but the Red Sox, probably reacting to press comments to the effect that Johnson ought to be allowed the chance to stop Wood's winning

streak, advanced him a day and started him against Johnson on Friday afternoon. To the local and national media this pitching matchup was an event of magnificent proportions, and it owned the headlines for several days. As Wood remembered it in later years, the newspapers treated the matchup as it would a championship fight; the papers were filled with the tales-of-the-tape of the two pitchers, and revealed all their physical measurements.

The Red Sox were playing their first season in the new Fenway Park, and for this game a crowd of more than 30,000 overflowed the Fens. While the fans were not unruly, they did press up so closely to the field that the Red Sox and Senator players had to abandon their dugouts and set up benches along the foul lines.

Johnson, who was on the way to a 32 and 12 record for the 1912 season, and Wood, who would finish the season with a 34 and 5 record, rose to the occasion, as everyone had expected. Johnson gave up only five hits and struck out five. Wood gave up six hits and struck out nine. The only run of the game was scored in the bottom

PRECEDING PAGES: *Joe DiMaggio breaks a record as he hits safely in his 42nd straight game.* RIGHT: *Boston's Joe Wood, 22-year-old phenom whose 1912 pitching record was 34 wins, 5 losses.* OPPOSITE LEFT: *Wood was a hero in the 1912 World Series against the Giants.* OPPOSITE RIGHT: *Wood with a bat.*

of the sixth inning when Tris Speaker hit what was called a ground-rule double (the ball rolled into the crowd along the foul line) and then scored on another double by Duffy Lewis. The final score was Boston 1, Washington 0. For Johnson, a 1-0 loss was nothing unusual; in fact, he lost 26 1-0 games during his great career. On the other hand, he won 38 games by the score of 1-0, too. Harry Hooper, the Hall of Fame outfielder for the Red Sox, said later that the Wood-Johnson matchup was the "most exciting" game he had ever played in, or had ever seen.

Wood's sterling pitching helped propel the Red Sox, who were supposed to have finished well down in the American League standings but easily outdistanced the Philadelphia Athletics of Connie Mack, into the World Series against John McGraw's New York Giants.

There are not many people alive today who remember much about that 1912 Series, but some baseball historians still maintain that it rates as the best World Series of all time.

The Red Sox pitched Smokey Joe in the first game and rallied from a 2-0 deficit after five innings to win 4-3, scoring one run in the sixth inning and three in the seventh. In the bottom of the ninth the Giants scored once to bring the score to 4-3 and had men on second and third with only one out. Wood should have been weary, but he somehow reached back for that little extra and struck out the last two Giants to preserve his victory. In game two the Giants wiped out a 4-2 Red Sox lead with three runs in the top of the eighth, but the Red Sox tied the score in the bottom of the eighth. The Giants then recaptured the lead with a run in the top of the tenth, only to have the Red Sox tie the score at 6-6 in the bottom of the tenth. There were no night games in those days, because there were no lights, and the game was called because of darkness an inning later.

In game three the Giants tied the series at one game apiece, Rube Marquard beating the Red Sox by a 2-1 score. Smokey Joe got the ball for Boston when the Series moved to New York, and he beat the Giants 3-1. Then the Red Sox took a three games to one lead by beating Giant ace Christy Mathewson 2-1. But the Giants were not dead yet. In game six New York scored five runs in the first inning and held on for a 5-2 victory, and in game seven—not the final game, remember, because game two was never finished—the Giants tied the

Series at three games apiece by scoring six runs in the first inning and walloping the Red Sox 11–4.

The eighth and final game of the Series was a classic. The Giants scored one run in the third and seemed certain to score another run in the fifth when Larry Doyle hit a long drive to deep right center field that was headed over the railing. But Hooper, running all out, tracked down the ball, dove over the railing and into the crowd—and came up with the ball in his glove. The Red Sox, given new life, tied the score at 1–1 in the seventh, but neither team could score in either the eighth or the ninth.

In the top of the tenth the Giants took a 2–1 lead on a hit by Fred Merkle, but they couldn't hold it. In the bottom of the tenth, Clyde Engle, pinch-hitting for Wood, hit what appeared to be the most routine of fly balls to left center field. Fred Snodgrass moved over and called for the ball, but, unbelievably, he dropped it—and Engle ended up at second base. Hooper was the next Boston batter, and the Giants were prepared for the bunt they felt certain Hooper would attempt. Snodgrass, in fact, moved in from his normal center field position and assumed a position just behind second base to guard against any overthrows or wild pickoffs. But Hooper confounded the Giants by swinging away, and

he hit the ball far over Snodgrass's head. Snodgrass had just dropped the easiest of fly balls, but now he raced back and miraculously made an over-the-shoulder catch of Hooper's ball on the dead run. Engle, running at the crack of the bat, was well around third when Snodgrass caught the ball, but he was able to get back to second safely in the time it took Snodgrass to recover his balance, turn, and throw the ball in.

Mathewson walked the next batter, and then Tris Speaker came to the plate. The Red Sox star hit what looked to be a harmless foul pop, a certain out, but the Giants inexplicably let the ball drop. Given new life, Speaker then smashed a single into right field to score Engle with the tying run and send the Series-winning run to third base. Mathewson issued another walk, to Duffy Lewis, and then Larry Gardner, the Boston third baseman, hit a long sacrifice fly to score pinch-runner Steve Yerkes with the run—unearned—that won the Series for the Red Sox.

Oh, yes. Smokey Joe Wood never was much of a pitcher after that great season of 1912. He hurt his arm and later had to quit pitching. He then took up outfielding, and in 1920 he played there for Cleveland in the World Series.

I say Walter Johnson. Except for 1912.

ABOVE: *Smokey Joe Wood (left) shakes hands with New York Giant pitching ace Christy Mathewson. Both pitchers worked in the 1912 World Series.* OPPOSITE: *Eddie Cicotte was one of the eight Chicago White Sox whose questionable activities in the 1919 World Series led to the Black Sox scandal.*

THE GAME'S BLACKEST DAYS

The 1919 World Series: the scandal of the Chicago Black Sox, who didn't play to win

Mention the year 1919 to a baseball addict and the immediate retort will be: the Black Sox scandal. There was nothing great about the Black Sox scandal, except for the fact that the baseball authorities reacted so immediately and with such severity that the reputation of the game suffered only minimally. Without a doubt, the single blackest moment in baseball history was the 1919 World Series. The American League-champion Chicago White Sox were solid favorites to beat the Cincinnati Red Stockings in the best-of-nine-games Series, but the Red Stockings ultimately prevailed by a margin of five games to three. Sadly, it later became apparent—and, in fact, it may well have been apparent at the time of the Series—that a number of Chicago players, at least eight, were involved in a gambling scheme and apparently contrived to throw the Series to the Red Stockings. In all, eight White Sox players—now known in infamy as the Black Sox—were indicted by a grand jury and charged with throwing the Series to the Reds. Today, when baseball officials or baseball fans mention the name of a player on the roster of the 1919 Chicago team, that player is identified as a Black Sox or a Lily White, depending on whether or not he was connected to the gambling scam.

The eight so-called Black Sox: pitchers Eddie Ci-

cotte and Claude Williams, outfielders Shoeless Joe Jackson and Oscar Felsch, shortstop Charles Risberg, first baseman Arnold Gandil, third baseman Buck Weaver, and utility infielder Fred McMullen. Cicotte and Williams were the mainstays of the Chicago staff, posting records of 29–7 and 23–11, respectively, during the 1919 season. Jackson was an outstanding hitter and one of the game's best outfielders. Today, though, no one remembers anything about their records, only that they were the infamous Black Sox.

According to various printed reports of the scandal, Gandil was the main man, the initial contact and then the intermediary between the many gambling factions and the Chicago players. Gandil and Cicotte reportedly were approached by several groups of known gamblers and asked if they were interested in forming a syndicate of sorts of many Chicago players to throw the Series. The gamblers reportedly offered each of the players some $10,000 to participate in the betting scam. Gandil reportedly jumped at the opportunity to make a quick financial killing. Later, Cicotte apparently was approached by still another group of gamblers from a foreign country and offered large sums to put together a similar scam. It was reported that Gandil and/or Cicotte had little trouble convincing several teammates to join them in the conspiracy; indeed, of the eight so-called Black Sox, only one, Buck Weaver, apparently did not contrive to throw the games. But Weaver was aware of the conspiracy, and he reportedly failed to inform the Chicago management or the league president. Thus, he, too, has been forever linked with the Black Sox. According to reports, the Black Sox had some funny ideas of their own. One of the Black Sox reportedly suggested that the players get all their payoff before the start of the World Series and then play the games to win.

Whatever, there was considerable suspicion in the Cincinnati air as the White Sox prepared to open the Series against the Red Stockings. There were reports of hordes of known gamblers walking around the hotel where the White Sox were staying and waving fistfuls of bills—all large denominations—in the air, signifying they were looking for action. These known gamblers were so blatant in their approach that they became the subject of jokes. But in those days gambling on baseball was fairly routine, if illegal in most places, and not that many people were turned off by the brashness of the gamblers.

Cicotte was the starting pitcher for the White Sox in game one, and the Chicago team was a heavy on-paper favorite to beat the Red Stockings that day. But Cincinnati KO'd Cicotte by scoring five runs in the fourth inning and rolled to an easy 9–1 victory. After the game, Cicotte and Chicago catcher Ray Schalk reportedly had a heated argument in the clubhouse, with Schalk charging that Cicotte had confused him repeatedly by ignoring his signals and throwing pitches that the catcher did not expect. Like, when Schalk called for a curve, Cicotte threw a fast ball across the heart of the plate.

The next day Chicago manager Kid Gleason started his number two hurler, Claude Williams. Again, the White Sox were heavy favorites on paper, but the word was that the gamblers reportedly were doing a heavy number on the Red Stockings. Williams gave up only four hits, but in the Cincinnati fourth he surrendered three walks, a single, and a triple—and the Red Stockings scored three runs. Cincinnati eventually won the game 4–2 to take a two-games-to-none lead in the Series.

By now, everyone suspected that something funny was going on—and in this case funny had no connection to humor. Still, baseball authorities could find no evidence to link any of the players with the suspected betting conspiracy, and the Series went on.

The third game was played in Chicago on October 3, and the White Sox, with Dickie Kerr on the mound, shut out the Red Stockings 3–0. But the next day the Red Stockings beat Cicotte again, this time by a 2–0 score. While Cicotte seemed to pitch effectively, the way in which the Red Stockings scored their runs only added more fuel to the fire. Both Cincinnati runs resulted from errors made by—that's right—Eddie Cicotte. First, Cicotte overthrew first base after fielding a routine ground ball to the mound. Second, Cicotte needlessly deflected an outfielder's throw to the plate that, according to most printed accounts, would have arrived there in time to beat the runner coming from third base.

In game five the Red Stockings trounced the White Sox 5–0, beating Williams for the second time. For five innings Williams pitched marvelously, but in the sixth he suddenly gave up three hits and a walk. He also was not helped by the play of his teammates in the field; Felsch made a poor throw on one play, and Jackson

never got to a fly ball that most observers thought he should have caught easily. "Jackson was slow getting to the ball . . . his mind appeared to be puzzled," read part of one account of the play.

Now Cincinnati was ahead four games to one and needed only one more victory to wrap up the Series. But the White Sox rallied behind Kerr's pitching to win game six by a 5–4 score, and then Cicotte won his first game in three Series starts by a 4–1 score. Later, people tried to figure out why Cicotte had pitched so well, and why the White Sox had played so well—after their dismal performances in the earlier games. One theory was that the gamblers had welched on their financial commitments to the players and that the players now were playing strictly to win. Another theory was that there were so many gambling groups involved in the scam that none of the players quite knew whether they were supposed to win or lose—or what. It was all terribly confusing.

However, the word seemed to be out as the two teams prepared to play game eight. The word was that the Red Stockings would win the Series on the strength of a big first inning, that they would blow the White Sox right out of the park. Well, whatever the word hap-

12

ABOVE: *Shoeless Joe Jackson, outfielder for the infamous Chicago Black Sox. Eight Chicago players allegedly threw the 1919 Series for cash from gambling interests.* OPPOSITE: *1919 World Series, Game 2, won by the Cincinnati Red Stockings. The eight Chicago players were banned from baseball.*

pened to be, the Red Stockings pounded Williams for four straight hits after he had retired the Cincinnati leadoff hitter and manager Gleason had to remove him from the game. Cincinnati went on to rout Chicago by a 10–5 score and win the Series five games to three.

Shortly thereafter an intensive investigation was launched to determine what had happened, if anything, in the Series. Nearly 12 months later, during the final week of the 1920 regular season, evidence was presented to a grand jury in Chicago. Eight Chicago players—immediately labeled the Black Sox—were charged with being criminals, in that they had allegedly contrived to throw the 1919 World Series. Also, many known gamblers admitted their involvement to various degrees. And three of the so-called Black Sox—Cicotte, Williams, and Jackson—reportedly signed confessions of their guilt, although they later retracted those confessions in court.

When the state of Illinois brought its case to court, a trial jury acquitted the players, some of whom apparently never were paid off by the gamblers. But the state had to present a weakened case because most of its papers pertaining to the betting scam, as well as the minutes of the grand jury and the confessions of Cicotte, Jackson, and Williams, had mysteriously disappeared from the offices of the district attorney. Once that innocent verdict came in, the indicted Chicago players had a victory party, and made plans to resume their baseball careers.

But Judge Kenesaw Mountain Landis, who had recently been appointed as the game's first commissioner, with orders to be dictatorial, would have none of it. "Regardless of the verdict of juries," Judge Landis announced, "no player that throws a ball game, no player that entertains proposals or promises to throw a game, no player that sits in a conference with a bunch of crooked players and gamblers where the ways and means of throwing games are discussed, and does not promptly tell his club about it, will never again play professional baseball."

And so, despite their heated protests, the eight Black Sox never put on baseball uniforms again. And baseball's image was on the way back to respectability—after a year in the black.

"THAT'S 60 HOME RUNS . . . 60 . . . COUNT 'EM"

The mighty Babe Ruth hits a 'knockdown' pitch for his record 60th home run

There's not much you can say about George Herman Ruth that the Babe didn't say himself on any number of occasions. The Babe was not an egomaniacal wonder on the order of Muhammad Ali, but the Babe was never one to suppress a bit of information if it had anything to do with the Babe himself, particularly his accomplishments. And the Babe had plenty of accomplishments to talk about. At one point in his career the Babe was the owner of more than 50—yes, 50—major-league records, most of which had something to do with home runs.

The Babe was, of course, "the Sultan of Swat," "the King of the Home Run Hitters," "Mr. Long Ball," you name it. In 1918 the Babe was a part-time pitcher, part-time outfielder, but he still tied for the American League home-run championship with 11; the baseball season was abbreviated that year because of World War I. The following year, 1919, the Babe stuck pretty much

to hitting and this time led the American League, indeed the entire major leagues, with 29 home runs. Then, in 1920, baseball introduced a livelier ball, all the better for sluggers like the Babe, and over the next 12 seasons the Babe led the major leagues in home runs 10 times; he missed in 1922 and 1925, mainly because he sat out several weeks of the playing season both of those years. He hit 54 home runs in 1920, 59 in 1921, 41 in 1923, 46 in 1924, 47 in 1926, 60 in 1927, 54 in 1928, 46 in 1929, 49 in 1930, and 46 in 1931, a year in which he shared the home-run championship with New York Yankee teammate Lou Gehrig.

The Babe didn't win the home run crown in 1932, but in the World Series that season he hit one of his most spectacular and most controversial homers. The Chicago Cubs inexplicably figured they could rattle the Babe by subjecting him to all sorts of verbal abuse be-

New York, September 30, 1927. In the second to last game of the season in his last time at bat in the game, Babe Ruth hits his record-breaking 60th home run. The pitch was a curve, up and in, but Ruth got wood on it and pulled it out.

fore, during, and after the Series games. This treatment didn't set well with the Babe, so he decided to put a halt to all the bench jockeying in the best way he knew. Stepping out of the batter's box, with the count at two balls and two strikes, the Babe—or so the legend has it—waggled his arm and pointed to a spot in dead center field. Now, there are some people who maintain that the Babe was pointing not at center field but at the Cubs' pitcher, Charley Root, telling Root in no uncertain terms that he was going to smash the next pitch right down his throat. Did he or didn't he? Well, Root delivered the next pitch and Ruth took a mighty cut. The ball exploded off his bat and screamed over the head of the Chicago pitcher, who probably was thanking his lucky stars that the ball had not hit him, and carried all the way over the fence in dead center field, finally touching down in a spot that no baseball had ever reached before. Needless to say, the Babe laughed all the way around the bases.

Except for his teammate Gehrig, Babe rarely had much competition for the home run championship each season. In fact, he usually was competing against himself, which was certainly the case late in the 1927 season when the Babe beat his own major-league record of 59 home runs, set in 1921, by hitting number 60 on the second to last day of the regular season.

The Babe had the good fortune that season to play on a Yankee team that totally dominated the American League—all of baseball, in fact—and over the years has always been rated as one of the two or three best teams in history. Ruth hit .375 and drove in 164 runs, as well as hitting his 60 home runs. Gehrig hit .373 and had a league-leading 175 RBIs, as well as hitting 47 home runs. Earl Coombs hit .356; Bob Meusel hit .337 and had 103 RBIs; and Tony Lazzeri hit .309 with 102 RBIs. And the Yankee pitching staff was deep and talented, heavy with starters, and relievers who really weren't needed that often.

For the first four months of the season Ruth and Gehrig, who batted third and fourth in the Yankee order, staged a private duel for the home-run lead, and early in August Gehrig led the Babe by three, 38 to 35. But then Gehrig went into a homer slump and hit only nine more during the rest of the season. The Babe, though, was just warming up. Over the next month Ruth hit 15 home runs, and with 17 games to play, he was up to 50. It's tough to get excited about records when the record you are chasing happens to be your own, but the Babe was clearly psyched up about getting 60 home runs, one more than his record 59. But then the Babe

went into a slight slump himself, hitting just three home runs in the next eight games, and with nine games left to play he needed seven home runs to break his record.

As it turned out, the Babe was not in a slump. He hit three home runs in the next three games, giving him 56 homers with six games to play. Like all hitters, Babe was just a little bit superstitious; he had bats that he liked, shoes that he liked, etc. He happened to like the bat he was using while trying to crack his home run record, and when he did hit a home run, he would carry that bat around the bases with him, so it would not be stolen, or lost. After hitting his fifty-sixth homer, Babe carried his bat around the bases, and as he approached third base a fan suddenly appeared in his path and tried to grab the bat from his hands. The Babe was a powerful man, and he had no use for such hijinks. So, barely breaking his stride, he grabbed the fan and lugged him down the third base line to home plate, all the while holding onto his bat.

The Babe failed to connect for a homer in either of the Yankees' next two games, but then hit number 57— a grand slam off Lefty Grove—and now needed only three in the last three games. He got two home runs the next day, one of them another monstrous grand slam,

New York, September, 1927. Babe Ruth watches the ball sail over the fence for home run number 59. The homer came in the third to last game of the season and was one of two that he hit in the game. The other was a patented Ruth monster grand slam.

15

and tied his own record with 59. He needed only one more home run, and the Yankees had two games to play. But in typical Ruth fashion, the Babe didn't wait until the last minute to break his record.

In the Yankees' second to last game of the season, facing pitcher Tom Zachary, the Babe walked his first time at bat, but then had two singles in his next two trips to the plate. On his last visit to the plate in the game, the Babe knew that Zachary, a cool craftsman, would never give him a decent pitch to hit, not wanting to be the pitcher who served up the pitch that broke the record. So Zachary threw the Babe a curve ball that seemed more like a knockdown pitch than anything else, traveling as it was in the direction of the Babe's head.

Somehow, though, the Babe manufactured a way to hit the pitch—probably before it hit him—and he powered it down the right field line. It would leave the playing field, there was no question about that. But would it stay fair long enough to be a home run? Zachary kept screaming that it was a foul ball, but the umpire properly ruled it a home run. Babe strolled triumphantly around the bases, proud that he had broken his own record.

After the game Zachary said that he could not believe Ruth had hit the curve ball for a home run. As for Ruth, he said, "That's sixty home runs, count 'em. Sixty. Let's see some other S.O.B. hit sixty home runs."

Thirty-four years later another Yankee, Roger Maris, would hit 61 home runs.

ABOVE: *George Herman Ruth, known as "Babe," "the Bambino," and "The Sultan of Swat." After his 60th home run in '27 he said, "Let's see some other S.O.B. hit sixty home runs."* OPPOSITE: *Carl Hubbell, who struck out the Hall of Fame Murderer's Row in the 1934 All-Star Game. Hubbell perfected the screwball.*

K, K, K, K, K

*King Carl Hubbell strikes out Murderer's Row—Ruth, Gehrig, Foxx, Simmons and Cronin—
one after the other in the 1934 All Star Game*

Lamentably, one of the casualties of the expansion boom that has placed so-called major league sports franchises in every nook and cranny of North America is the All-Star Game. The idea of any All-Star Game, of course, is to collect the absolute best players from a particular league and have them play a game, or a series of games, against the absolute best players from a rival conference, a rival division, a rival league, whatever. American League versus the National League. East versus West. NFC versus AFC.

Nowadays, however, there are 26 baseball teams in the major leagues, not 16; there are 21 hockey teams, not six; there are a few dozen basketball teams (the number seems to change almost by the week), not a handful; there are 28 pro football teams, not 8 or 10.

And now the rules for the selection of All-Star Game personnel have changed—for the worse. In most sports, each team in a particular division or conference or league must be represented by at least one player in the All-Star Game. Also, in most sports the All-Star squads are picked not by the players, not by the coaches, but by the fans, as part of the merchandising tactics of some official league sponsor. The fans submit their ballots at an arena, and a computer tabulates them; trouble is, fans can vote as often as they like, and fans tend to be ignorant and notoriously provincial when filling out an All-Star Game roster. Consequently, many deserving players never get to play in an All-Star Game, while many journeymen do.

Such was not the case, thank goodness, in the early years of baseball's All-Star Game. It was the best against the best, no expansion automatics allowed. And if you were selected to play in an All-Star Game, you considered it an honor, a privilege—not a burden. In 1979 true baseball fans everywhere were outraged when Garry Templeton, a shortstop for the St. Louis Cardinals who cannot carry Marty Marion's glove, but makes more money in half a season ($350,000) than Marion probably made in his entire career, decided that he would not play in the All-Star Game. Templeton, you see, had not been selected by the fans but had been picked as an alternate by the manager of the All-Star team. "If I don't start, I don't go," Templeton said. So he took his bat and glove and stayed home.

The players on the 1934 National League All-Star team would have laughed Templeton right out of baseball, that's for sure. There was no room in the game for any prima donnas, thank you. No way.

The 1934 All-Star Game was played on July 10 at the Polo Grounds, the home field of the New York Giants, and a crowd of more than 52,000 turned out to see the best of the National League battle the best of the American League. The names were very impressive: Bill Terry, Frankie Frisch, Pie Traynor, Ducky Medwick for the Nationals; Babe Ruth, Lou Gehrig, Joe Cronin, Jimmy Foxx, Al Simmons for the Americans. The mighty Americans were favored to win this second All-Star Game ever played.

Terry, who managed the Giants and also played first base, was the manager of the Nationals, and before the game he assembled his All-Stars to discuss the

17

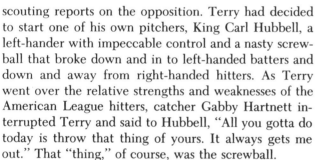

scouting reports on the opposition. Terry had decided to start one of his own pitchers, King Carl Hubbell, a left-hander with impeccable control and a nasty screwball that broke down and in to left-handed batters and down and away from right-handed hitters. As Terry went over the relative strengths and weaknesses of the American League hitters, catcher Gabby Hartnett interrupted Terry and said to Hubbell, "All you gotta do today is throw that thing of yours. It always gets me out." That "thing," of course, was the screwball.

Hubbell, who was a product of the Oklahoma prairie, seemed nervous and edgy when he went out to pitch to the American stars in the top of the first inning. And he got off to a bad start when leadoff hitter Charlie Gehringer rapped a single to the outfield. Then Hubbell's usually flawless control failed him and he walked Heinie Manush, putting runners at first and second.

If any baseball team ever had a real, live Murderer's Row of hitters, it was the 1934 American League All-Stars. Try these names: Babe Ruth, Lou Gehrig, Jimmy Foxx, Al Simmons, and Joe Cronin. Each is a member of the Hall of Fame. They batted third, fourth, fifth, sixth, and seventh in the American League lineup. To the Giant fans in the Polo Grounds, it looked like curtains for their star pitcher. Two men on, nobody out,

and five of the greatest hitters in the game itching to take their swings. It was never like this in Oklahoma.

Terry suspected that Hubbell might not be in the proper frame of mind, so he walked to the pitcher's mound and summoned the other infielders—second baseman Frankie Frisch, shortstop Travis Jackson, third baseman Pie Traynor—to join him for a conference with Hubbell.

"You all right?" Terry asked Hubbell.

"Yup," said Hubbell, never a man to use two words when one would do.

Terry hemmed and hawed for a few moments, killing time, and then the infielders all resumed their positions. They didn't know it at the time, but they would soon be watching perhaps the greatest exhibition of pitching in the history of the game.

In the early 1930s, baseball people used Walter Johnson as their frame of reference when the topic of a discussion became "great moments in pitching." Twenty years earlier, in a critical game between Washington and Detroit, Johnson had artfully pitched out of a bases loaded, no outs situation in the ninth inning by striking out, in order, Ty Cobb, Bob Veach, and Sam Crawford. That, the experts all believed, was an exhibition of pitching that would never be matched.

Now, in the Polo Grounds, Babe Ruth, the home run king, stepped into the batter's box, and the crowd was buzzing. Why, the way Hubbell was pitching, the Babe would probably belt one into the seats for a three-run homer. But Hubbell had regained his control, and he quickly ran the count on Ruth to one ball and two strikes as the Babe watched each pitch go by without lifting the bat off his shoulder. Was Babe playing possum? Maybe he was, maybe he wasn't, but the bat stayed on his shoulder as the next pitch from Hubbell whizzed across the plate for a called strike three. So much for the mighty Ruth, who walked back to the bench wearing a funny look.

Gehrig, the so-called "Prince of Punch," was next. Hubbell was now locked into private combat, and he went with his number one weapon, the screwball. Gehrig, a left-handed batter, dug in at the plate, but all he saw was one screwball after another, each one twisting wickedly towards him. The count was one ball and two strikes, the same as it had been on Ruth. Gehrig knew what pitch Hubbell would throw next, and sure enough, it was another screwball. Gehrig tried desperately to get his bat on the ball, but failed to do so. Strike three. Two outs.

Jimmy Foxx, whose 26 home runs led the entire major leagues at the All-Star break, was next. One thing in Foxx's favor was that he was a right-handed batter, unlike both Ruth and Gehrig, and Ol' Jimmy would be waiting to yank a pitch into the seats. Once again, though, Hubbell needed only four pitches, three of which Foxx swung at mightily, to get the strikeout. Foxx managed to get his bat on one of Hubbell's pitches, something that neither Ruth nor Gehrig accomplished, but that was it. The side was out.

Carl Hubbell had struck out Babe Ruth, Lou Gehrig, and Jimmy Foxx in order.

In the top of the second, Hubbell, whom the Giants called "Meal Ticket," because he put bread on their tables, struck out Al Simmons and then he struck out Joe Cronin. That made it five strikeouts in a row: Ruth, Gehrig, Foxx, Simmons, and Cronin.

Murderer's Row? Forget it.

According to the rules of the All-Star Game, Hubbell could pitch only three innings, and he departed accordingly. Once Hubbell had left, the American League went on to outscore the Nationals by a 9–7 score. But no one remembers any of the details of the game, except for the fact that Carl Hubbell set five of the best hitters in the history of the game down on their ears—one by one.

ABOVE (left): Ruth batted 3rd in the 1934 All-Star lineup.
ABOVE (right): Jimmy Foxx, shown here in 1940, batted 5th.
OPPOSITE (left): Al Simmons, shown here in 1930, batted 6th.
OPPOSITE (right): Lou Gehrig batted clean-up for the "Row."

19

THE DOUBLE NO-HIT KID

On the occasion of the first night game in Brooklyn,
Johnny Vander Meer of the Cincinnati Reds puts the lights out on the Dodgers
by pitching his second consecutive no-hit, no-run game

It was the early spring of 1934, a time when people in the United States were trying to recover from the crippling Depression. In Dayton, Ohio, a minor-league baseball manager named Ducky Holmes approached a 19-year-old left-handed Dutchman from New Jersey and said to him, "Hey, kid, I want you to pitch the opening game of the season." That statement should have been the sincerest form of flattery for the kid pitcher; indeed, baseball teams traditionally reserve the "opening day" assignment for their number one pitcher. But the young lefty was not doing handstands over the words he had heard from his manager. "First, you'll have to give me all the money you owe me from last year," the kid told the manager. "You promised me at the end of last season that I'd be paid all the money I was owed. So where is it?"

Holmes was not accustomed to hearing such threats from teenaged players, and he wasted little time in disposing of this one—Johnny Vander Meer. Holmes sold Vander Meer to a team in Scranton, Pennsylvania, and Vander Meer had a highly successful season. So successful, in fact, that the Brooklyn Dodgers called him up to the major leagues near the end of the season. Unbeknownst to the Dodgers, though, Vander Meer had been sold—not reassigned, not loaned, not traded—to Scranton, and as a result they no longer owned his major-league rights. Scranton turned around and sold Vander Meer to the Boston Braves, but the Boston franchise immediately came upon hard financial times and sold Vander Meer to a minor league team in Nashville, Tennessee. The Cincinnati Reds had a working agreement with the Nashville team, and in time they acquired young Vander Meer and brought him to Cincinnati.

Vander Meer enjoyed very limited success in his early games as a Red, mainly because he could not consistently deliver his pitches from an overhand motion. Too often he dropped his arm while going through his motion and ultimately delivered the ball from a sidearm motion that made his pitches all too hittable. Then one day Vander Meer suddenly fell into a groove from which he delivered all his pitches from a very high overhand motion.

Early in June of 1938 Vander Meer, now 23, was given a start against the New York Giants and pitched a three-hitter for the victory. His next start was on Saturday, June 11, against the Boston Braves, managed then by Casey Stengel, at Cincinnati's Crosley Field. Before a crowd of about 10,000, the majority of whom were members of the local Knothole gang and didn't even pay for a ticket, Vander Meer not only beat the Braves

3–0 but he also pitched a no-hitter.

Five days later, on June 16, Vander Meer made his next start in a game against the Brooklyn Dodgers at Ebbets Field. This was never going to be your ordinary, run-of-the-mill baseball game. No, this was going to be the first game ever played at night and under the lights in Brooklyn, and the Dodger management had gone to extremes to provide pregame entertainment for the crowd, which totaled 38,747. The gates opened at 5 P.M., almost four and one-half hours before the first pitch, and the fans were serenaded by not one, not two, but three bands on the field. Jesse Owens, the hero of the 1936 Olympics at Berlin, was also on hand as a special attraction, and he received a series of thunderous ovations even though he lost two races to Dodger players. In one, he spotted Ernie Koy 10 yards in a 100-yard dash and barely lost; in the other, he lost a special 120-yard race to Gil Brack, who ran on a flat track while Owens had to do the regulation 120-yard high hurdles. As game time approached, the 615 floodlights—the candlepower was 92,000,000—turned the field into a silky green, then some bombs exploded behind second base, the national anthem was sung, and the game—at last—began.

The fans in Flatbush didn't realize it, but the real show was just getting underway.

When the Dodgers came to bat in the first inning, their fans—always the most raucous in baseball—immediately began to mimic Vander Meer's pitching style, which best could be described as "Rocking Chair." And the Flatbush faithful did it by the numbers—loudly. As Vander Meer bent forward to start his motion, the crowd would yell, "One." Then it would be "two"—as he raised his arms over his head; "three"—as he kicked his lead right leg; "four"—as he moved forward; and, finally, "five"—as he released the ball. 1 . . . 2 . . . 3 . . . 4 . . . 5 . . . The numbers echoed through Brooklyn all night.

The Reds took an early lead on Frank McCormick's three-run homer. Meanwhile, Vander Meer was pitching with the same command that he had enjoyed against the Giants and the Braves in his two previous starts. He was slightly wilder in this game than he had been in the others, but no one was doing much with his pitches. One by one the Dodgers went out, and through six innings Vander Meer had a no-hitter on the board. And now he showed that the Flatbush faithful were really faithless; in fact, the crowd was cheering Vander Meer's every pitch, hoping that perhaps they were sitting in on history—a second consecutive no-hit, no-run game.

Johnny Vander Meer, 23 years old, pitched a no-hitter for the Cincinnati Reds on June 11, 1938, against the Boston Braves. The Reds won 3–0. In his next start against the Brooklyn Dodgers on June 16, the first night game ever played at Ebbets Field, he pitched a second no-hitter as the Reds won 6–0.

21

Struggling with his control, Vander Meer walked two Dodgers in the bottom of the seventh but then neatly pitched his way out of trouble. In the eighth inning Vander Meer easily disposed of Woody English, Kiki Cuyler, and Johnny Hudson, getting both English and Hudson on strikeouts. Through eight innings not one Dodger had come close to getting a hit off Vander Meer.

The game no longer was in doubt, Cincinnati was leading 6–0, as Vander Meer strolled out for the bottom of the ninth. Not one fan had left the premises, and all the lights were still burning brightly. Johnny Vander Meer was at center stage, staring history in the face, and the crowd was on its feet and cheering his every move. Buddy Hassett, the Dodgers' leadoff hitter in the ninth, topped a ball down the first-base line, but Vander Meer reacted quickly, scooped up the ball, and tagged Hassett out. One down, Two to go.

Vander Meer had walked five Dodgers in the first eight innings, and now he walked another—Babe Phelps. Then he walked Cookie Lavagetto. And then he filled the bases with Dodgers by walking Dolf Camilli. Suddenly the crowd was quiet as Cincinnati Manager Bill McKechnie trotted from the dugout and headed for the mound to settle down his young pitcher.

"You're trying to put too much on the ball, trying to throw it too hard," McKechnie told Vander Meer. "Just throw your regular stuff, the way you've been doing for the last couple of games. And don't give them anything cheap."

Ernie Koy was the next Dodger batter, and he hit a sharp grounder to third base. Lew Riggs fielded the ball cleanly and fired to catcher Ernie Lombardi, forcing Goody Rosen, who was running for Phelps. Bases still loaded, two down, one to go. But the one was none other than Leo the Lip, Leo Durocher, the man who supposedly coined the phrase, "Nice guys finish last."

Vander Meer quickly ran the count on Durocher to one ball and two strikes, and he thought that the game was over on his fourth pitch. But umpire Bill Stewart never raised his right hand in the traditional gesture for a strike; he called the pitch a ball. "That pitch was a strike," Vander Meer said later. "He lost it, that's all." But Stewart insisted that the pitch was too high to be a strike. "I had to call it a ball," the umpire said. "I was pulling for the kid as much as anyone. It was mighty lonely behind the plate, believe me. But I'd've kicked myself in the pants if Durocher had got a hit."

Vander Meer stood on the mound for an extra second, trying to regain his composure. Then he was ready. With the crowd roaring, he pitched to Durocher, and the Lip swung away. For a second the crowd was breathless, but then the roar resumed as center fielder Harry Craft moved under the ball and caught it easily.

It was over. Johnny Vander Meer had pitched his second consecutive no-hit, no-run game, a feat that stands alone in baseball history.

After the game the Flatbush faithful rushed on the field to engulf Vander Meer, who eventually needed a police escort to get to the Cincinnati dressing room, where he also was mobbed by well wishers, one of whom was a fairly bulky man named Babe Ruth. "Nice game, kid," the Babe told the Double-No-Hit Kid.

Earlier in the evening another well wisher had sent a telegram to Larry MacPhail, the boss of the Dodgers, wishing him success in the first night game in Brooklyn. The telegram came from Ducky Holmes, the manager who had sold Johnny Vander Meer out of the Brooklyn organization. MacPhail ripped it up.

Vander Meer's no-hit streak ended at 21⅔ innings when he gave up a single to Deb Garms of the Braves with one out in the third inning of his next start. He finished that 1938 season with a 15–10 record, but the next season he was named the biggest disappointment in the majors and two years later, in 1941, at the age of 26, he was back in the minor leagues, searching for the control that he had misplaced—forever, as it turned out.

OPPOSITE AND ABOVE: *Johnny Vander Meer. Vander Meer's two consecutive no-hit games is a feat that has never been matched. The final out in the second no hitter was a pop fly to center field by the Dodgers' Leo Durocher. Vander Meer finished 1938 at 15–10, but wound up in the minors in 3 years.*

"HE GLORIFIED THE HORSEHIDE SPHERE"

Joltin' Joe DiMaggio captures the hearts and minds of an entire nation as he hits in a record 56 straight games

It was in the mid-1960s, in a hugely successful film called *The Graduate,* starring Dustin Hoffman, Ann Bancroft, and Katherine Ross, that songwriter Paul Simon sentimentally posed the question, "Where have you gone, Joe DiMaggio? . . . a nation turns its lonely eyes to you . . . oohoohooh . . . oohoohooh . . ."

Joltin' Joe hadn't really gone anywhere; he had just been maintaining a rather low profile since the death of his former wife, film queen Marilyn Monroe. Still, the question hit home, touching millions of Americans, just as Joltin' Joe himself had touched millions of Americans back in the spring and summer of 1941 when he had the entire nation—except for about 175 baseball players on the seven American League teams that had to play against DiMaggio's New York Yankees—cheering his every time at bat.

From May 15, 1941, until July 16, 1941, Joe Di-Maggio—number 5 in the pinstripes, the Yankees' center fielder, the man who on the occasion of baseball's centennial in 1969 was named the game's greatest *living* player—hit safely in 56 straight games, a record that no player has ever seriously threatened. Boston Red Sox star Ted Williams, perhaps the greatest pure hitter ever to play baseball, and the last player ever to hit better than .400 in a season, something he did, ironically, in the same year of 1941 when he batted .406, said of Di-Maggio's 56-game hitting streak, "It may be the greatest batting achievement of them all."

For DiMaggio and, indeed, the nation, it all started innocently on May 15 when DiMaggio had one hit in four at-bats in a game against the Chicago White Sox, the lone hit being a single to left field off Edgar Smith. The next day he had two hits against the White Sox and the day after that he had one. On May 18 DiMaggio had a perfect three-for-three day against the St. Louis Browns, two singles and a double, and then he had one hit in each of the next two games against the Browns. On May 21 DiMaggio had a two-hit game against the Detroit Tigers, and over the next four games, one against Detroit and three against Boston, he managed to get one hit a game—all singles. On May 27, following an off day for the Yankees, DiMaggio exploded for four hits in five at bats against the Washington Senators, hitting three singles and a home run. His streak was now at 12 games, but not too many people were counting.

Joe DiMaggio lines a single past Cleveland pitcher Al Milner in the first inning of a game at Cleveland on July 16, 1941. DiMaggio started a streak on May 15 against the White Sox, and, with this hit, he extended that streak to a record 56 straight games.

Over the next six Yankee games DiMaggio officially batted 20 times—official at bats exclude any bases on balls—and got six hits, but he spread those hits over each game. And the streak was at 18 and counting, although the nation still was not turned on. DiMaggio was, after all, still 23 games away from tying the American League record of 41 games, set by sweet-swinging George Sisler in 1922. On June 2 DiMaggio went up against one of the toughest hurlers in the game, Cleveland's Bob Feller, who owned a fast ball that traveled at laser speed, but he more than met the challenge, getting

two hits—including a double—in four at bats. After two more one-hit games, extending his streak to 21, DiMaggio broke loose. On June 7 he had a three-for-five game against the St. Louis Browns, then the next day he went two for four again, one of the two hits being a home run, in a doubleheader against the same Browns. DiMaggio, his streak now at 24, had to be sorry to see the end of the series against St. Louis; in all, he had seven hits in 13 at bats in the three games.

Chicago and Cleveland provided the opposition for DiMaggio and the Yankees over the next seven games, and DiMaggio didn't exactly pound the ball, getting only eight hits in 26 trips to the plate. He had one hit in five at bats against Chicago on June 10, two hits in four trips the next day against the White Sox, then got a hit a game for the next five, prolonging what the nation now,

at last, was calling "the Streak" to 31 games. DiMaggio now was becoming superstitious, too; when some spectators grabbed his Yankees cap one day as DiMaggio trotted off the field, Joltin' Joe responded angrily and recaptured the hat. He wouldn't talk much about the incident, but word was that DiMaggio had worn the same hat every day since "the Streak" had started, and, well, now was not the time to switch.

The National League record was 33 games, set by Rogers Hornsby in 1922, the same year, coincidentally, that Sisler established the American League record, and DiMaggio quickly whizzed past Hornsby with a three-for-three game, including a home run, against the White Sox, a smashing four-for-five performance against Detroit, and a one-for-four game against Dizzy Trout of the Tigers. He was now at 34, only seven games from

Sisler's record.

Les Brown, the orchestra leader, popularized a song for DiMaggio, and his Band of Renown played it all over the country. A one . . . and a two . . . and a three . . .

> He started baseball's famous streak,
> That's got us all aglow.
> He's just a man and not a freak,
> Joltin' Joe DiMaggio.
>
> He'll live in Baseball's Hall of Fame.
> He got there blow by blow.
> Our kids will tell their kids his name,
> Joltin' Joe DiMaggio.
>
> Coast to coast that's all you hear
> Of Joe the one-man show.
> He's glorified the horsehide sphere,
> Joltin' Joe DiMaggio.

On June 22 DiMaggio made it 35 games by going two for four against the Tigers, then he quickly whipped through 36, 37, and 38 by going one-for-four in each game, with the one hit in game number 37 a three-run homer against Denny Galehouse of the St. Louis Browns. Two hits in three at bats against the Philadelphia Athletics on June 27 extended "the Streak" to 39 games, and in game number 40 DiMaggio probably got more than a little kick from the first of his two hits against the Athletics. Johnny Babich, a Philadelphia pitcher who by modern-day standards would probably be called a pop-off, was the starter against the Yankees, and he wasted few words in telling the press before the game exactly how it was that he, Johnny Babich, was going to put an end to "the Streak" that was captivating the nation. "I'll get DiMaggio out the first time," Babich said flatly, "and then I'll walk him every time after that."

Joltin' Joe was never one to reject a challenge on the field, of course. His first time at bat, the time Babich was going to get him out, DiMaggio hit an absolutely vicious smash back at Babich, and before the A's pitcher could react, the ball whizzed through his legs and into center field for a base hit. So much for Johnny Babich and his predictions. "If DiMaggio's shot had ever hit Babich on the leg, they'd have had to amputate it," said one baseball writer of the base hit that moved "the Streak" to 40, just one shy of Sisler's record.

On June 29 the Yankees had a double-header against the Washington Senators. In the first game Di-

Maggio tied the record with a hit off Dutch Leonard. Between games DiMaggio's favorite bat was lost somehow; it was not in the Yankees' bat rack when the players came out for the second game. Using one of his other bats, DiMaggio failed to get a hit in his first three at bats in that second game. Tommy Henrich, seeing, perhaps, that DiMaggio was not comfortable with the new bat, offered Joltin' Joe one of his own bats, figuring it might bring him good luck. After first refusing the offer, DiMaggio finally accepted, and in his fifth and last at bat of the day he got a single to break Sisler's record.

But wait. There suddenly was a new record to be broken. It was discovered that Wee Willie Keeler, the 5-foot 4-inch, 130-pound batting master of the nineteenth century, once had hit in 44 straight games for the Baltimore Orioles back in 1897. DiMaggio wasted little time wiping out Keeler's record; he tied it with two hits in the first game and one in the second of a double header against Boston on July 1, and the next day he hit a home run against the Red Sox to run "the Streak" to 45 games. The record was his, and his alone.

Most men would have been exhausted, physically as well as emotionally, after setting such a record amid such pressure and fanfare, but not DiMaggio. He was, indeed, just warming up. Over the next 11 games DiMaggio went on a hitting tear, getting 24 hits—four in two games, three in two games, two in three games, one in four games. Suddenly his record streak stood at 56 games as the Yankees met the Indians in Cleveland on the night of Thursday, July 17, 1941.

A crowd of 67,468, the largest night audience in baseball history, poured into Municipal Stadium to watch Joltin' Joe go for number 57. In the stands, too, were representatives of a soup company with a brand line called "57"; if DiMaggio got a hit against the Indians, the soup company was prepared to give him $10,000 for an endorsement of its soups.

DiMaggio had started his streak against one pitcher named Smith, Edgar, and now he was facing another Smith, this one named Al, a left-hander. In the first inning DiMaggio turned on an inside pitch and lined it down the third base line. Ken Keltner, the Cleveland third baseman and an excellent fielder, moved with the crack of the bat, stopped the ball on his backhand, and fired to first base to get DiMaggio. On his next at bat, in the fourth, DiMaggio received a base on balls. Then, in the seventh, DiMaggio once again smashed a ground ball to third base. Once again, though, Keltner scooped up the ball cleanly and threw DiMaggio out at first base on a very close play. DiMaggio came to bat again in the top of the eighth, this time against Jim Bagby. The Yankees were leading the Indians 4–1, and the crowd was practically breathless, realizing that "the Streak" was there on the line.

On a two-balls, one-strike pitch, DiMaggio hit a hard ground ball that at the crack of the bat seemed destined to end up in center field for a single. But Lou Boudreau, who as a fielder relied not on swiftness but on positioning, got a great jump on the ball, picked it cleanly, and turned it into an inning-ending double play.

After 56 games—after 91 hits in 223 at bats for a .408 average, after 55 RBIs, after 15 home runs, 4 triples, 16 doubles and 56 singles, after 21 bases on balls, 7 strikeouts and two hit-by-pitches—"the Streak" was over. As for the $10,000, it was no soup.

The Yankee Clipper, Joe DiMaggio, rounds first base on his way to the double that tied George Sisler's record for hits in 41 consecutive games. Ted Williams lauded Joltin' Joe's ultimate 56-game streak with the phrase, "It may be the greatest batting achievement of them all." The record still stands.

27

TEDDY BALLGAME DID IT HIS WAY

On a cool day in Philadelphia, Ted Williams becomes, as they call him today, the 'last of the .400 hitters'

Theodore Samuel Williams was his name, but most people called him "Ted." Some called him "Terrible Ted." Some called him "the Kid." Some called him "the Splendid Splinter." Some called him "Lefty." Some called him "Number 9," which was his uniform number with the Boston Red Sox. Some called him "Teddy Ballgame." And some called him names that cannot be printed. You could call him Ted or you could call him anything else, but by any name Ted Williams rates as one of the three or four best pure hitters ever to play the game of baseball.

Williams had the purest of swings, one that youngsters and, indeed, oldsters have long attempted but failed to duplicate, and he had eyes that never betrayed him when he was at the plate. If the Splendid Splinter passed on a pitch because he judged it to be a silly millimeter off the corner of the plate, the umpire would al-

most automatically call the pitch a ball. And he was a proud hitter, too, one so stubborn that it probably cost him a couple of batting championships—he won a total of six, as it was—during his career. Williams joined the Red Sox in 1939 and retired in 1960, but during that time he also missed the equivalent of almost six baseball seasons because of his military commitments during World War II and the Korean War.

Williams was a natural pull hitter who, with a snap of his powerful wrists, would rifle shots over, under, through, and around the first and second baseman; or slam drives between the right fielder and the foul line, the right fielder and the center fielder; or power the ball over the fence—he hit 521 home runs in his career. He challenged the pitcher mano-a-mano; he was not a Punch-and-Judy hitter who would hit the outside pitch to the opposite field or try to fool the defense with a

bunt. No, sir, Teddy Ballgame came to play.

And so it was one day after World War II that Lou Boudreau, the crafty player-manager of the Cleveland Indians, devised what immediately became known as "the Williams Shift," because, after all, it was used against only one hitter—Ted Williams. Boudreau, who played shortstop, watched Williams rake Cleveland pitchers for several hits in the first game of a double-header in the 1946 season. Between games he told his Indians that in the second game they would defense Williams differently: the first baseman would hug the line, the second baseman would play midway between first and second, the shortstop would play to the right, not left, of second base, and the third baseman would play in about the shortstop's normal position. As for the outfielders, the right fielder would shade the line, the center fielder would play well over in right center, and the left fielder would move well over toward left center.

"When I came to bat," Williams said, "it seemed that everyone was over on the right side. I said, 'What the hell is this? Boudreau's trying to make a joke of the game.'" The Williams Shift was no joke, though, and Williams lost a couple of seemingly routine base hits in that second game because the ball suddenly was fielded by an Indian who would not have been there if not for Boudreau's shrewd shift. Other American League teams immediately picked up on the Shift, and soon Williams was facing it every time he came to bat. Today Williams likes to insist that he regularly beat the Shift by hitting balls to the vacant areas on the left side of the diamond, but those who watched him and remember him maintain that it was on the rarest of occasions that the Splendid Splinter would honor the Shift by hitting to left field.

There was no such thing as a Williams Shift in use during the 1941 season, though, and pitcher after pitcher after pitcher paid dearly for it. By baseball standards, one would have to say that 1941 was a very good year. Joe DiMaggio compiled his record 56-game hitting streak, Lefty Grove became the sixth pitcher in history to win at least 300 games, and Ted Williams— the Splendid Splinter at his best—became the first player since 1930 to hit .400, finishing the season with an average of .406. No player has hit .400 since then.

It is difficult to compare a .400 batting average with any other statistic in sports, because, as Williams likes to say, "The hardest thing in all sports is to hit a round object with a round bat, which is the name of the game in baseball." The fact that no player since Williams in 1941 has hit .400 should attest to its difficulty.

Indeed, the players today use livelier bats, hit livelier baseballs, play under conditions—lightning-quick synthetic surfaces, etc.—that favor hitters and are physically more fit than their predecessors, but only a handful has made a serious challenge at .400. One of the funny things of any baseball season is the first mention of the fact that some hitter is "ahead" of Williams's pace when he hit .406; in fact, that usually happens in early June, and by the time summer is out, that same hitter is struggling to keep his average over .300.

Williams started that 1941 season somewhat slowly, spending the first few weeks on the bench, his participation limited to the role of pinch hitter, because of a severe ankle injury incurred during spring training. The sore ankle prevented Williams from running and also from playing in left field, but it didn't keep him from standing at the plate. Each day he would hit for almost an hour against Red Sox pitchers, particularly Joe Dobson, trying to get their work in while awaiting a future start.

By the middle of June, Williams was hitting .436, but not many people were paying much attention to the

OPPOSITE: *Ted Williams blasts the 499th homer of the 521 in his career. Williams' devastating pull hitting caused Lou Boudreau of Cleveland to invent the "Williams Shift" as a countermeasure.* ABOVE: *Ted Williams, whose eagle eye was legendary, was the last hitter in baseball with a .400 average.*

29

feats of the Splendid Splinter. The eyes of the nation were on Joe DiMaggio, who had started his record 56-game hitting streak back on May 15 and would continue his at-least-a-hit-a-game pace until the middle of July. In fact, the first real notice that Williams attracted came in the All-Star Game at Detroit, where he hit a prodigious home run to lead the American League to victory.

The heat and humidity of summer took its expected toll on Williams, however, and at the end of August he was hitting only .402. DiMaggio's streak was over, in the record books, and now it was Ted's time. Fans everywhere suddenly warmed to him after treating him mainly with boos ever since he came up to the major leagues in 1939; DiMaggio was an idol, Williams was an enigma.

Once into September, the summer heat began to give way to the coolness and crispness of early fall, and Williams returned to the offensive. In one game he rapped three straight hits against the Yankees, and when an exasperated Lefty Grove gave Williams absolutely nothing to hit on his fourth time at bat and walked him, the crowd in Yankee Stadium booed the Yankee pitcher. The last American Leaguer to hit better than .400 had been Harry Heilmann, who finished the 1923 season with an average of .403. Heilmann was a

A young Ted Williams raps out a triple for the Red Sox in 1941. While Joe DiMaggio was putting together a 56-game hitting streak, Ted was on his way to a .406 season for the Red Sox. Williams left baseball to serve in World War II and in the Korean War.

radio broadcaster for the Tigers in 1941, and when Williams came to Detroit on the Red Sox's last western swing, Heilmann took him aside for some avuncular advice. "Listen, kid," Heilmann said, "hit your pitch and you can do it." By mid-September Williams's average was at .413, but then he went into a slight slump and on the eve of the last day of the season his average was at .3996.

Rounded off, that .3996 would have become a .400 in the record books, since baseball averages are carried to only three decimal places. The Red Sox were scheduled to conclude the schedule with a double-header against the Athletics in Philadelphia, and the night before the games Boston manager Joe Cronin asked Williams, "Do you want to play tomorrow or do you want to sit it out? It's up to you." The Splendid Splinter wasted not even a second before he gave the manager his reply. "I'll play. I never want anybody to say that I got in the back door." Later that night Williams, obviously on edge, walked through the deserted streets of Philadelphia with Johnny Orlando, the Red Sox equipment manager and one of his best friends. They covered some 10 miles, with Williams stopping on a few occasions for a chocolate milk shake.

It was a nasty Sunday afternoon in Philadelphia, but more than 10,000 braved the cold and rain to watch Williams make his final assault on .400. In his first at bat in the opening game, Williams lined a single to right field against Dick Fowler. Philadelphia manager Connie Mack had told his players not to let up on Williams, but no one had told Williams to let up on the Athletics. In his next turn at bat Williams blasted a home run off Fowler. For his third at bat Williams got to face a new pitcher, left-hander Porter Vaughan. But Vaughan was no more of a mystery than Fowler had been, and Williams got his third straight hit by singling up the middle. Williams made it four hits in four at bats with another single, then reached base on an error his last time at bat. At the end of the first game his average was at .404.

Cronin asked Williams if he wanted to sit out the second game. Ted's cherished .400 was secure, but still he wouldn't take a seat. He played that second game and got two hits in three at bats, giving him six hits in eight at bats for the day and pushing his final average to .406. Williams's sixth and last hit was one for the memory books: a smash that clanked against the horns above the right field fence, the impact of the ball cracking one of the horns. Even today Ted Williams will tell you it was probably the hardest ball he ever hit.

Yes, Teddy Ballgame was some hitter.

THANKS, JACKIE

Jackie Robinson, a legend in his time, cracks baseball's color barrier in 1947 . . . and it isn't easy

"Every time I look in my pocketbook, I think of Jackie Robinson."

— *Willie Mays*

Jackie Robinson had been a brilliant running back at UCLA. He had been a United States military officer during World War II. And he had been the batting champion of the International League, baseball's top minor classification, in 1946 while playing for the Montreal Royals, a farm team of the Brooklyn Dodgers. But now, in the early spring of 1947, it was obvious that none of his previous accomplishments in life would be much help to 28-year-old Jackie Robinson. He was on the roster of the Dodgers, and barring a calamity, he would soon become the first black ever to play in the major leagues—to crack the color barrier, as they said in those days—but Jackie Robinson was living in an isolation booth.

While all the other Dodger major leaguers were ensconced in the lap of luxury in a four-star Havana hotel that spring, Robinson, along with two other blacks, minor-league prospects Roy Campanella and Don Newcombe, resided in a fourth-rate hotel on the outskirts of the city—an outcast from his teammates. Many of the Dodger regulars did not want Robinson for a teammate, something they made quite clear to owner Branch Rickey.

Hard-hitting outfielder Dixie Walker, a southerner, wrote to Rickey before spring training and asked to be traded, indicating that he could not play on the same team with Robinson. Rickey promptly granted Walker his wish and dispatched him to lowly Pittsburgh; later, Rickey said that Walker's actions cost him the Dodger manager's job when it became open in 1948.

Several other southerners also officially protested Robinson's appearance on the roster, and Rickey called all of them into his office. In blunt words, Rickey told the players that he didn't care about the color of a man's skin. If that man could go farther to his right and farther to his left than someone else, he was going to play. And no one was ever going to tell Branch Rickey who could play.

Among Dodger personnel, the anti-Robinson protest movement also spread to relatives of the players. Pee Wee Reese was a Kentuckian, from Louisville, and

the star shortstop of the Dodgers in those days; in fact, he would quickly become one of Robinson's allies. But Reese's sisters apparently wrote to Rickey and requested that he trade their brother because they didn't want him playing on a team with Jackie Robinson. Rickey laughed it off.

Robinson had a good spring training with the Dodgers and was in their regular lineup, at first base, as they barnstormed north to open the 1947 season. But he could not escape the racism, or the isolation. In most towns he had to eat apart from his teammates and stay in separate quarters. Once, in Atlanta, Robinson stepped onto an elevator with a couple of other Dodgers and suddenly the elevator operator said, "This thing just went out of order, and it's going to stay out of order as long as he is on it." Robinson walked the four flights of stairs to his room.

Jackie Robinson, the man who smashed big league baseball's "color barrier," as he looked in 1947. Robinson was voted Rookie of the Year that year in the National League, and went on to win the league batting title two years later with a .342 average.

The Dodgers opened the regular schedule on April 16 with a game against the Boston Braves at Ebbets Field in Brooklyn, and history was made as Robinson started at first base; he later would move to second base and remain there for most of his career. Johnny Sain, a crafty right hander, pitched for Boston, and when Robinson came to bat in the bottom of the first inning, Sain got him to ground out third base to first. In the third inning Robinson skied to the left fielder, and in the fifth inning he hit into a shortstop-to-second-to-first double play. In the seventh Robinson executed a successful sacrifice bunt and reached base safely himself when the Boston first baseman mishandled the ball. So, for the day, Robinson officially went 0-for-3. "All I saw from Sain was curve balls—curves of different sizes, shapes and speeds," Robinson said after the game. "I never saw curve balls like the ones he was throwing."

The next day Jackie got his first major-league hit, a bunt single against Boston's Glenn Elliott, and in his third game he hit his first home run against Dave Koslo of the hated New York Giants. Jackie Robinson was here to stay.

Robinson's debut was, on the whole, well received by the people of New York, with the cheers drowning out the boos. But it was another matter when the

ABOVE: *Robinson began his career with the Brooklyn Dodgers at first base, but soon became a permanent fixture at second.*
OPPOSITE: *Robinson steals second in the 3rd game of the 1947 World Series against the Yankees. Rizutto missed the ball, but Stirnweiss backed up the play and Jackie was tagged out.*

Dodgers went on the road. When the Brooklyn team went to Cincinnati, Robinson received three letters containing threats on his life. The hotel in which the Dodgers had stayed for years in St. Louis suddenly said there was no room for the team if Robinson tried to register. The St. Louis players even threatened to pull a collective no-show, a strike, if Robinson appeared on the field with the rest of the Dodgers. Baseball Commissioner Ford Frick responded immediately to the strike threat of the Cardinal players by announcing he would suspend for life any player who refused to play in a game against Jackie Robinson.

Before the Dodgers' first trip to Philadelphia, the owner of the Phillies called Rickey and pleaded, "Don't bring Robinson here, Branch. We're not ready for it yet in Philadelphia, and we might have a riot. We just won't take the field if you play Robinson against us."

Rickey, as always, had the perfect squelch.

"It's fine with me if your team won't take the field. We'll just take the forfeit."

When the Dodgers arrived in Philadelphia, though, they were barred from their hotel of long standing. They finally found lodging, but when they took the field at Shibe Park, Robinson was subjected to the worst harassment he had ever received. Philadelphia Manager Ben Chapman, a legendary bench jockey, kept chattering away at Robinson on the field, suggesting that he ought to "go back and pick cotton" and that he ought to rejoin "the monkeys in the jungle." The word Robinson heard most in Philadelphia and most other cities was "nigger"; it followed him everywhere.

As the taunts and the racial slurs continued, rival players developed a new form of harassment for Robinson: the beanball. Indeed, Robinson was getting it from every direction. "What Jackie Robinson had to put up with was unbelievable," said one Dodger. "Most people would have cracked, but Jackie kept pretty good check on himself." In time, the vicious anti-Robinson, anti-black tactics began to turn the stomachs of the other Dodgers. One day early in the season Pee Wee Reese, the Kentuckian, decided he had had enough. When some rival players began to taunt Robinson with some racial slurs, Reese walked over, put his hand on Robinson's shoulder and said, "This is my teammate, whether you like it or not."

What also irritated Robinson's opponents was the way in which he played the game. Robinson performed only one way: hard. All the time. He was aggressive at the plate. He stole bases. He stole home plate. He was fiery on the field, in the dugout, in the locker room. He was a winner. When Robinson would steal a base and take out the second baseman, knocking him head over heels in the process, rival managers or players would say that he was bush. Robinson laughed at the charge, which he heard almost daily. "For forty years players have done what I'm doing and it's been called smart baseball," he said. "Now I do it . . . and it's bush."

Robinson also refused to tolerate beanball pitchers. When Sal Maglie knocked Robinson down or hit him with a pitch, Robinson would subsequently bunt the ball down the first base line so the pitcher would have to field it. Then there would be the ultimate collision between the full-speed-ahead Robinson and the pitcher. Score one for Jackie.

Joe Garagiola, the baseball telecaster, was a catcher for several National League teams during Robinson's years with the Dodgers, and he still remembers how Robinson played havoc with Dodger opponents. "Before each game we used to have a meeting to discuss the other team," Garagiola said. "Well, when we'd play the Dodgers, the manager would say, 'When Robinson's on first base we gotta keep him close because he'll steal second. When Robinson's on second base we gotta keep him close because he'll steal third. And when Robinson's on third base we gotta keep him close because he'll even try to steal home plate.' " Garagiola laughed for a moment. "When you went over one player base by base," he said, "you knew he was trouble."

Although he had to fight as many battles off the field as on, Robinson hit .297 in 1947 and was voted the

National League's rookie of the year. He won the league batting championship two years later, hitting .342. Over his 10 years with the Dodgers, Robinson stole 197 bases, including home plate 20 times, and had a career batting average of .311. Six times he was named to the National League All-Star team. Better still, Robinson's Dodger teams won the pennant six times in 10 years. Oh, yes, one other statistic: during his career Robinson was hit by pitches some 70 times.

Before the 1957 season the Dodgers traded Robinson, then 38, to the New York Giants. But as much as he was perhaps the biggest giant of them all, Jackie Robinson could never be a New York Giant, and he announced his retirement. By then almost every team in baseball had at least one black on its roster, and most major-league teams were scouting and signing black players by the dozen.

Five years later, in 1962, Jackie Robinson, the man who had broken baseball's color barrier, a man of dignity, was eligible for election to baseball's Hall of Fame. He made it. Easy. Unfortunately, that was about the only thing that had been easy for Jackie Robinson in his baseball career. Jackie died in 1972, but his memory will always live on. Someday, maybe Dave Winfield, the outfielder who in 1981 signed a $1.5 million per-year, ten-year contract with the New York Yankees—or exactly $1.475 million more than Jackie Robinson made in any season—will repeat these words of Willie Mays: "Every time I look in my pocketbook, I think of Jackie Robinson."

THE HOME RUN HEARD 'ROUND THE BOROUGHS

*Bobby Thomson's incredible home run in the bottom of the 9th inning of the third-and-final
playoff game caps the Giants' amazing comeback and gives them the National League pennant over the hated Dodgers*

ABOVE: *A sequence showing Bobby Thomson heading for home
plate after his pennant-winning home run for the 1951 New
York Giants. Leo Durocher, Giant manager, cavorts on the
sidelines as Dodger 3rd baseman Cox is frozen in dejection.*
OPPOSITE: *Thomson is welcomed home by the jubilant Giants.*

Leo "the Lip" Durocher, the king of the second
guessers, generally has been acknowledged as the individual who first uttered the remark "Nice guys finish
last." As a ballplayer, Leo was more of a pest than a
star; he survived mainly on guts, guile, and chatter,
along with a realization of what his place really was,
and as a result he enjoyed a productive, if not a Hall of
Fame, career. Durocher was one of those players, too, of
whom it was always said, "Someday he'll make a good
manager."

Sure enough, Durocher did indeed become a
major-league manager. If not a great manager, he was a
good one, always outspoken and controversial and second guessing everyone in sight. Durocher managed the
Brooklyn Dodgers from 1939 to 1946, winning the National League pennant in 1941, and also for a time in
1948. He later took over as manager of the New York
Giants in 1948—going from manager of the Dodgers to
manager of the Giants was a trick worthy of Houdini;
indeed, the Dodgers and the Giants were always at war
with each other—and remained with them through the
1955 season, winning two pennants and the 1954 World
Series. Leo later turned to broadcasting baseball games
on television, and that enabled him to manage not one
but two teams each game from his second-guessing seat
in the press box. In 1966 Durocher came out of retirement to manage the stumblebum Chicago Cubs, and he
nearly won the pennant for them in 1969; unfortunately, in keeping with their tradition, the Cubs collapsed in September that season. He left the Cubs in
1972 and finished that year as manager of the Houston
Astros. In all, he managed for 23 seasons.

For Durocher, though, no season produced as many
thrills, as many upsets, as many great moments, as many
nervous attacks as did 1951, when he was managing the
New York Giants. Philadelphia's Whiz Kids had stunned
the baseball world by winning the 1950 National
League pennant, but everyone expected that order
would be restored in 1951 and that the Giants and the
hated Dodgers would battle it out for first place. On
paper, the Dodgers had a pat and powerful lineup, fea-
turing Jackie Robinson, Gil Hodges, Roy Campanella,
Duke Snider, Carl Furillo, Peewee Reese, and Don
Newcombe, and were clearly stronger than the Giants,

who listed Wes Westrum, Sal Maglie, Bobby Thomson, Don Mueller, and the double-play combination of Alvin Dark and Eddie Stanky as their main men. But the Giants had Durocher, and every Dodger knew that Leo the Lip would be worth a couple of victories himself during the 154-game season.

Nothing went right for Leo and the Giants at the start of the schedule. While the Dodgers rolled up one-sided wins practically every day, the Giants were losing 11 straight games in April and falling well back into the pack. Many of the Polo Grounds regulars were already writing the season off, believing there was no way their Jints could ever catch Dem Bums from Brooklyn. The Giants continued to swoon in May, playing lackluster ball, and even Durocher seemed incapable of arousing them from their lethargy. Then, on May 24, the Giants made a move that was very unpopular in Minneapolis when they recalled a 19-year-old center fielder by the name of Willie Mays from their farm team in that city. Mays was hitting a powerful .477 for Minneapolis and luring large crowds to home games, and when Giants' owner Horace Stoneham announced that he was bringing Mays to New York, howls of protest were heard in Minneapolis. Indeed, Stoneham had to take out large ads in the Minneapolis-area papers explaining his decision to recall Mays.

Durocher immediately inserted Mays into the lineup in center field, but the youngster from Alabama broke in not with a bang but a whimper, getting only one hit in his first 26 at bats against major-league pitching. Back in Minneapolis the fans were hoping, in fact praying, that the Giants would return the young phenom for more seasoning. In New York, though, the Giants had no such plans.

While Mays was not exactly wowing people with his hitting, he had everyone cheering his fielding, which bordered on the sensational. In one game he put on his jets to track down a fly ball, and while running after it he lost his cap. Without breaking his stride, Mays reached out and caught his hat with his right hand while almost simultaneously catching the ball with the glove on his left hand. After watching Mays for several weeks, Leo the Lip uttered another famous Durocherism, "I wouldn't trade Willie Mays for anyone, and that includes DiMaggio, Williams, Musial, Robinson, Snider, you name it."

Late in May the Giants finally reached the .500 mark, but the Dodgers were still very much in a league of their own. June and July passed somewhat uneventfully, and early in August even the most rabid Giant rooter was all but ready to concede the pennant: on August 11 the Giants were in second place, but they were 13½ games behind Dem Bums.

Not many people in New York will ever forget what happened over the next seven weeks; on the other hand, not many people in Brooklyn want to be reminded of it.

Starting on August 11 the Giants launched a 16-game winning streak, including a three-game sweep of the Dodgers, and on September 11—exactly a month later—they found themselves just 5½ games behind the Dodgers. Then the Giants and the Dodgers both took extended train trips to the west—Cincinnati, Chicago, and St. Louis being the wild west in those days—and when they returned home nine games later, the Brooklyn lead was down to 4½ games. Then, with seven games to play, the Dodgers led the Giants by six games in what they call the all-important loss column.

The Dodgers split a series against Philadelphia, winning one and losing one. Meanwhile, the Giants swept a three-game series from the Boston Braves. The Dodger lead was only 2½ games. On Tuesday, September 25, the Giants—with all New York watching—cut the Dodger lead to a single game by beating the Phillies 5–1 while the Braves, thanks to the pitching of Warren Spahn and Jim Wilson, were taking both ends of a double-header from the Dodgers, 6–3 and 14–2. Yes, there was not much doubt about it: the Dodgers were choking.

The Giants and the Dodgers both won their games the following day, but on Thursday the Braves beat the Dodgers 4–3 with a stormy finish at Boston; the Dodgers protested the Braves' winning run in the eighth inning so vehemently that Roy Campanella, Jackie Robinson, and Preacher Roe all were fined for their volatile outbursts. Whatever, the Dodgers led the Giants by a mere ½ game.

The Giants had another off-day on Friday, but the Dodgers had to play the Phillies at Shibe Park in Philadelphia. Brooklyn squandered an early lead in that game, and in the bottom of the ninth Phillies catcher Andy Seminick fired the shot that was heard all the way back in New York; he crashed a bases-empty home run to give the Phillies a 4–3 win and the idle Giants a tie for first place. That once seemingly unassailable 13½-game lead had been wiped out.

Still, there were two games to play. On Saturday, Sal ("the Barber") Maglie and Don Newcombe both pitched shutouts, Maglie 3–0 over the Braves and Newcombe 5–0 over the Phillies. On Sunday Larry Jansen five-hit the Braves as the Giants won 3–2, and then everyone looked to Philadelphia where the Phillies were routing the Dodgers. The score was 6–1 for Philadelphia after three innings and 8–5 for Philadelphia after five, but the Dodgers scored three times in the eighth inning and the game went into extra innings.

In the Phillies' twelfth Jackie Robinson saved Brooklyn with a tremendous catch of a ball hit by Eddie Waitkus, but he momentarily KO'd himself in the process. Robinson stayed in the game, and in the fourteenth inning he cracked a home run off Robin Roberts to give the Dodgers a 9–8 victory and force a best-of-three games playoff for the pennant against the Giants. The winner would then get to play the Yankees in the World Series.

Game one of the playoff at Ebbets Field was a home-run battle, with Andy Pafko's homer giving the Dodgers a 1–0 lead that Bobby Thomson of the Giants wiped out with a two-run homer. Monte Irvin later hit another homer, a bases-empty shot, and the Giants won 3–1. The next day, though, the Dodgers' Clem Labine quieted the Polo Grounds by pitching a shutout as Dem Bums, getting home runs from Robinson, Pafko, Gil Hodges, and Rube Walker, romped to a 10–0 victory and tied the playoff.

For game three, it was Sal Maglie for the Giants against Don Newcombe of the Dodgers in a battle of pitching aces before 34,320 at the Polo Grounds. The Dodgers took an early lead of 1–0 on Robinson's single in the second, and Newcombe kept the Giants in check until the seventh when Thomson, who had hit the decisive home run in game one, tied the score with a sacrifice fly. Then, in the eighth, the Dodgers went ahead 4–1, scoring three runs on a wild pitch and singles by Pafko and Billy Cox.

Now, in the bottom of the ninth, Leo the Lip and the Giants were down to their last three outs. Al Dark, the shortstop, led off with an off-field single to right, and Don Mueller doubled to right, sending Dark to third. Newcombe, sweating profusely, got Monte Irvin on a foul pop to the catcher, but Whitey Lockman doubled home a run to make the score 4–2. That was all for Newcombe. The new Dodger pitcher was Ralph Branca.

Branca's first pitch to Thomson was a fast ball that hummed across the middle of the plate for a strike. His second pitch to Thomson was another fast ball that also hummed across the middle of the plate. Thomson swung from his heels and made perfect contact, launching the ball into an orbit toward left field. As the crowd went bonkers it landed in the bottom deck of the left-field stands for a three-run homer—and the Giants, miracle of miracles, had won the pennant.

Forever etched in the memory of millions of New Yorkers will be the sight of Leo the Lip jumping into the arms of Eddie "the Brat" Stanky as Thomson made his triumphant journey around the bases before being swamped under by teammates and fans when he finally reached home plate. The Giants went on to lose the World Series to the Yankees, but to tell the truth not many people really cared. Or as they said, "This was the year when the pennant was bigger than the World Series."

Bobby Thomson has the biggest smile of all as he steps on home plate. His home run came in the 9th inning of the final playoff game between the Giants and the Dodgers, held at the Polo Grounds on Oct. 3, 1951. Brooklyn led 4–2 until Thomson's 3-run homer.

DEM BUMS ARE DEM CHAMPS

The Dodgers were zero-for-history in the World Series until a 1955 day at Yankee Stadium when Johnny Podres'
masterful pitching and Sandy Amoros' stunning catch in left field end the misery for Brooklyn

During the postwar 1940s and the early 1950s thousands—indeed, hundreds of thousands—of young New Yorkers grew up listening to "the Ol' Redhead" describe the doings of Dem Bums, the Brooklyn Dodgers, from his perch in the catbird seat at Ebbets Field or some enemy ballyard. "Let me set the Dodgers for you defensively," Red Barber would intone as the Dodgers took the field. "At first base, number fourteen, Gil Hodges. At second base the incomparable Jackie Robinson. At shortstop, the Louisville colonel, Mr. Peewee Reese. And at third base the flawless-fielding Billy Cox. Carl Furillo, the Reading Rifle, in right field. Duke Snider, number ten on the all-time homer list, in center. And young Gene Hermanski in left. Campy behind the plate . . . and Big Newk on the mound." When you were young, and a Dodger fan, or even when you were old and a Dodger fan, your day or night was made when you tuned in the Ol' Redhead.

And the Dodgers in those days were some powerhouse. They won the National League pennant in 1947, 1949, 1952, and 1953, and as anyone who has ever been to Brooklyn well knows, the Dodgers also tied for the pennant in 1951 but then lost a playoff to the hated New York Giants on Bobby Thomson's memorable home run off Ralph Branca. But every time those Dodgers won the pennant, they lost the World Series— and always to that other team people from Brooklyn hated so passionately, the New York Yankees. In fact, through that 1953 season the Dodgers had participated in seven World Series and lost all seven, including five to the miserable Yankees.

Certainly, these modern-day Yankees—that is, of the late 1940s and early 1950s—seemed to have a hex on Dem Bums, as the Flatbush faithful liked to call their Dodgers. In the 1947 Series the Dodgers and the Yankees split the first six games but the Yankees won the deciding seventh game by a 5–2 score at Yankee Stadium. The next time they met, in 1949, the Yankees routed the Dodgers four games to one. In 1952 the Dodgers won the pennant, somehow blotting out the memory of the tragic 1951 collapse that saw them blow a 13½-game lead to the Giants and lose the pennant playoff, and for a time it appeared that they finally

The sequence shows the Brooklyn Dodgers' Johnny Podres pitching against the Yankees in the final game of the 1955 World Series. Podres, who had just turned 23, had been the winning pitcher in Game 3, and went on to win Game 7 and the Series.

would win the World Series. The Dodgers took a three games to two lead back to Ebbets Field, but the Yankees won game six by a 3–2 score and then took the Series with a 4–2 victory in game seven. Then the next season, the Yankees won the Series from the Dodgers four games to two, and that old Brooklyn refrain of "Wait 'Til Next Year" was being sung all over Flatbush.

Neither the Dodgers nor the Yankees won a pennant in 1954, but they both were back on top of their respective leagues in 1955 and once again met in the World Series. For the Dodgers, this would probably be their last fling together; age was setting in, and management was ready to install a youth movement. Billy Cox already had been discarded; Jackie Robinson no longer was Jackie Robinson four times a game anymore; Preacher Roe had retired; and Pee Wee Reese was preparing young Don Zimmer for the day, not too far off, when Reese would be retiring to Kentucky.

Sure enough, in game one at Yankee Stadium it was the same old story for the Dodgers. Brooklyn manager Walter Alston, making his Series debut, started his ace right-hander, Don Newcombe, who had finished the season with a 20–5 record; New York manager Casey Stengel pitched his ace left-hander, Whitey Ford. The Dodgers jumped on Ford for two runs in the top of the second, but the Yankees responded immediately with two runs in the bottom of the second on a home run by Elston Howard, the first black player ever to wear a Yankee uniform in the Series. The Dodgers scored another run in the third, but so did the Yankees. Then it became the Joe Collins show as the left-handed Yankee slugger smashed one home run in the fourth and another in the sixth to give the Yankees a 6–3 lead. Duke Snider and Carl Furillo answered with two home runs for the Dodgers, but both came with the bases empty—and the Yankees won the game 6–5. The next afternoon they took a two-game lead in the series when Tommy Byrne, like Ford a crafty left-hander, outpitched Billy Loes. Not only were the Yankees two games up, they also had won both games without the benefit of Mickey Mantle's bat; the young outfielder from Oklahoma had suffered a leg injury and would appear in only three Series games, two as a regular and one as a pinch hitter, and get just two hits in 10 at bats.

For game three the subway went to Brooklyn, not the Bronx, and Alston had a surprise for the Yankees: the Dodger starter would be a young left-hander named Johnny Podres, whose record that season had been an undistinguished 9 wins and 10 losses. Podres, in fact, had not completed a start in almost three months. But it was

Podres's twenty-third birthday, something Alston apparently had discovered when he heard some of the Dodgers serenading Podres in the locker room, and Alston was desperately looking for something—anything—to ignite his Dodgers. Maybe the birthday boy would pitch the game of his life. Which, as it turned out, he did. Podres stopped the Yankees on seven hits and the Dodger bats rapped Yankee pitchers for eight runs in an 8–3 victory. Dem Bums weren't dead yet.

The next day Roy Campanella, Duke Snider, and Gil Hodges all hit home runs as the Dodgers tied the series at two games apiece with an 8–5 romp, and the day after that Snider hit two home runs, Sandy Amoros hit one, and the Dodgers won 5–3, with Roger Craig and Clem Labine pitching effectively. Suddenly, the Dodgers were only one victory away from their first World Series championship. Of course, they had been in the very same position just three years before, and as people kept reminding them, they had blown it.

That may well have been on the minds of the Dodgers during game six at Yankee Stadium as the Yankees routed them 6–1 to tie the Series at three games apiece.

There were 62,465 people in Yankee Stadium for game seven on October 4, and the great majority of them probably still don't believe what they saw. First of all, Alston bypassed his ace, Newcombe, who was well rested, and pitched Podres, and this time it was not Podres's birthday. Alston's thinking was sound. Newcombe was a right-hander and the Yankees' left-handed sluggers—Mantle, Berra, Collins, and friends—usually feasted on such pitchers because of the short home-run porch in right field. Podres, on the other hand, was a left-hander who kept the ball moving away from left-handed hitters, thus taking away their power. Who cared what right-handed hitters did? The left field and left-center field areas in Yankee Stadium were graveyards for right-handed power hitters, reachable usually only by express train.

Podres immediately established a strong command over the Yankee bats. Meanwhile, in the top of the fourth inning, Gil Hodges gave the Dodgers a 1–0 lead when he singled home Roy Campanella, who had doubled to left field. Then, in the sixth, Hodges put the Dodgers ahead 2–0 with a sacrifice fly to center field that scored Pee Wee Reese, who had singled to open the inning. Still, a two-run lead was not much against the mighty Yankees.

As the Dodgers trotted onto the field for the bottom of the sixth, Alston craftily made a couple of defen-

sive changes, moving Junior Gilliam from left field to second base and replacing him in left with Sandy Amoros, who would have to play the toughest sun field in baseball. And now the Yankees launched their first—and only, as it turned out—serious threat, putting runners on first and second with only one out. Yogi Berra, one of the greatest clutch hitters of all time, was at bat.

Podres kept the ball away from Berra, but Berra reached out and drilled a long fly into the left-field corner. Amoros was playing Berra over in left center, and when the ball took off it appeared that it would either drop into the left-field stands for a three-run homer or land in the corner for a two-run double or triple. There was no way that Amoros would ever catch it. No way.

But the young Cuban never stopped charging for the corner, and the ball—luckily for the Dodgers—

seemed to hang in the air endlessly. Then, suddenly, there was Amoros—the glove on his right hand fully extended, his feet moving as fast as they could—reaching out desperately for the ball and grabbing it in the webbing of his glove, just a few feet from the seats. He stopped, pivoted, and fired the ball back to the infield, doubling Gil McDougald off first base. So ended the inning.

Instead of tying the game, or even taking the lead, the Yankees were still trailing 2–0.

And that is how it ended. Podres stifled the mighty Yankees for the last three innings, and when he disposed of the final Yankee, the borough of Brooklyn became the scene of one of the wildest and longest parties on record. For days Dem Bums paraded around Brooklyn in triumph. Yes, at long last Brooklyn owned the world.

Sandy Amaros makes a heroic catch in the last game of the '55 World Series. With Yankees on first and second in the bottom of the 6th, Yogi Berra drove the ball to the left field corner, but somehow Amaros was there, the relay of his throw doubled up McDougald at first, and the Yankee threat evaporated.

39

IT WAS A PERFECT DAY

Don Larsen's baseball career was mediocre at best . . .
in 1956 when he faced 27 Dodger batters in a World Series game except for that October afternoon
and put down all 27 . . . a Perfect Game

"Do you ever get tired of talking about it?"

"No, why should I?"

The "it," of course, is probably the only reason why anyone outside of his immediate circle of family and friends knows of Don Larsen. In 1953 Larsen was a 22-year-old rookie pitcher-outfielder from Michigan City, Indiana, who had the misfortune of performing for baseball's worst team, the St. Louis Browns. Larsen, a right-handed pitcher and hitter, finished that season with a 7–12 record and a .284 batting average. The following season the St. Louis franchise moved to Baltimore, and the Browns became the Orioles. Larsen became strictly a pitcher, and he had a record of 3 wins and 21 losses for the Orioles. Then Larsen got lucky in 1955 when the Orioles included him in a massive 17-player deal they made with the New York Yankees, the perennial American League champions; suddenly Larsen found himself wearing pinstripes. He had a 9–2 record for the Yankees that season, and over the next four seasons his Yankee records were 11–5, 10–4, 9–6 and 6–7. The Yankees won the pennant each of Larsen's first four years in New York, although no one ever said that Larsen won any pennant for them, but they lost the pennant to the Chicago White Sox in 1959 and decided to clean house over the winter. So Larsen was traded to Kansas City, and in 1960 his record was 1–10. He subsequently made pitching stops at Chicago, San Francisco, Houston, Baltimore, and Chicago once again, and in 1967 he retired. His career record was 81 wins and 91 losses, nothing to write home about.

Except for "it." In the 1956 World Series, in game five, played on the afternoon of October 8, Don Larsen, who at the time was known more for his wild living off the field than for anything he had done on it, pitched the first and so far only perfect game in Series history, beating the Brooklyn Dodgers 2–0 before a boisterous crowd of 64,519 at Yankee Stadium. A perfect game: no hits, no runs, no walks, no baserunners, no nothing. Oddly, Larsen pitched his so-called "gem" while using a no-windup pitching technique for only the second or third time in his career. Late in the regular season Larsen became convinced that he was tipping off his pitches to Boston Red Sox third base coach Del Baker,

and thus was born a new delivery—the no-windup motion.

And now, let's go to Yankee Stadium for the play by play.

In the Dodger first, Junior Gilliam led off and took a ball. Oh, well, the crowd probably thought, Larsen was going to be wild today. Then Gilliam bounced a foul ball wide of first base. Larsen missed with the next pitch, but evened the count at two-and-two by getting a called strike. His next pitch caught Gilliam looking for a called strike three. Pee Wee Reese, the Dodger captain and shortstop, was up next and Larsen quickly ran the count on Reese to one ball and two strikes. Then Larsen missed with his next two pitches, running the count full at three-and-two. His next pitch caught Reese looking at a called strike three. Duke Snider, the center fielder, one of baseball's top home-run hitters, was the third batter in the Brooklyn lineup, and on a two-balls, one-strike pitch Snider flied out to Hank Bauer. No hits, no runs, no Yankee errors.

In the Dodger second, Jackie Robinson, with a count of one strike, hit a shot off the glove of third baseman Andy Carey, and for a moment everyone in the park thought Robinson had a hit. But the ball caromed directly to Yankee shortstop Gil McDougald, and McDougald's throw to first nailed Robinson by a flash. One out. Larsen then struck out Gil Hodges on a bad pitch, a curve that was well outside. Then Larsen had his second great escape of the inning. Sandy Amoros, one of the heroes of Brooklyn's 1955 World Series win over the Yankees, popped a ball into short right field. It looked like a hit but Yankee second baseman Billy Martin, backpedaling, caught the ball over his head and then fell to the ground. He held the ball. No hits, no runs, no Yankee errors—two very close calls.

In the Dodger third, Larsen didn't waste his time. He got Carl Furillo on a fly ball to Bauer, struck out Roy Campanella swinging, and got his pitching opponent, Sal ("the Barber") Maglie on a liner to Mickey Mantle. No hits, no runs, no Yankee errors.

In the Dodger fourth, Larsen faced the top of the Brooklyn batting order for the second time. Gilliam swung at the first pitch and grounded to Billy Martin, whose throw to Joe Collins at first base beat him by a wide margin. Pee Wee Reese tried to check his swing on Larsen's first pitch but bounced out the same way, Martin to Collins. Larsen then fell behind Snider two balls and no strikes. Not wanting to go deeper into the hole, Larsen threw a fast ball across the plate and Snider ripped it into the seats—foul. Larsen ran the count to two-and-two with a called strike, then Snider hit another foul ball before taking a called third strike. No hits, no runs, no Yankee errors.

In the Dodger fifth, Larsen was now working with a 1–0 lead. On a one-and-two pitch he got Robinson on a long fly to Bauer. On a two-and-two pitch he got Hodges for the second out on an even longer fly to Mantle, who had to make a fine, one-handed running catch in the left-center field alley. Then, on a one-and-one pitch, Amoros hit a shot into the lower deck in right field that Ed Runge, the American League umpire who was working in right field, signaled foul after taking the longest of looks. It could not have been foul by more than a few inches. As the announcers all said, "Baseball is certainly a game of inches." Larsen then got Amoros on a ground ball to Martin, whose throw to Collins at first beat him easily. No hits, no runs, no Yankee errors—three more very close calls.

In the Dodger sixth, Larsen got the first two Dodgers—Furillo and Campanella—on simple pop-ups

to Billy Martin on the outfield grass. He then struck out Maglie on a two-and-two pitch after Maglie twice had fouled off good pitches. No hits, no runs, no Yankee errors.

In the Dodger seventh, Larsen now owned a 2–0 lead as he faced the top of the Brooklyn order for the third time. Gilliam grounded out, McDougald to Collins, then Reese flied out to Mantle in deep center field. Larsen gave Snider nothing good to hit, and the Duke flied out to Enos Slaughter. No hits, no runs, no Yankee errors.

As the Yankees returned to their bench after the Dodgers batted in the seventh, the home crowd stood for the seventh-inning stretch. Those fans who were not aware that they were sitting in on a no-hitter suddenly became quite aware of what was happening. But the television announcer, Vin Scully, maintained the tradition of the sport by refusing to acknowledge that Larsen was working on a no-hitter. All Scully said on the air was this, "Mr. Don Larsen, through seven innings, has retired 21 men in a row." It was supposed to be bad luck to mention "no hitter" over the airwaves. Meanwhile, the Yankee players also were honoring the rules of superstition as they rested on their bench. They sat in the same seat in which they had sat the previous inning; they put their gloves in the same spots they had put them

ABOVE: *Don Larsen, pitching in the top of the eighth inning, Game 5 of the 1956 World Series between the Yankees and the Brooklyn Dodgers.* OPPOSITE: *With Billy Martin playing at second, Larsen delivers a third strike pitch for the last out of a miraculous, unprecedented World Series perfect game.*

Yankee pitcher Don Larsen receives ebullient congratulations from his catcher, Yogi Berra, after Larsen had just completed the only perfect game in World Series history. Larsen won the game 2–0 and the Yankees went on to win the Series in the 7th game. No Series pitcher has matched Larsen's feat.

the previous inning; they didn't say a word to Larsen.

In the Dodger eighth, Jackie Robinson led off and on a two-strike pitch bounced back to the mound, Larsen throwing him out at first base. Hodges was up next, and on a two-and-two pitch the Dodger first baseman hit a shot toward third base that seemed certain to end up in left field for a single. But Andy Carey again made a superb stop, going to his left, intercepting the ball, and rifling it to Collins at first in time to beat Hodges. Amoros, an old Yankee tormenter, was next, and he flied deep to right center but Mantle tracked the ball down and made the catch. No hits, no runs, no Yankee errors—one more close call.

The tension was unbelievable as Larsen walked to the mound for the Dodger ninth. Larsen said later that a perfect game was not "first place in my thoughts. I was after the game first, and anything else I could get after that. The series was tied at two games apiece. We had to win."

Carl Furillo led off for the Dodgers. He fouled off the first pitch, fouled off the second, then took a pitch that was too high before fouling off two more pitches. With a one-and-two count, Larsen then got Furillo on a fly ball to Bauer. Campanella was next, and after fouling off Larsen's first pitch, he grounded out to Martin at second base. Maglie was scheduled to bat next, but Dodger manager Walter Alston went to his bench for a pinch batter and sent up Dale Mitchell, an experienced left-handed hitter. Larsen's first pitch was a ball, just outside. Mitchell then took a pitch for a strike. He swung and missed at the third pitch, bringing the count to one ball and two strikes. Mitchell then fouled off Larsen's next pitch, the count remaining one ball and two strikes.

Babe Pinelli of the National League was umpiring behind the plate; he had been an arbiter for 22 seasons and would be retiring at the end of the Series. Larsen's one-and-two pitch to Mitchell was on the outside of the plate and the Dodger batter did not offer at it. Pinelli raised his right arm and signaled strike three. Mitchell tried to offer a mild protest, but hitters should never take such a close pitch in such situations. Once Pinelli called strike three, Yankee catcher Yogi Berra raced out to the mound and jumped in Larsen's arms, soon to be followed by the other 23 Yankee players, manager Casey Stengel, and all the coaches. No hits, no runs, no Yankee errors.

"It" was the greatest moment of Larsen's career, and the greatest pitching moment in World Series history. No wonder that Don Larsen doesn't get tired of talking about "it."

THE BUCCOS HAD THE LAST LAUGH

*The Yankees scored more runs and had more hits, but the Pirates won
more games in the 1960 World Series . . . thanks to Bill Mazeroski's last-gasp home run*

Today, the people of Pittsburgh think of their city as a winner's town, and of themselves as winners, and with good reason. The Pittsburgh Pirates won two World Series championships and several National League divisional titles during the 1970s. The Pittsburgh Steelers have dominated the world of professional football, winning the Super Bowl championship in 1975, 1976, 1979, and 1980. And the University of Pittsburgh has resurfaced as a collegiate football power, with the 1976 national championship and several major bowl victories to its credit. As Willie ("Pops") Stargell, the captain and slugger of the Pirates, likes to say, "All we got in Pittsburgh is winners."

Maybe so. But let's go back to 1960, a year when not many people in Pittsburgh even knew how to spell the word "win." The big word in Pittsburgh those days was "lose," something all of the city's sporting representatives did all too often. The Steelers were a ragtag outfit; the Pitt Panthers were pushovers; and the Pirates had not won a National League pennant in 33 years or a World Series championship in 35.

Then, miracle of miracles, the Pirates—rallying behind the daily heroics of shortstop Dick Groat, the batting champion and MVP of the National League, and right fielder Roberto Clemente, the hitter and daredevil extraordinaire—won the 1960 pennant and suddenly found themselves playing in the World Series against those winners of all winners, baseball's reigning dynasty, the New York Yankees. Ironically, the Pirates had last played in the Series in 1927, and their opponents also had been the Yankees. Babe Ruth, Lou Gehrig, and friends won that Series for New York in four straight games, and most baseball people figured that the 1960 Yankees would sweep the Bucs in four straight games, too. "Pittsburgh may even decide to wave the white flag after the third game," crowed one American Leaguer.

But, surprisingly, the supposedly outmanned Pirates got the series jump on the Yankees with a 6–4 victory in game one at old Forbes Field. The highlight of that game was some curious managerial strategy by Casey Stengel, the 70-year-old skipper of the Yankees. In the top of the second inning Stengel stunned everyone by using a pinch hitter for his starting third base-

man, Clete Boyer. When asked later why he had done such a thing, Casey responded in typical Stengelese, "Well, now, you see, my third baseman, he's got a brother who was a pitcher, and he couldn't hit his brother, and I didn't think that because we were in Pittsburgh, with all them television cameras, and, you know, I know that he . . ." Sure, Casey.

The next afternoon form prevailed in game two as the Yankees pounded the ball all over Forbes Field while scoring a 16–3 triumph. Two days later the Series resumed at Yankee Stadium, and the New Yorkers continued their cannonading against Pirate pitching by erupting for six runs in the first inning—four of them coming on a grand-slam home run by little Bobby Rich-

1960 World Series, Pittsburgh Pirates vs. the Yankees, 7th game, bottom of the ninth, score tied at 9–9. Yankee fielder Yogi Berra watches a Bill Mazeroski homer sail over the wall of Pittsburgh's Forbes Field for the Pirate victory.

43

ardson, the second baseman who had hit only one home run during the regular season—and then coasting to an easy 10–0 win. But the next day the Pirates evened the series at two games apiece with a 3–2 win.

Catch these comparative statistics for the first four games: New York won two games by a total of 23 runs; Pittsburgh won two games by a total of 3 runs.

And then, in game five, Pittsburgh beat New York 5–2 and flew home with a three-games-to-two lead in the Series; indeed, the Bucs were only one game away from their first world championship since 1925. Game six was another laugher, with the Yankees—Mickey Mantle, Roger Maris, Yogi Berra, Elston Howard, Bill Skowron, Tony Kubek, Richardson, and friends—running up 12 runs while Whitey Ford held the Pirates scoreless. So, the Yankees had outscored the Pirates 46 runs to 17, but the series was tied at three games apiece.

In the history of baseball, there have not been many games any wackier or wilder than game seven, which was played on October 13. Stengel started his ace right-hander, "Bullet" Bob Turley, and Pittsburgh manager Danny Murtaugh, the smiling Irishman, countered with right-hander Vernon Law. Turley's fast ball was no mystery to the Pirate hitters. In the first inning Glenn ("Rocky") Nelson, who for years had been a legendary minor-league slugger in Montreal, belted a two-run homer for the Pirates, and in the second inning center fielder Bill Virdon, a one-time Yankee prospect who never could beat out Mickey Mantle, singled home two more runs to give the Bucs an early 4–0 lead—and Turley an early shower.

Of course, the Yankees were not dead—yet. Bill Skowron homered for one New York run, and the Yankees busted through for four runs in the sixth inning to

Bill Mazeroski gallops in with the 1960 World Series winning run after slaming a homer for the Pirates in the seventh game against the Yankees. The Yankees had scored 55 runs in the Series, the Pirates 27; and the Yankees out-homered the Pirates 10 to 4, but the shot they remember is Big Bill's.

take a 5–4 lead. Two more runs in the eighth inning put New York ahead 7–4, and the champagne was on ice in the Yankee dressing room. Some of the Pirate fans even began to head for the exits so they could beat the traffic. Still, the Pirates would have at least two more turns at bat.

Gino Cimoli, a career substitute, opened the Pirate eighth with a single against Bobby Shantz, the diminutive and wily left-hander. Shantz featured a sinkerball pitch that batters tended to beat into the ground, and, sure enough, he got Virdon to beat a sinker into the ground to shortstop. It was a tailor-made double play ball, and the pro-Pirate crowd let out a huge groan. Now there was no hope. Tony Kubek, the Yankees' fine-fielding shortstop, moved in front of the ball, ready to initiate the double play. But as Kubek bent over to scoop up Virdon's grounder, the ball took a bad hop in the infield dirt, bounced up, and struck Kubek on the Adam's apple, knocking him to the ground. The ball rolled away and both runners—Cimoli at second, Virdon at first—were safe. Shantz should have found himself in a two-outs, nobody-on-base situation; instead, there were no outs and Pirate runners were on first and second.

Dick Groat was the next Pirate batter, and he rapped the obviously rattled Shantz for a single that scored Cimoli from second base, cutting the Yankees' lead to 7–5. Exit Shantz, who got a pat on the back and a shrug of the shoulders from Stengel, and enter right-hander Jim Coates. Bob Skinner successfully sacrificed Virdon to third and Groat to second, but Coates then managed to retire the next two hitters. For Pittsburgh, it was now all up to Clemente, and he beat out a hit as Virdon scored, further reducing the Yankees' lead to 7–6. The next Pirate hitter was Hal Smith, the backup catcher, who was batting for only the eighth time in the Series, and he stunned the Yankees by walloping a three-run homer over the wall in left field. Now the Pirates led 9–7, and they were only three outs away from a great celebration.

Bobby Richardson opened the Yankees' ninth with a single, and pinch-hitter Dale Long, a former Buc, followed with another single. Harvey Haddix, a crafty left-hander, came on to relieve Bob Friend for the Pirates and he immediately forced Roger Maris to foul out. But Mantle, who enjoyed one of his finest Series with three home runs and a .400 batting average, singled home Richardson, pulling the Yankees to within one run at 9–8. Yogi Berra then lashed a ground ball to first base and Nelson made a spectacular stop, back-handing the ball and rushing to force Berra at first. Nelson then tried to get Mantle for a game-ending double play, but Mickey slid safely back into first while Gil McDougald, running for Long, raced home to tie the score at 9–9.

Stengel had just about run out of pitchers and now had to call on one of his starters, Ralph Terry, to face the Pirates in the bottom of the ninth. Leading off for the Pirates was Bill Mazeroski, the second baseman who was the master of the pivot on the double play; indeed, Mazeroski was said to have the quickest hands of any second baseman in baseball. He had joined the Pirates in the mid-50s, when they were regular losers, and his teammates liked to kid him about the days when he played for the Hollywood Stars, a Pittsburgh farm team, and wore a uniform that featured short pants and knee socks. "You should have stayed in Hollywood and gone right into the movies," the Pirates used to tell Mazeroski. "You could have been a child actor."

Terry's first pitch to Mazeroski was a ball. Terry's second pitch to Mazeroski was down the heart of the plate, a fast ball that had straightened out. Mazeroski had a compact swing, and he took a good rip at Terry's pitch. The ball came off his bat with a crack and kept rising and rising and rising. Out in left field the Yankees' Yogi Berra kept running back and back and back . . . until suddenly he found himself against the wall. Yogi looked up . . . and the ball flew over his head and over the wall. A home run!

Mazeroski, who said he knew the ball was a home run the moment he hit it, doffed his cap when the ball disappeared over the wall and started hopping around the bases. The Pirate bench emptied, fans started to invade the field, and when Mazeroski reached home plate he was swamped by happy Pittsburghers.

The Pirates were the World Champions.

The Yankees had outscored the Pirates 55 runs to 27, outhit them 91 to 60, outhomered them 10 to 4. The Yankees hit .338 as a team, the Pirates hit .256. The Yankees' staff earned-run average was 3.54, the Pirates' was 7.11. "The Yankees set all the records, but we won the most games," Murtaugh crowed. "And since I was a wee lad, they've always paid off on games won—not records."

The biggest loser of all, though, was Casey Stengel. A few days later the Yankee management unceremoniously fired Stengel, who had led the Yankees to victory in seven of ten World Series during his 12 years as New York manager. They said Casey was too old. Bill Mazeroski made him too old.

ROGER AND THE BABE

On the last day of the 1961 season, Roger Maris hits home run No. 61 to break
the Babe's record . . . but all he got for it was an asterisk

In the history of sports, perhaps no great athlete ever enjoyed his success more than Babe Ruth. The Babe owned New York. He was a celebrity. The people never let the Babe forget that he was a celebrity, and the Babe never let the people forget that he was a celebrity. There was always a table—front row center—waiting for him at every nightspot in town. And every restaurant owner worth his prime filet with mushroom caps would conveniently forget to present the Babe and his party with a check for the meal—and then phone the gossip columnists to report that the Babe had just eaten at his place. So popular was the Babe that it used to take him half an hour to cover a single block on Fifth Avenue; the autograph seekers and the hand shakers would be lined up 50 and 60 deep to meet the man who hit a record 60 home runs for the New York Yankees in 1927.

And then there was Roger Maris. Roger hated New York. He was a celebrity, but he refused to play the part. A country boy from Fargo, North Dakota, Maris had enjoyed peace and quiet when he played for Cleveland and Kansas City, but then the Yankees acquired him and all the peace and quiet ended. He played on pennant-winning teams and hit home runs, but he did not celebrate his celebrity in New York. For that matter, he did not celebrate it anywhere. Indeed, Maris was practically a recluse when the Yankees were in New York; he usually shared an apartment with Mickey Mantle but would move to a quiet, out-of-the-way hotel when his wife and family came to visit from their home in the midwest.

But now, as the 1961 season wound down, here was Roger Maris, 26 years old, chasing the Babe's home-run record. Mantle and Maris both had been on a season-long home run binge, and for a time it looked as though both of them would shatter the Babe's record. But with two weeks to play in the season, Mantle, his home run total at 54, was in such terrible pain because of his many injuries—he had chronically bad knees, for one thing—that he went to the bench to rest for the World Series. Maris would chase the Babe alone. And in a swirl of controversy. And before the prying eyes of baseball writers and syndicated columnists from all over the

country. Roger Maris was the hottest item in the U.S.

The controversy was this: baseball commissioner Ford Frick had pompously decreed that if Maris broke the Babe's record after the one hundred fifty-fourth game of the season—the 1927 season consisted of 154 games, the 1961 season of 162—the record books would show an asterisk after Maris's name to indicate that there were records and there were records. As such, Yankee teammates began to call their right fielder Roger Asterisk. And the pressure definitely was on Maris to break the record in 154 games.

He had 58 home runs through game number 153, and in game number 154 the Yankees played the Orioles in Baltimore, the birthplace of the Babe. Back in New York Claire Ruth, the Babe's widow, watched the game on television. In the third inning, facing Baltimore right-hander Milt Pappas, who gave up more than his share of gopher balls, Maris, a left-handed hitter, cracked number 59 over the wall in right field. But that was it. In a later at bat Maris made a gallant bid to tie the record at 60, but his long drive to right curved foul. And so, thanks to Ford Frick, the Babe's record survived. "I'm glad Maris didn't equal it," Claire Ruth said after that game. "The Babe loved that record. He wanted to be known as 'the King of Home Runs' forever."

Still, there were eight games to play in the season, asterisk or no asterisk. A notorious streak hitter, Maris slumped for a few games, hitting nothing that even resembled a home run. The nation's sporting press was reporting on Maris's every move, television cameras and microphones were everywhere, and it all seemed to be getting to Maris, who suddenly was acting more snappish—and becoming more withdrawn—with each passing game. To some, though, it appeared that the press was making Roger pay for the sin of not getting the record over with. After all, the longer it took Maris to achieve his asterisk, the longer the press had to follow him.

Then, in game number 158, Maris tied the record against the Orioles at Yankee Stadium. Fat Jack Fisher, who had given up a home run to Ted Williams on the

Yankee Stadium, October 1, 1961. Roger Maris hits
his 61st home run to break Babe Ruth's record set in
1927. Maris, hitting against the Red Sox' Tracy
Stallard in the fourth inning, put the ball in the
right field stands near the spot Ruth hit #60.

47

Splendid Splinter's last time at bat in 1960, was on the mound for the Orioles. Like his teammate Pappas, Fat Jack had a reputation for gopher pitches. He tried to fool Maris with a curve ball, but the ball seemed to hang in the middle of the plate and Maris whacked it into the friendly right-field seats. He now had four games—15 or 16 at bats—in which to break the record and win himself an asterisk.

Maris was weary when he showed up for game 159, also against the Orioles, and asked Yankee Manager Ralph Houk for the day off. Steve Barber, a wily left-hander whose pitches broke wickedly away from left-handed hitters, was the Baltimore pitcher that day, and Maris had never enjoyed much success against Barber. So Houk gave Maris permission to sit out; Yankee owner Dan Topping then suggested that Maris *really* take the day off and leave the ballpark while the game was in progress, which Maris did.

The Boston Red Sox then came into Yankee Stadium for the final three games of the season, which the Yankees planned to use as warmups for the upcoming World Series against the Cincinnati Reds. Except for the injured Mantle, all the other Yankee regulars—including such stars as Bobby Richardson, Tony Kubek, Elston Howard, Yogi Berra, Clete Boyer, Bill Skowron, Tom Tresh, Johnny Blanchard, and Hector Lopez, along with such pitchers as Whitey Ford, Ralph Terry, Luis Arroyo, and Bob Turley—would be playing in the three games against the Red Sox. (The 1961 Yankees won 109 games during the regular season, a total exceeded by only one previous club, and won four of five games against Cincinnati in the World Series. They are rated as one of the four or five best teams to play the game.)

When the Red Sox announced their pitching rotation for the final three games, it seemed certain that Maris would break the Babe's record with ease. The Boston starters would be three right-handers—Bill Monbouquette, Don Schwall, and Tracy Stallard. Advantage Maris. He had hit 48 of his 60 home runs off right-handed pitchers, including two off Monbouquette. In game number 160 Monbouquette, obviously not wanting to go down in history as the pitcher who served up the homer that broke the Babe's record, gave the anxious Maris nothing good to hit, masterfully keeping the Yankee slugger off balance by feeding him an assortment of off-speed breaking pitches. Maris came away empty. In game number 161 Schwall, a rookie who had a good sinking fast ball, also gave Maris nothing decent to hit, keeping the ball down at Maris's knees—or even lower. Once again Maris came away

empty, and now there was only one game to play.

A $5,000 reward had been promised to the fan who caught Maris's sixty-first home run—if indeed Maris ever hit it—but only 23,154 showed up at Yankee Stadium on Sunday, October 1, to watch his final try in the final game. Stallard, the Boston starter, was an inexperienced youngster with only one solid pitch: a live fast ball. And Maris, of course, feasted on live fast balls. Better still, Stallard had so little faith in his ability to get his breaking pitches across the plate that Maris could wait him out and make him throw his fast ball.

In the bottom of the first inning Maris came to bat and hit a long fly to left field for an out, bringing a groan from the crowd and also from the press box. Then, in the bottom of the fourth, he came to the plate for the second time. There was no Yankee on base, so the confrontation was essentially a private duel between pitcher and hitter—Stallard versus Maris.

Stallard's first pitch was a ball, and that produced boos from the fans. His second pitch was another ball, and that, too, produced a loud chorus of boos. A two balls-no strike pitch is called a hitter's pitch; the pitcher cannot afford to miss the plate again, thus going to three balls and no strikes, and usually will try to get his third pitch somewhere in the strike zone. Advantage Maris.

Sure enough, Stallard's next pitch was a waist-high fastball dead across the heart of the plate. It probably looked the size of a watermelon to Maris, whose eyes seemed to light up as the ball approached the plate. Maris owned a classic swing, and this time he attacked the ball in a powerful but seemingly effortless motion. He made solid contact and the ball took off in the direction of right field. There was no question about its ultimate destination: the right field seats. Suddenly, the thousands of fans who had packed those seats in hopes of catching what they called the $5,000 ball were elbowing one another out of the way and trying to reach the ball. A young man named Sal Durante got to it first, and he later gave it to Maris and collected the $5,000 reward.

As Maris trotted triumphantly around the bases, the crowd tendered him a tremendous ovation, and when he reached the Yankee dugout his teammates pounded him on the back and shook his hand. Then Maris bounced up the dugout steps to wave his hat to the cheering multitudes.

Home run number 61 was the only run that the Yankees scored that day, but it gave them a 1–0 victory and also gave Maris the RBI championship of the American League.

NO. 715

Hammerin' Henry Aaron breaks the Babe's career record
for home runs by smashing No. 715 on Opening Night in Atlanta in 1974

Babe Ruth was a 20-year-old pitcher for the Boston Red Sox in 1915 when on May 6 in New York he hit the first home run of his major-league career against a Yankee pitcher by the name of Warhop. Twenty years later, in 1935, Babe Ruth was a 40-year-old outfielder for the Boston Braves when on May 25 in Pittsburgh he hit the seven hundred fourteenth and last home run of his major-league career. It was his third home run of the day—against a Pirate pitcher by the name of Guy Bush.

Henry Aaron was a 20-year-old outfielder for the Milwaukee Braves in 1954 when on April 23 in St. Louis he hit the first home run of his major-league career against a Cardinal pitcher by the name of Vic Raschi. Over the next 20 seasons Henry Aaron—"Hammerin' Hank," number 44—raised his career home-run total from 1 to 713, and at the start of the 1974 schedule he

needed just one home run to tie the Babe's career record and two to break it. And so, over the winter between the close of the 1973 season and opening day of the 1974 season, one had plenty of time to review the home-run career of Henry Aaron.

For one thing, Aaron hardly looked like a home-run hitter. He was 6 feet tall and weighed a tad under 190 pounds, certainly not the physical characteristics of a mighty home-run hitter. But Aaron had whiplike wrists, strong hip movement, and a powerful leg drive, and he unleashed the bat at the ball with great quickness and force. Some home run hitters depended on long, lazy fly balls for their homers, but not Aaron. Hammerin' Hank's home runs "jumped" off the bat, as they say; they departed over the fence or into the seats on a low, blurred line. As one infielder once said, "You

Hank Aaron, Number 44 for the Braves. Aaron was 20 in 1954 when he hit his first home run in the major leagues for the Milwaukee Braves. He was tall and slim, not at all the barrel chested shape of Ruth. But Aaron generated great bat speed with his stride, hip rotation, and whip-lash wrists.

never want to get in the way when Henry hits one of his shots. It could take your head off."

For another, Aaron, being a right-handed hitter, should have been a piece of cake when he came to bat against right-handed pitchers who threw from the side. Tell that to Don Drysdale, who not only threw from the direction of third base but also was generally considered to own the best spitball in the game. Aaron hit more home runs off Drysdale—17—than he did against any other pitcher; in fact, of Aaron's nine favorite victims, seven threw right-handed—Drysdale, Bob Friend (12), Don Cardwell, Roger Craig, and Larry Jackson (all 10), and Vernon Law and Robin Roberts (both 9)—while only two threw left-handed, Claude Osteen (13) and Mike McCormick (9).

As for the breakdown of those 713 home runs, Aaron hit 128 in the first inning, 30 in the second, 95 in the third, 89 in the fourth, 57 in the fifth, 100 in the sixth, 83 in the seventh, 74 in the eighth, 45 in the ninth, 6 in the tenth, 4 in the eleventh, 1 in the twelfth; and 1 in the fourteenth. He hit 372 home runs with the bases empty, 235 with one man on base, 92 with two men on base, and 14 with the bases loaded.

Aaron also spent some time mentally researching his career, and produced the following list of his most memorable home runs:

ABOVE: *At the beginning of the 1974 season, Aaron needed one homer to tie Ruth's lifetime record of 714. Shown here with Johnny Bench catching, Aaron hits number 714 against the Reds in the season opener at Cincinnati.*

1) The two-run homer over the center field wall at County Stadium in Milwaukee that won the 1957 pennant for the Braves.

2) The homer that enabled him to become only the eighth player in baseball history to hit 500 home runs, a three-run smash off McCormick at Atlanta Stadium.

3) The homer off Gaylord Perry in the 1972 All-Star Game; Atlanta Stadium was filled to capacity and it broke into a thunderous and interminable ovation for its home-town hero.

4) The first homer he ever hit in the major leagues, the one off Vic Raschi.

But when he hit number 715, Aaron admitted, that would go right to the top of his list—and, indeed, all lists.

So, all eyes were on Aaron when the Braves arrived in Cincinnati to open the 1974 season with a three-game series against the Reds. The Atlanta management was understandably miffed that the Braves had not been scheduled to open the season at home; the Braves were not a good draw in Atlanta, and the Atlanta brass correctly felt that Aaron's chase for number 715 would pack the park for as many games as Aaron needed to beat the Babe's record. To protest the scheduling, the Braves planned to keep Aaron on their bench for all three games in Cincinnati and save him for their home opener the following week in Atlanta. No dice, said baseball commissioner Bowie Kuhn. Kuhn told the Braves that they were obliged to put their best lineup on the field at all times, and if they didn't, he would penalize them severely.

Thus warned, Atlanta manager Eddie Mathews, who had been Aaron's home-run-hitting sidekick for years with the Braves, penciled Aaron into the lineup on opening day. Then, with his first swing of the new season, Aaron hit number 714. I've only tied the record," Aaron cautioned his followers, "but it's almost over." The next day, though, Mathews ignored the commissioner's edict and kept Aaron on the bench. Though he didn't play, Henry had some fun that day.

Some of the Braves were having an argument about who should play Aaron when they made the movie of his life.

"Well," said Ralph Garr, an outfielder, "the guy'll have to be black."

The names of Sidney Poitier, Harry Belafonte, and Bill Cosby were tossed out for discussion.

"Nope, none of those people," said Aaron. "I'll play myself. I'm a better actor than any of those guys."

Aaron's relaxed manner surprised some of the hundreds of members of the media who were trailing him during the chase for number 715.

"What's the matter with Aaron?" one writer asked Mathews.

"What do you mean?" the manager said.

"Well, Henry doesn't seem excited at all. He doesn't show anything. It's just like it's going to be another home run."

"Maybe," Mathews said, "Henry should do like I told him. I told him to lie on his back and kick his feet and scream. Then everyone might be convinced he's excited by it all."

Aaron's idleness on that Saturday in Cincinnati aroused Kuhn's ire, and he made it very clear to the Braves that Aaron had better play on Sunday. Henry did, for six and one-half innings, but he never came close to hitting number 715—striking out twice and grounding out to the third baseman. Then Mathews removed him from the game.

It was a rainy Monday night in Atlanta as the Braves opened their home season against the Dodgers before a crowd of 53,775. Noting the turnout, one Atlanta official said, "We normally don't get this many people for 10 games. We could get lucky, too. Maybe Henry won't hit number 715 until September. We'd have a packed house every game." No such luck. The Atlanta fans had signs—MOVE OVER BABE—everywhere and the scoreboard kept flashing the name HANK. Before the game the Braves staged a "This Is Your Life" program in Aaron's honor, and it seemed that anyone and everyone who ever knew Aaron was there. Pearl Bailey sang the national anthem, and among the politicians who had front row seats were Maynard Jackson, the mayor of Atlanta, and Jimmy Carter, then the governor of Georgia, but soon to become the president of the United States.

Al Downing, a left-hander, started for the Dodgers. "I will pitch to Aaron no differently tonight," Downing said. "I'll mix my pitches up, move the locations. If I make a mistake, it's no disgrace. I don't think the pitcher should take the glory for number 715. He won't deserve any accolades. I think people will remember the pitcher who throws the last one he ever hits, not the seven hundred fifteenth."

Aaron did not bat in the bottom of the first inning, but led off in the bottom of the second. Downing obviously did not want to give Aaron anything good to hit, and walked him, thus provoking loud boos from the home-town crowd. Aaron later came around to score a run on a Los Angeles error, and thus broke Willie Mays's National League record for runs scored (2,063).

Aaron came to bat again in the bottom of the fourth, with a Brave already on base. Downing had to pitch to Aaron now; he could not afford the luxury of a base on balls. However, his first pitch did not even get to home plate, bouncing in the dirt. The next pitch . . . "It was a fastball down the middle of the upper part of the plate," Downing said. "I was trying to keep it down, but I didn't. He's a great hitter. When he picks his pitch, he is pretty certain that it's the pitch he's looking for. And chances are he's gonna hit that pitch pretty good. When he did hit it, though, I thought it was going to be caught by either Jimmy Wynn or Bill Buckner. But the ball kept carrying and carrying and . . ."

Wynn and Buckner both raced to the fence, right at the 385-foot sign, but then Wynn gave up, obviously realizing that what he was doing was hopeless. Buckner seemed ready to climb the fence in a valiant effort to keep the ball in play, but soon he, too, realized that such an effort was a waste of time. The ball flew over the fence and landed in the Atlanta bullpen, where an obscure relief pitcher named Tom House gained the only real measure of fame in his major-league career by winning the battle for the ball.

Number 715 was history. Number 715 was in the record books.

The game was then delayed for a long time while Aaron's accomplishment was celebrated. Henry shook hands with his father, Herbert, and he hugged his mother, Estella. The list of people who came onto the field to shake his hand, or to embrace him, was endless. One man was missing, though. Bowie Kuhn, the commissioner. The man who had ordered Aaron to play the games in Cincinnati never showed up in Atlanta to see number 715. He was in Cleveland, of all places; nobody in Cleveland was going for 715 home runs. Henry Aaron properly considered Kuhn's absence as a slight, and it is something that he has never forgotten.

And then Aaron had a word for the crowd, for the millions watching on national television, for everyone. "I just thank God it's all over," he said.

At the end of that 1974 season Aaron, partly at his request, was traded by the Braves to the Milwaukee Brewers of the American League, so he could conclude his career in the city where he had achieved his greatest fame. Henry retired at the end of the 1976 season. He hit the seven hundred fifty-fifth (one home run every 16.38 times at bat) and last home run of his major-league career on July 20, 1976, in Milwaukee against a California Angels pitcher by the name of Dick Drago.

"HAI, GAMBATTE"

*It was a summit meeting of home run champions from
different worlds, and when all the hitting was done . . . score one for Henry Aaron*

Henry Aaron may hold the major-league record with his 755 career home runs, but according to the Japanese, the leading home run hitter in baseball history is not Henry Aaron but Sadaharu Oh, the legendary left-handed slugger of the Yomiuri Giants who in 1980 finished his 21-year career in the Japanese major league with a total of 868 home runs, 113 more than Aaron. Mind you, Aaron, for one, does not recognize Oh's achievement as being on a par with, or even better than, his. "I don't think there is any comparison with the home runs he hit in Japan and the ones I hit in the United States," Aaron once said.

While most everyone in the United States would certainly agree with Aaron on that point, the people in Japan have always felt that their Mr. Oh ranks second to none as a home-run hitter. So it was that at the end of 1974 a sharp CBS television producer by the name of Frank Chirkinian arranged what turned out to be the first and only home-run-hitting contest in history between the American champion, Henry Aaron, 40, and the Japanese champion, Sadaharu Oh, then 34. To get Aaron to travel from Atlanta to Tokyo for the contest, CBS paid him $50,000 and picked up all his expenses. Oh lives in Tokyo, and he came considerably cheaper

ABOVE: *Hank Aaron's seemingly effortless swing is captured
in this photo as he cracks his 600th homer against the San
Francisco Giants.* OPPOSITE: *There is another Giants' team
in the world, the Yomiuri Giants of Japan. Their slugger,
Sadaharu Oh is shown here after hitting his 756th homer.*

than Aaron, getting some six million yen ($20,000) for his services. The prize for the winner was not a Toyota, not a Ford, but—drum roll, please—a plain silver bowl.

The site of the home-run contest was Tokyo's Korakuen Stadium, the home field for Oh and his Yomiuri Giants. Like most Japanese parks, it is considerably smaller than an average stadium in the U.S., measuring just slightly more than 290 feet down each of the foul lines; the typical American stadium measures approximately 340 feet down the foul lines. Also, the power alleys in left and right center are much shorter in Japan than in the U.S.; indeed, there are no fences 440 feet away in Japan, as there are in the U.S.

Still, baseball fans everywhere recognized Oh's talents as a home-run hitter. Oh always looked more like a singles hitter than a slugger, standing barely 5 feet 10 inches tall and weighing just 170 pounds, but he generated his considerable power by means of a Mel Ott-style swing, cocking his lead (right) leg in the air as the pitcher threw the ball and then, with a mighty snap of his wrists, uncoiling into the ball as it reached the plate. It was a batting style that hitting instructors would never suggest to their pupils, but Oh used it effectively throughout his career.

The New York Mets happened to be in Japan on an exhibition tour during that fall of 1974, and the Aaron–Oh contest was held before one of the Mets' games against the Japanese all stars. The two sluggers met in a room—SPECIAL, read the sign on the door—under Korakuen Stadium a few hours beforehand.

"We'll begin the show with you wishing Oh good luck," producer Chirkinian said to Aaron.

"Fine," said Aaron.

Trouble was, neither Aaron, nor Chirkinian, nor any of the other Americans in the room knew how to say "good luck." Suddenly, Oh came to the rescue.

"Hai, gambatte," he said, the gambatte sounding suspiciously like gom-bah-tay.

Aaron nodded his head. "Gom-bah-tay," he said.

Yes, Henry was ready.

Aaron had forgotten to bring any of his own bats with him, but that morning, during a private batting practice at Korakuen, he had tested several of the Met bats and selected one belonging to Ed Kranepool, a first baseman for the New York team who never was much of a home-run hitter during his 17 years in the major leagues. The Kranepool model was one ounce lighter and one-half inch longer than Aaron's regular bat, but Aaron said not to worry, that "the handle feels good to me."

Both Aaron and Oh got to select their own pitcher. Oh brought along his usual batting practice pitcher with the Giants, a right-hander named Kiniyasu Mine. Aaron hit against two Met coaches, Rube Walker and Joe Pignatano, in batting practice, then opted for Pignatano, who threw the ball with an overhand motion that was to Aaron's liking. As for the contest itself, each player would get to hit a total of 20 fair balls; one would hit five fair balls, then the other. Mr. Oh had the honor.

One thing about batting practice pitchers is that they serve up only the juiciest of baseballs. Their pitches don't travel too fast, they don't travel too slow; they travel at just the right speed and pace. Batting practice pitchers are not employed to "work over" hitters; they are employed to keep hitters happy. As such, hitters can dig in against a batting practice pitcher, knowing full well that the upcoming baseball will arrive across the heart of the plate. It is a comforting feeling, indeed.

Sure enough, Oh's preferred pitcher, Kiniyasu Mine, gave Oh only excellent pitches on the first round of five fair balls, and Oh smashed the ball once, twice, three times into the right field seats, bringing a tremendous roar from the partisan crowd of more than 50,000.

Aaron, wearing his familiar Atlanta uniform—actually, Aaron would be traded from Atlanta to Milwaukee before the start of the next season—with number 44 on the back, took a few practice swings to unlimber his muscles and sharpen his wrists, then stepped into the box against Pignatano. Peculiarly, Aaron was hitting against a right-handed pitcher, not a left-hander; according to baseball psychology, right-handed hitters should have a tougher time against right-handed pitchers than against left-handed pitchers. Whatever, Henry just wanted Pignatano to throw the ball across the plate. Now, the crowd in Korakuen became absolutely silent; there was not a Nikon or a Yashica to be heard.

Aaron unleashed his bat at Pignatano's first pitch and smashed it into the left field seats. Suddenly, the crowd, which groaned, was obviously in awe of Aaron; the fans could not understand how such an effortless swing had produced such a prodigious home run. Aaron failed to get a home run with his second swing, but then hit home run number two into the seats before concluding the first round with two routine hits. So, the score at the end of round one was: Sadaharu Oh 3, Henry Aaron 2. The Japanese fans were going wild, while the Met players and their wives were very quiet.

Oh started the second round with a home run and then hit two more, one of which crashed against a wall some 30 rows up. So, as Aaron took his second round, he was trailing Oh by a 6–2 count. "Okay, Piggy, good pitches now," the Mets yelled to their coach on the mound. And good pitches they were. Aaron took five swings and hit four monstrous home runs, barely missing a rousing five-for-five performance when another ball landed less than five feet from the fence. Aaron and Oh now were tied at 6–6. But it seemed that the advantage clearly belonged to Aaron, because even the legendary Oh was wide eyed in amazement each time Aaron hit the ball in round two.

Nevertheless, Oh started the third round with a home run, taking a 7–6 lead. But after that he hit one harmless ground ball after another, finishing the round with just one home run in five swings. The Japanese fans were nodding to one another, saying that it certainly didn't look very good for their man.

Aaron failed to hit a home run on his first swing in round three, but tied the score at 7–7 with his second swing. Then he took the lead for the first time at 8–7 with what people in the U.S.—and who knows, maybe in Japan—call a Chinese home run, the ball just clearing the left-field fence. Aaron seemed embarrassed to have hit such a chintzy home run, so he gave the fans something to remember on his next swing, cracking a prodigious home run deep into the seats to take a 9–7 lead.

Now the pressure rested squarely on the shoulders of Oh, and he responded with a home run on his first swing in the final round, cutting Aaron's lead to 9–8. On his next swing Oh hit a long fly that was lost in translation. The Japanese umpire in right field signaled that it was a home run, and the scoreboard lit up with 9–9—indicating that Oh had tied the score. But Chris Pelekoudas, the National League umpire who had been assigned to home plate, immediately overruled the Japanese arbiter and declared that the ball was a foul, motioning accordingly with his hands. Oh did not argue the issue; he knew that the ball had been a foul. Whatever, the home-country advantage had not been a problem. Oh still had four more fair swings, and he managed to hit one more home run, tying him with Aaron at 9–9. But Henry now had five more swings, and needed only one home run to win the contest.

His first hit on the last round was a long fly to left, a routine out. His second was a soft ground ball to shortstop, another routine out. Only three swings to go. Then Aaron smashed a long drive to left that had home run written all over it. The only question was: fair or foul? The answer was: fair. Henry Aaron then dropped his bat. The contest was finished.

Later, Aaron accepted the silver bowl, and as he looked at it he noticed that something was wrong. Henry Aaron's name read Henry Arron.

Oh, well, Aaron or Arron, by any name Henry was the champ, baseball's number one home-run hitter, no doubt about it.

In 1974 the stage was set for a home run contest between Sadaharu Oh and Hank Aaron in Tokyo. Oh is shown as he participates in the event. The distance to the fence down the foul line in the Tokyo stadium is 290 feet. Aaron won, 10 homers to 9.

GAME SIX

*When baseball fans begin to reminisce, they start with Game Six
of the 1975 World Series between Boston and Cincinnati ... or as Pete Rose calls it,
"The greatest game I've ever seen or played in"*

Checking through the baseball history books, one notices with great fascination that each decade seems to have produced one great World Series moment. For instance, the eighth and final game of the 1912 Series, when the Red Sox parlayed an error, some timely hits, and a sacrifice fly into an extra-inning victory. And what about the 1926 Series, when Grover Cleveland Alexander, supposedly over the hill, struck out the Yankees' Tony Lazzeri with the bases loaded. Or the 1932 Series, when Babe Ruth called, or didn't call, his tremendous home run against Charley Root of the Cubs. In 1947, it was Dodger Cookie Lavagetto's down-to-the-last-out two-base hit that broke up Yankee pitcher Floyd Bevens's no-hitter. Don Larsen's perfect game in the 1956 Series overshadowed the Dodgers' Series triumph the previous year. And in the 1960s, Bill Mazeroski provided enough heroics to last for all ten years with his home run in the bottom of the ninth inning in game seven that lifted the Pittsburgh Pirates over the Yankees in 1960.

However, all those Series moments, as great as they were, must take second place—a six-way tie for second place, if you will—to the great Series moment of the 1970s: game six. Ask any baseball fan what the term "game six" means, and he or she will answer: Cincinnati versus Boston, October 21, 1975, Fenway Park. And then the kicker: Carlton Fisk's home run. Pete Rose, the star of the Reds that year, says that game six was "the greatest game I have ever seen and the greatest game I have ever played in. It was a game for the ages. We'll never see another game like it."

Maybe not.

For starters, game six was rained out not once, not twice, but three times. It was scheduled to be played in Boston on Saturday, October 18, but was not played until Tuesday night, October 21. The Reds led the Red Sox three games to two, and both teams were hungry for a championship; Cincinnati had not won a World Series in 35 years, Boston in 47 years. The Reds and Red Sox had split the first two games in Boston, then the Reds had taken two of three in Cincinnati. (One of the Reds' home-field victories, a 6–5 triumph in game three, was hotly disputed by the Red Sox, who claimed, with some

justification, that the home-plate umpire made the wrong call on an apparent interference maneuver by a Cincinnati hitter—leading to the decisive run in the tenth inning.)

Back to game six. Bill Lee, the eccentric left-hander, was scheduled to start for the Red Sox, but manager Darrell Johnson bypassed Lee at the last minute and went with his right-handed ace, ancient Luis Tiant, who had won games one and five. Gary Nolan, a once-brilliant prospect who had endured arm miseries for several seasons, started for the Reds. Tiant, as he had done in his earlier victories, baffled the Reds in the top of the first inning with his usual assortment of hesitation pitches, sidearm pitches, overhand pitches, underhand pitches, three-quarters pitches, loop-de-loop pitches— you name it. He threw one pitch to Rose when his face was looking at the center-field seats.

Boston struck quickly in the bottom of the first, with rookie sensation Fred Lynn, who later would be named both MVP and rookie of the year, hitting a monstrous three-run homer into the right-center field bleachers. Boston went bonkers as Lynn trotted around

1975 World Series, Cincinnati Reds vs. Boston Red Sox, Game Six, Oct. 21, Fenway Park, Boston. The Reds led the Series three games to two going into the sixth game. The tone of the game was set as Yastrzemski made this sliding, first-inning catch.

the basepaths. But Tiant suddenly fell upon harder times than he had experienced in his earlier outings, the Reds having apparently figured him out. Or maybe Luis, whose age was somewhere between 35 and 50, was just getting tired. Cincinnati tied the score at 3–3 in the fifth. Ed Armbrister, who had been at the center of the interference controversy in game three, walked and Rose advanced him with a single. Ken Griffey, the right fielder, then teed off on a Tiant fast ball and smashed it toward the wall in deep center field. Lynn, a brilliant outfielder, made a valiant effort to catch Griffey's hit by throwing himself—glove outstretched—against the wall. The sound of Lynn's body striking the cold green wall could be heard on Cape Cod. Lynn bounced off the wall and lay stunned on the ground, and the Reds merrily trotted around the basepaths, Armbrister and Rose scoring and Griffey winding up at third. Lynn received medical attention on the field but remained in the game. However, Johnny Bench then rattled a shot off the left-field wall to score Griffey from third with the tying run.

Boston, meanwhile, was unable to generate much of an attack against the Cincinnati pitching, and in the seventh inning the Reds took the lead. Griffey singled and so did Joe Morgan, who later would be named the National League's MVP. George Foster, the power-hitting left fielder, then drove home both Griffey and Morgan with a ringing double off the centerfield wall. Cincinnati 5, Boston 3. In the eighth, the Reds extended their lead to 6–3 when Cesar Geronimo KO'd Tiant with a home run that barely made it into the seats down the right-field line.

OPPOSITE: *Fred Lynn's 3-run homer in the 1st inning, Game 6.* ABOVE LEFT: *With the Reds leading 6–3 in the bottom of the eighth, Boston's Bernie Carbo pinch-hit this 3 run homer to tie the game.* ABOVE RIGHT: *And Carlton Fisk, shown here hitting a homer in Game 3, was waiting in the wings.*

The people of Boston, especially the BLO-HARDS—the Benevolent Loyal Order of Honorable and Ancient Red Sox Diehard Sufferers—had been in this situation before. Once again, all looked lost. Wait 'til next year. But the Red Sox weren't dead yet.

Lynn led off the Boston eighth with a sharp single that bounced off the leg of Cincinnati's fifth pitcher of the game, flashy Pedro Borbon. When Rico Petrocelli then walked, Reds' manager Sparky Anderson, ol' Captain Hook himself, yanked Borbon and replaced him with Rawly Eastwick, who already had won two Series games for the Reds in relief. Eastwick, a right-handed

pitcher, fanned Dwight Evans and got Rick Burleson to fly out. Boston's last hope, it seemed, was pinch hitter Bernie Carbo, a former Red, who had pinch-hit a home run in game three. On a two-balls, two-strikes pitch, Eastwick fooled Carbo and seemed to have him struck out, but Carbo just got his bat on the ball and dribbled it foul. Then, on Eastwick's following pitch, Carbo drilled a shot into the center field seats for a three-run homer, tying the score at 6–6. Once again Boston went bonkers. Carbo did not run around the bases, nor did he walk; he danced and leaped and, well, he would have done handstands if he could.

Now revived, the Red Sox quickly disposed of the Reds in the top of the ninth, and in the bottom of the inning they just as quickly loaded the bases with none out. A fly ball, a base on balls, an error, a hit—any hit— and the Red Sox would win. And who was at bat? Fred Lynn. Lynn looped a lazy fly down the left-field line, and three Reds converged on it. Foster grabbed it, near the stands, perhaps 200 feet from home plate. For some reason Denny Doyle, the Boston runner at third base, thought he heard the "go go" order from third base coach Don Zimmer. Actually, what Doyle didn't hear was Zimmer yelling "no . . . no . . . no." But Doyle tried to score, was thrown out easily, and when Petrocelli grounded out to Rose, the inning—unbelievably—was over.

Boston went on the defensive to thwart the Reds in the eleventh. Fisk, the catcher, scooped up a Ken Griffey bunt, ignored the safe out at first base, gambled that he could get Rose running for second—and did, by an eyelash. Then Morgan, or "Little Joe," as they called him, hit a long fly deep to right field, and everyone in the park thought it was a home run. Everyone except

57

58

Dwight Evans, the Boston right fielder, maybe the best player at that position in baseball. Evans raced back to the low wall, stuck out his glove, and plucked the ball out of the seats, practically tumbling into them himself in the process. No Cincinnati player believed what had happened, certainly not Griffey, who kept running around the bases, thinking Morgan had a home run, and then was doubled off first base when Evans recovered from his visit to the seats and threw the ball to the infield. Double play.

Now, as the clock in right field approached 12:30 A.M., the Red Sox came to bat in the bottom of the twelfth. Fisk led off against the eighth—and last—Cincinnati pitcher of the night, right-hander Pat Darcy. Fisk swung at Darcy's second pitch and hit a long, high fly ball down the left field line. As the ball curved toward the foul pole atop the left-field wall, Fisk, a study in anxiety as he tried to body-English the ball into fair territory, stayed pretty close to home plate, his eyes trained on the ball; if it stayed fair, he knew it would be a home run, the game winner. Then, as the sound of thousands and thousands of cheering Bostonians told the

world watching on television, the ball struck the foul pole—the fair pole, really—and the left-field umpire gave the signal for a home run.

Once again, there was bedlam in Boston as Fisk, having rounded the bases in celebration, was mobbed at home plate by his teammates. Some fans were so captivated by the events of the game that they didn't leave the park for hours, and when they did they found their friends and neighbors dancing and drinking in the streets around Kenmore Square.

"I don't think anybody in the world could ask for a better game than this one," Fisk said in the Red Sox dressing room. "Pete Rose came up to me in the tenth inning and said, 'This is some kind of game, isn't it?' Pete Rose said that to me!"

Yes, it was some kind of game. Cincinnati won the Series the next night by beating the Red Sox 4–3 on Morgan's bloop single in the top of the ninth. The Red Sox may not have won the Series, but ask anyone in Boston, anyone in New England, anyone anywhere, and they will tell you that the Red Sox didn't lose the Series either. They'll tell you that the Red Sox won game six.

OPPOSITE: *Carlton Fisk led off for the Red Sox in the bottom of the 12th, Game 6. As his long fly carried down the left field line, Fisk, shown here, used body English to make it stay fair. It hit the pole. Home run.* ABOVE: *Fisk, greeted at home plate by his teammates after his game-winning shot.*

59

Golf

THE DAY GOLF WENT PUBLIC

Francis Ouimet's classic playoff victory over a pair of esteemed
British professionals in the 1913 U.S. Open stimulated the masses and altered the nature of the sport

In 1913 golf in the United States was mainly a game for two classes of people—the rich and the very rich. No one else need apply. At that time the sport had no links to the great majority of Americans, no common ground. The rich and the very rich were properly delivered to their club on a Saturday or Sunday afternoon, played 9 or 18 holes, dined, chatted, chatted some more, and then were chauffeured home. As they used to say, golf was a blue-blooded game.

Perhaps *THE* bastion of blue-blooded elegance and sophistication and old money in those days was The Country Club in Brookline, Massachusetts, and don't forget that the "T" in "the" is capitalized, please. Besides golf, polo was also an "in" sport at The Country Club in the early years of the twentieth century, and what better way to spend a day than to play 18 in the morning and follow that with a friendly polo match against the chaps from, oh, Myopia Hunt.

The Ouimet family lived across the street from The Country Club at the turn of the century. The senior Ouimet was a gardener, a working man, and there were no gardeners and few working men among the members of The Country Club. One of the Ouimet children, Francis, used The Country Club as a shortcut between the family home and the Putterham school; in fact, it cut his trip in half. Occasionally young Francis would find a golf ball in the deep grass bordering the neat fairways, and he would put it in his pocket and take it home. Behind the Ouimet residence was a meadow, and one day when he was nine Francis borrowed an old golf club from a neighbor, went out to that meadow, and flailed away at some of the old golf balls he had found in the rough at The Country Club. In time young Francis had four or five clubs at his disposal, and he soon was able to hit those old golf balls straight and far—all the way across the small pond 180 yards out in the meadow. Then he began to caddie at The Country Club, earning the princely sum of 28 cents for lugging one golf bag for 18 holes.

One day a club member invited Francis into the locker room after a round and gave him an almost complete set of slightly used clubs as a present. Francis now was completely hooked on the game. After caddying, at dusk, Francis would sneak out onto The Country Club

course and play those holes not in view of the clubhouse until the greenskeeper showed up and shooed him off. Many a day Francis's mother would hear directly from some club official of her son's golfing activities "on private property," and she would tell him, "Francis, the game of golf will ruin you." On those days when he didn't caddie, Francis, now in his early teens, would travel to Franklin Park—a trip that required a complicated series of transfers from one car line to another—and play until it got dark; he usually managed to get in at least six 9-hole rounds, or 54 holes in all, each day at Franklin Park.

Francis was indeed dedicated to the game. After school, or after caddying, he would hit balls for endless hours, and he began to compete in amateur tournaments throughout the Greater Boston area. He won schoolboy and other local competitions, and soon his golfing itinerary included tournaments throughout New England and into New York. In 1910 he won the prestigious The Country Club Cup, beating a field the equal of that for the U.S. amateur, and in 1913 he won the Massachusetts state amateur championship. In that latter tournament, Ouimet found himself two-down with six holes to play in the semifinals, then finished 2-3-3-3-3-3 (six under) to win the match. The next day he scored a smashing 10-and-9 victory in the finals. That same summer Ouimet took a week's vacation—his only week—from his job with a Boston sporting goods firm to play in the U.S. Amateur at the Garden City Golf Club on New York's Long Island, but he lost in the second round to the legendary Jerome Travers of the host club. Still, the Travers–Ouimet match was considered to be the best of the tournament, with each player producing one marvelous golf shot after another.

The 1913 U.S. Open was scheduled to be played at The Country Club in the middle of September. The Open had always been played in the summer, but it had been switched to the later dates in order to attract the entries of the leading British and Scottish professionals, particularly Harry Vardon and Ted Ray. Ouimet had entered the tournament, but as the Open approached, it appeared that he would be unable to participate. He had used up his only vacation week, and he would need a week off to play in the Open. Fortunately, at the last

PRECEDING PAGES: *Spectators watch Francis Ouimet chip out of clover and onto the green.* OPPOSITE: *Francis Ouimet in 1913 at "The Country Club," Brookline, Massachusetts, where he won the U.S. Open by beating experienced British professionals. Until Ouimet, golf had been an exclusive game for the rich.*

minute Ouimet's boss, hearing of his young employee's dilemma, told him, "Francis, you had better play. That's an order."

On the weekend before the Open, Francis journeyed out to the Wellesley Country Club to practice. On Sunday he shot an 88 in the morning, and followed that dismal round with still another 88. (Earlier that summer Ouimet had set the Wellesley course record with a 66.) So, it was hardly a confident Ouimet who showed up at The Country Club for the 36 holes of Open qualifying. But Francis, who, remember, had tramped over this very course en route to grade school, shot a fine 74 the first day, added a comfortable 78 the

second, and qualified easily.

The Open proper began with 36 holes on Thursday, and Ouimet bettered his 152 qualifying score by one stroke, finishing the day at 151, four strokes behind Vardon and another English professional, Wilfred Reid. The next day Ouimet shot a strong 74, and suddenly he found himself tied for the 54-hole lead with Vardon and Ray. The day of the final round brought rain, but masses of Bostonians—proper and otherwise—turned up at Brookline to cheer the 20-year-old native son—an amateur, no less—who would be fighting the best professionals in the world for the Open title.

Ouimet kept regular check on the progress of Ray

and Vardon during the final round, and as he stood on the tenth knee, having played the front side in 43 strokes, he knew he would have to play the back side in 36 to finish the round with a 79, which would tie him with Vardon and Ray, who had already finished the tournament at 304. Then, on the short tenth hole, disaster struck Ouimet as he made a double-bogey 5. He recovered with a par at the eleventh, but a bogey at the twelfth seemed to write finis to his Open dreams. Now he would have to play the last six holes in two under par to get into a playoff. He made one of the necessary birdies at the short thirteenth, chipping in for a 2. A routine par followed at the fourteenth, but Ouimet needed a good greenside recovery and a delicate putt to save par at fifteen and a long putt to save par again at the sixteenth. Now he needed to birdie one of the last two holes—or else.

Francis spanked his second shot on the long, par-four seventeenth to within 15 feet of the cup, and studied the putt carefully. As he stood over the ball, horns were tooting in the background as the result of a traffic jam on the street that ran alongside the seventeenth hole. Ouimet said later that he never heard any horns, so great was his concentration. He stroked the ball and it rolled dead into the cup. A birdie. One more hole to play. Ouimet drove straight down the middle on the eighteenth hole and hit his second shot onto the bank fronting the green. He chipped to within five feet, then calmly sank the putt to finish at 304 and tie Vardon and Ray, thus forcing an 18-hole playoff the next day.

Once Ouimet's ball dropped into the cup, he was mobbed by hundreds of elated Bostonians and carried off the green on their shoulders. The scene was hardly fitting of the usual tranquility and sophistication of The Country Club; after all, the mob, of all things, was carrying off one of the club's former caddies, of all people, in absolute jubilation. Why, things like that had never happened at The Country Club before.

The next morning Ouimet, accompanied by his trusty caddie, 10-year-old Eddie Lowery, who had taken an unrequested and unpermitted leave from school to carry Ouimet's bag (Lowery later was a prosperous automobile dealer in California and helped sponsor the careers of former U.S. Open champion Ken Venturi and former U.S. Amateur champion Harvie Ward), arrived early for the playoff, having just walked across the street from the family residence. "I was an amateur who played golf for fun," Ouimet wrote many years later, recalling the moment, "and I looked on professionals as magicians who knew all the answers. This

ABOVE: *Francis Ouimet, a native of Brookline, Massachusetts, was the first American amateur to win the U.S. Open.* OPPOSITE: *Ouimet with one of the several trophies he won in his career. Ouimet was the son of a carpenter, and his U.S. Open win suddenly brought golf to the attention of many Americans.*

was to be a match between Vardon and Ray. I was there by mistake."

Ouimet drew the longest straw and thus had the honor on the first tee. "When I saw the crowd, I was terribly excited," Ouimet wrote. "If I could only get my tee shot away. Eddie handed me a driver and said, 'Be sure and keep your eye on the ball.'" Ouimet heeded his caddie's advice and drove the ball long and straight through the rain.

Ouimet had to drop a testing four-foot putt to hold par on that first hole, but he did. On the fifth hole Francis hit a shot out of bounds, but Vardon played the same hole poorly, too, and through five holes Ouimet and Vardon led Ray by a shot. Vardon pulled a stroke ahead of Ouimet and two ahead of Ray at the sixth, and Ray regained a stroke on both Ouimet and Vardon at the seventh. On the 380-yard eighth Ouimet drilled his second shot to within 12 inches of the cup, then tapped in for his birdie 3; Ray, too, made birdie, canning a 40-

foot putt, while Vardon settled for a par 4. So, through eight holes, the three players were dead even, and they preserved the tie with matching fives at the ninth.

The pro-Ouimet crowd had cheered their favorite loud and clear every shot of the way, and now the noise was deafening as Ouimet took the lead for the first time at the par-three tenth when he made a routine par while Vardon and Ray were taking bogeys. As it developed, Ouimet was in the lead for good. He extended his margin to two strokes at the twelfth, making a 4 while

the two Englishmen had to settle for fives. Vardon birdied the thirteenth to close within a stroke of Ouimet, and stayed that way through the sixteenth. Ray, meanwhile, fell out of the chase, dropping five strokes behind Ouimet after suffering a series of mishit shots. So it was really Ouimet versus Vardon with two holes to play, Ouimet leading by a stroke.

Vardon's tee shot on number seventeen landed in a bunker and stopped so close to the bank that he had no shot to the green; indeed, Vardon had to play a safety recovery out onto the fairway. Ouimet's tee shot landed safely to the right, and his second shot stopped 15 feet from the pin. Vardon eventually made a bogey 5, as did Ray. Seeing this, Ouimet—leading by a stroke, remember—just wanted to lag his putt close to the hole, take his four and extend his lead to two shots. But his putt was true and firm . . . and the ball rolled into the middle of the cup. The noise from the crowd was heard miles away in downtown Boston.

The Englishmen were beaten now, beaten by a mere amateur, a 20-year-old homebody from Brookline, and the crowd was going wild. On the last hole Ouimet negotiated a safe par, while Ray took a bogey and Vardon a double bogey, so the young American finished with a 72—five shots better than Vardon, six better than Ray. Once again Ouimet was carried from the green on the shoulders of hundreds of Bostonians, carried to a reception that never seemed to end. Single-handedly, Francis Ouimet had taken the game of golf and brought it to the masses; no longer would the game be the private preserve of the rich and the very rich. Golf was now a game that could be played by all Americans.

As Ouimet was being carried off that eighteenth green at Brookline, a little lady fought through the crowd and suddenly appeared at his feet. "Francis," she called up to the Open champion. Hearing that voice, Ouimet looked down and then spotted the lady who had once told him, "Francis, the game of golf will ruin you." It was a tender scene—mother congratulating son, son accepting his mother's congratulations—and as the crowd tugged him off, Francis said, "Thank you, Mother, I'll be home soon."

										THE SCORECARDS (September 20, 1913)										
Hole	1	2	3	4	5	6	7	8	9	Out	10	11	12	13	14	15	16	17	18	In	Total
Ouimet	5	4	4	4	5	4	4	3	5	38	3	4	4	4	5	4	3	3	4	34	72
Vardon	5	4	4	4	5	3	4	4	5	38	4	4	5	3	5	4	3	5	6	39	77
Ray	5	4	5	4	5	4	3	3	5	38	4	4	5	4	5	6	4	5	3	40	78

BOBBY JONES AND CALAMITY JANE

*It has been more than 50 years now, and still no golfer
has been able to win the Grand Slam . . . as Bobby Jones did in 1930, his last year as a competitor*

One by one, the legends of earlier eras have seen their records fall by the wayside, shattered by athletes bigger and stronger, athletes enjoying equipment technologically superior in every way to that which their predecessors had to use, athletes employing techniques devised and refined by such modern-day wonders as computers and analysis systems, athletes enriched by diets specially prepared to fill their individual needs, athletes pampered by a society that demands winners and rewards them exorbitantly for their successes.

No one was ever going to break Babe Ruth's record of 60 home runs in a season. Roger Maris broke it.

No one was going to break the 4-minute mile. Roger Bannister did that in 1954, and now in the eighties the question is: who will be the first man to break the 3:45 mile?

No one was going to own Wimbledon. Bjorn Borg does.

No one was ever going to score more goals than the 50 that Maurice "the Rocket" Richard scored one season. Phil Esposito scored 76.

No one was ever going to match the incomparable Bobby Jones by winning golf's four major champion-

ships—the Grand Slam, including the U.S. Open and the U.S. Amateur, the British Open and the British Amateur—in one season, as Jones did in 1930. And you know what? No one has.

Today, golfers use supersonic-age equipment—clubs as well as balls—that powers shots prodigious distances, and they travel in luxury aboard commercial or, in many cases, personal jets. Jones, on the other hand, played in an era when clubs featured hickory shafts, not lightweight steel or even lighter weight graphite, and he traveled from tournament to tournament via automobile, train, or ocean liner. It was hardly an easy way to go.

Over the years the makeup of the Grand Slam has changed slightly, with the U.S. Amateur and the British Amateur having been replaced by the Masters and the P.G.A. championships. Bobby Jones was always an amateur—he never played the game for money—but the great majority of today's best players are professionals, and thus not eligible to play in "amateur" tournaments. Still, the Slam has really been challenged seriously only once; many players have won two legs of the Slam, but only one—Ben Hogan—has ever won three. In 1953

Hogan won the Masters, the U.S. Open, and the British Open, at Carnoustie, but never had a chance to complete the Slam because that year the British Open and the P.G.A. championship were scheduled in such a way that it was impossible to play in both of them. The Slam remains first and foremost on the minds of golfers everywhere; indeed, when a player wins the Masters tournament, the first of the Slam events held each season, he invariably is asked, "Do you think you can win the Grand Slam?"

Today's players like to suggest that one reason no one has ever duplicated Jones's achievement is that there is a larger number of so-called great players competing in every tournament. The implication, of course, is that Bobby Jones teed it up against a bunch of 10-handicappers. Sour grapes. Jones's competition included such skilled shotmakers as Walter Hagen, Gene Sarazen, Tommy Armour, Horton Smith, and Johnny Farrell. Bobby Jones was just better than all of them, starting with the driver, which he hit ramrod straight, and going to the putter, his famous Calamity Jane, a hickory-shafted blade that never failed Jones in time of need.

In all, Jones won a total of 13 major championships—major meaning those four tournaments included in the Grand Slam—during his brief career; he retired from competitive golf in 1930, at the age of 28, after winning the Slam. Only one player, Jack Nicklaus, has won more "majors" than Jones; Nicklaus, who grew up in golf with Jones as his idol, has won 19 majors, spread among four U.S. Opens, five Masters, three British Opens, five PGAs, and two U.S. amateurs. But he has never won more than two in any one year.

The first of the majors in 1930 was the British Amateur, played that year on the Old Course at St. Andrews, the home of golf, as the Scots like to call the historic links with the seven double greens; for instance, the fourth and the fifteenth holes at St. Andrews share a common putting surface, although that green—from one side to the other—is much more than 100 yards wide. Jones had won the 1927 British Open over the Old Course, and he was familiar with the layout. Sure enough, he started the Amateur brilliantly, going birdie, par, birdie, eagle (he holed a 150-yard shot from a fairway bunker), birdie—or 5-under par for the first five holes. This put him three up on Englishman Henry Roper, and Jones then played out the string to win 3-and-2.

Two days later Jones had to play two matches in a treacherous wind that roared in from the adjacent sea.

LEFT: *Bobby Jones is cheered by the crowd after sinking his last putt for a 287 and a victory at the U.S. Open.* ABOVE: *Jones swinging one of his hickory-shafted clubs in the British Open. Jones, an amateur from Atlanta, Georgia, won the event.*

In the morning he disposed of Dow Shankland 5-and-3, but in the afternoon he was forced to the nineteenth hole before beating defending champion Cyril Tolley 1-up. And it was a strange finish, indeed. In those days a player could what they called "stymie" his opponent by rolling his putt almost to the lip of the cup and stopping it in such a way that it blocked his opponent's route to the cup; he then could leave the ball there. Jones did exactly that, and won the match. (Today, the "stymie" is not legal; players must mark a ball if an opponent so requests.)

During Jones's era golf was an endurance contest as much as it was a shot-making competition. On the following day Jones had to play two more matches, win-

ABOVE: *Bobby Jones in the center of the picture, escorted by the crowd during the final round of the 1930 British Amateur Golf Championship at St. Andrews.* OPPOSITE: *Jones holds the trophy symbolizing his win of the British Open Championship in 1930. No one has duplicated his Grand Slam.*

ning by a 7-and-6 rout in the morning and by a tight 1-up in the afternoon. Then he had to play two more matches the next day, prevailing 1-up over Eric Fidder in the morning and 1-up again in the afternoon against fellow American George Voight. Jones found himself in what seemed to be a hopeless predicament against Voight—two down with five holes to play—but rallied brilliantly to even the match at the sixteenth hole. He stayed even at the seventeenth by making a long putt, then won on the home hole. Jones now had to play 36 holes again the next day in the finals, but as it turned out he needed only 30 holes to beat Roger Wethered by a 7-and-6 margin.

The world didn't realize it at the time, but the Grand Slam was on.

Three weeks later, following a vacation trip to Paris, Jones arrived at the Royal Liverpool links near Hoylake for the British Open, which was a stroke-play competition, not match play, as the British Amateur had been. Jones opened with a 2-under-par 70 and followed that with an even-par 72 to take a one-shot lead into the final day, when the players would have to go 36 holes. In the morning of that final day Jones played poorly, ballooning to a two-over-par 74, and lost his lead to Archie Compton. But in the afternoon Jones caught Compton early, established a lead, and protected it to the end, finishing with a comfortable 75 to sweep the championship.

When Jones arrived back in the United States, he was tendered a ticker-tape parade up Broadway in New York, his second such reception in four years. The U.S. Open was next. When Jones reached Minneapolis, the site of the host Interlachen club, the weather was hotter than a pistol; he had endured the chills, the winds, and the rains of England and Scotland, now he would have to suffer the wicked 100-degree heat of Interlachen. Jones opened with a safe 71 but trailed Macdonald Smith and Tommy Armour by a shot, and after a second-round 73 he trailed leader Horton Smith by two shots. As always, the Open closed with two rounds on Saturday, and for 36 holes Jones was even more scorching than the weather. In the morning he made six birdies during a round that featured only 27 putts and posted a 68 to take a five-shot lead on the field. Jones faltered at times during the afternoon round—about the only real criticism that Jones ever had to suffer during his playing career was comments to the effect that he too often turned a seemingly secure victory into a very tight victory because of so-called mental lapses down the stretch—and with five holes to play he had lost four

shots of his lead and led Smith by only one shot. But as Jones always did when the going got tough, he dropped a birdie putt on the fourteenth and then another at the sixteenth to widen his margin. Then, sure enough, with victory seemingly in his grasp, Jones lapsed again, taking a double bogey at the seventeenth. But whatever hope Smith may have had was dashed on the eighteenth hole when Jones rapped in a 50-foot putt and won the Open by two shots.

Three down, one to go: the U.S. Amateur at Merion, outside Philadelphia.

As it developed, the Amateur was a piece of cake for Jones. He was never behind at any time in any of his matches leading up to the scheduled 36-hole final against Eugene Homans, and he never gave Homans much of a chance, either, wiping him out on the twenty-ninth hole by an 8-and-7 count. On the eleventh tee of Merion there is a plaque that states that it was on this hole in the year 1930 that Bobby Jones completed his Grand Slam.

Jones announced his official retirement from regular tournament golf shortly after winning the Amateur. He was only 28, but he had left behind a record that still stands today. Indeed, the Grand Slam remains the most elusive conquest in sports.

THE STUFF OF MIRACLES

Ben Hogan miraculously survived a head-on collision on a
foggy Texas road . . . and even more miraculously, he returned to the golf course and dominated the game

It was a cold, rainy February morning in the Texas Panhandle and a pea-soup fog had settled in, turning the highways into semiblind passageways. Ben Hogan and his wife, Valerie, woke up in their motel room in El Paso and Ben soon began packing their luggage, including his trusty golf clubs, into their new Cadillac so they could continue on their trip from Phoenix, Arizona, to their home in Fort Worth. Hogan was in an understandably festive mood at the time.

The 1949 Professional Golfers Association tour was just a month old, but Hogan, 36, already was the leading money winner with more than $11,000. He had won two championships, and a few days before had tied

ABOVE: *Ben Hogan recuperates from a near-fatal accident, a head-on crash with a bus on February 2, 1949. OPPOSITE (top and bottom): Hogan's recovery was miraculous. Here he is shown competing in the 1950 Los Angeles Open. Hogan won the U.S. Open that year, the following year, and in 1953.*

Jimmy Demaret for first place in Phoenix, only to lose in a sudden-death playoff. But Hogan, no one else, all 135 pounds of him, was at the top of the golf world in those days. He had won the PGA Championship in both 1946 and 1948 and the United States Open title in 1948, and he was the favorite each week as the PGA tour played in 72-hole competitions around the country. Now he was going home to rest for a time in his new house.

The Hogans pulled onto highway 80 and headed east. The conditions were not conducive to easy riding; indeed, highway 80 was a two-lane road that featured sharp curves and unannounced dips, and, of course, there was that dense fog. In a later era, someone with the credentials of a Ben Hogan would not be driving from an El Paso to a Fort Worth; the trip would be made in the luxury of a private jet. But this was 1949, a time when golfers were still playing for peanut-sized purses.

As Ben Hogan drove through the fog, a large trailer truck and a large bus were heading for El Paso on highway 80. The truck led the bus in what was a slow procession, too slow for the driver of the bus. Suddenly, the bus driver pulled out of his lane and tried to pass the truck. Immediately, the bus driver found himself racing down a hill, picking up speed; his vision limited severely, the bus driver undoubtedly never knew that the road would go from level to downhill so abruptly.

The bright lights of the bus instantly focused on a car coming dead-on from the east. Ben Hogan's car. The bus and the car were on a collision course, and there was nothing that either driver—Ben Hogan or the bussie—could do to prevent it. The massive bus smashed into Hogan's new car, driving the steering wheel straight through the driver's seat and almost out the back. No way the driver of the car could have lived! Milliseconds before impact, though, Hogan, reacting with great instinct, tossed himself across the front seat and landed on his wife, hoping that he might protect her once the car began to break up, as he knew it would. As it turned out, Valerie Hogan emerged from the collision with remarkably few injuries. Her husband may well have been lucky to be alive, but his injuries were severe.

It took almost 90 minutes for an ambulance to

reach the site of the crash. During that time Hogan lay alongside the highway, his body a wreck. The Hogans's new car was damaged beyond repair, and their luggage was everywhere; Ben's golf clubs were scattered on the wet road, but it was doubtful that he'd ever be able to use them again. Finally, the ambulance arrived and carted Hogan on a three-hour ride to a hospital back in El Paso. By now reports of the collision were on the major newswires that served the country and the world, and more than one dispatch stated that Ben Hogan was dead.

"I am lucky to be alive," Hogan said in a soft, pained voice when he arrived at the hospital. He was indeed, but he also was very close to death. His injuries were many: a fractured pelvis, a broken collarbone, facial and eye bruises, a broken rib, a broken ankle, bladder complications, and severe contusions in his leg. Lying in his hospital bed, Hogan could not help but keep his eyes trained on his golf clubs; his wife had brought the clubs to the hospital and set them in the corner, hoping no doubt that they would serve as a psychological stimulant to her battered and bruised husband.

Then, there was more trouble: a blood clot passed to Hogan's lung and threatened his life. A second clot was discovered almost immediately, with doctors fearing that it would pass to Hogan's heart—and prove fatal. News of Hogan's condition—*grave* was the proper word for it—passed throughout the country in a flash; one major news service, preparing for official word that Hogan had passed away, transmitted his obituary to its subscribers around the world, instructing them to hold the obit until Hogan's death was official.

Doctors recommended a vena cava operation for Hogan, suggesting strongly that it was the only way his life might be saved. If successful, the vena cava would restrict the passage of that second clot and prevent it from reaching the heart. Hogan asked the doctors, "Will I be able to use my legs and play golf again?" When the answer came back in the affirmative, Hogan gave them the go-ahead for the surgery. A specialist was flown in from New Orleans via a U.S. military plane, and he performed the operation in El Paso. Following the two-hour surgery, Hogan was in a cast from his waist almost to his neck, his left leg was massively swollen, and he would need regular blood transfusions. But he was alive.

Ten months later, miracle of miracles, Hogan made his return to golf when he entered the 1950 Los Angeles Open. His body still ached and creaked in places, and

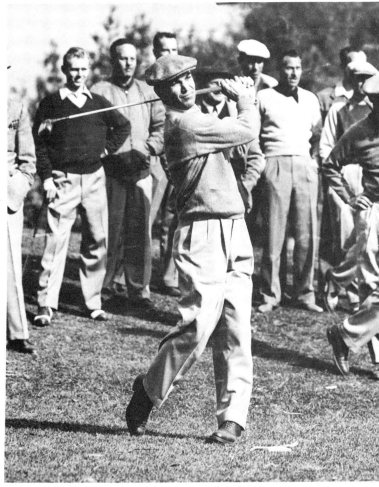

his legs ailed him at times, but he had the itch to play the game at which he was the best in the world. He had played three rounds at home in Fort Worth late in 1949, and he had hit practice balls on occasion, but now he wanted to try it again for real, to see if he could still play the game with any great skill.

Ben and Valerie did not drive from Fort Worth to Los Angeles; they took the train. And once Bantam Ben showed up at the Riviera Country Club, he was welcomed as the conquering hero returning home, for Riviera had been the site of two previous victories in the L.A. Open as well as his triumph in the 1948 U.S. Open. He shot a 69 in one early practice round, but he didn't really decide to compete in the tournament until he shot a stunning 67 in another practice round the day before the opening 18 holes of the championship proper.

Hogan's return to competition had aroused the emotion of the country, and all the leading sportswriters were there at Riviera to report on his comeback. As for the gallery, Hogan was followed by thousands of people each day, while the other pros in the field played their rounds in solitary splendor.

In the first round at Riviera Hogan shot a 73, and the next day he shot a splendid 69. But he was tired, and some said that he was tempted to withdraw from the tournament. Whatever, his game was not very, sharp during the third round, but then Hogan got a break: rain flooded the Riviera course and wiped out the round. Hogan needed the rest. The following day a refreshed Hogan shot another 69, and in the final round he had his third straight 69. In the Riviera clubhouse Hogan's four-round total of 280 seemed unbeatable, with only Sam Snead having any chance to catch him. Standing on the seventeenth tee, Snead realized he needed two birdies on the last two holes to tie Hogan—and he got them, forcing an 18-hole playoff, which was held a week later because the pros had a scheduling conflict involving the Bing Crosby tournament.

As it turned out, Snead won that playoff at Riviera, shooting a 72 to beat Hogan's 76, but there was no trace of defeat on Hogan's face when they gave Snead the trophy and the winner's check. Indeed, as Hogan said to the crowd, "I'm happy to be playing the game."

The L.A. tournament convinced Hogan that he would be able to play golf at his old skill level, but, in fact, he went on to perform at a level that exceeded his performance prior to the car crash on highway 80. Later in the summer of 1950, Hogan won the U.S. Open for the second time, beating George Fazio and Lloyd Man-

grum in a playoff after they had finished the regulation 72 holes at 287; Hogan shot a 69, while Mangrum had a 73 and Fazio a 75. He won the U.S. Open again the following year and also in 1953, and he took the Masters at Augusta in 1951 and 1953. It was in 1953, though, that Hogan scored one of his most brilliant victories when he made one of his infrequent forays abroad and won the British Open at treacherous Carnoustie in Scotland.

Today, caddies and other Scotsmen still love to tell how Hogan played the demanding par-5 sixth hole at Carnoustie each round. During practice, Hogan had discovered that the best way to birdie the sixth hole was to play your tee shot and your long wood shot down the left side, in the rough; by doing this, you would leave yourself with an open shot into the trick green, one without any bunkers in the way. The risk, though, was that there was an out-of-bounds fence all down the left side. Hogan was willing to court this disaster, however, and each round he played his shots down the left side, dropping them into perfect position from which to execute the next shot. He played the sixth hole in 4 under par. At Carnoustie they now call the left rough on number six "Hogan's Alley," and with good reason.

By virtue of that triumph at Carnoustie, Hogan today is one of only four golfers ever to win all four major championships—the U.S. Open, the Masters, the P.G.A. and the British Open; Gene Sarazen, Gary Player, and Jack Nicklaus are the others. He also is one of only four golfers to win the U.S. and the British Opens in the same year; Sarazen, Bobby Jones, and Lee Trevino are the others.

The story of Ben Hogan's remarkable recovery from the doorstep of death was, as they say in show business, a natural for Hollywood, and Glenn Ford was enlisted to play the role of Ben Hogan in the movie, which was called *Follow the Sun.* It brought tears to the eyes of millions.

Ben Hogan accepts the trophy for the U.S. Open Championship. Lloyd Mangrum, who finished second, applauds Hogan's victory. Hogan, Mangrum, and George Fazio were tied at 287 over 72 holes at Merion Golf Club, Ardmore, Pa. Hogan shot a 69 in the playoff, leaving Mangrum 4 strokes behind at 73.

THE COUP AT OAKMONT

*Arnold Palmer's reign as the King of Golf ended almost in his
backyard when a brutish youngster from Ohio by the name of Jack Nicklaus routed the King
from his throne by winning a playoff for the 1962 U.S. Open*

When golf nuts sit around with their favorite cocktails in their overlapping grips, sooner or later—usually sooner—they begin to play the old game of golf trivia. Like what was the name and the age of Bobby Jones's caddie when he completed his Grand Slam that day at Merion? Or what was the name of the man who was driving the bus that crashed into Ben Hogan's new Cadillac that foggy morning on highway 80? Or what percentage of the finishers in the 1955 U.S. Open used Spalding Dots? Or what did Arnold Palmer major in at Wake Forest? Now try this one: where, when, how, and why did Jack Nicklaus first convince the rest of the golfing world that he was not just some fat hotshot from the amateur ranks, that he was not just some cocky golden boy who could hit the ball out of sight, that he was on the road to success, fame, glory, and the multi-millionaire's club.

Where: the Oakmont Country Club in Pittsburgh.

When: in the 1962 U.S. Open.

How: by defeating the reigning king of golf, Arnold Palmer, in a tense 18-hole playoff for the Open crown.

Why: if you can win at Oakmont, you can win anywhere. Indeed, on any given day, there is no better golf course in the United States than Oakmont, with its 187 bunkers, including the famed "church pews," and its lightning-quick greens, of which one touring pro once said, "It's like putting down a flight of marble stairs and trying to stop your ball halfway down."

Now, let's go back to the month of June, in the year 1962, when Arnold Palmer was 32 and Jack Nicklaus was 22. Palmer was at the charismatic peak of his game; he had won 33 pro tournaments, including the Masters Tournament just two months before, and he was favored to win at Oakmont, too. Two years earlier Palmer, the master of the incredible, go-for-broke finish, had captured the hearts of people everywhere by coming from seven shots behind on the final day, when they played two rounds, to win the Open at Cherry Hills in Denver. Now he was at home, the general playing host to his legion of followers, the members of Arnie's Army. Indeed, Palmer has always made his home in Latrobe, Pennsylvania, about 40 miles east of Pittsburgh, and Oakmont was right there in his back yard.

In the late 50s and early 60s, Arnold Palmer was the king of golf. His energy, charisma, and ability to mount a charge on the final day of a close match endeared him to thousands of fans who came to call themselves Arnie's Army. His dominance ended in 1962 with the coming-of-age of Jack Nicklaus.

As for Nicklaus, he had turned pro at the start of the 1962 season after winning his second U.S. Amateur championship, but he had not won anything on the tour. At 5 feet 11½ inches and 205 pounds and wearing the baggiest of pants and shirts, Nicklaus looked more like the Incredible Hulk than any golf pro. In fact, the other players on the tour called him (behind his back) such fitting names as "Whaleman," "Sir Blob-O," and "Ohio Fats." By any name, though, Nicklaus, the Golden Bear from Columbus, Ohio, could play the game of golf; he just needed to win that first tournament, the one that would ignite his career.

Palmer, never one to mask his feelings, was obviously and understandably keyed up for this Open. "I want to win here at Oakmont more than I've ever wanted to win any tournament in my career," he said on the eve of the opening round. No one bothered to ask

the fat kid how he thought he'd play at Oakmont. No one really thought the fat kid had much of a chance. No one, that is, except for the fat kid's friends from Columbus, dubbed "the Silent Minority" by the members of Arnie's Army. Then Nicklaus launched his Open by making a birdie on each of the first three holes, and the hunt was on.

·Nicklaus eventually came back to earth and finished that first round with an even-par 72, while Palmer, with whom he was paired, turned in a 1-under 71. Then, the following day, Palmer had the Army going bonkers as he shot a strong, 4-under-par 68, two strokes lower than the score posted by Nicklaus, who had a 70. Palmer's 36-hole score of 139 tied him with Bob Rosburg for the halfway lead; Nicklaus was three shots behind the co-leaders.

In those days the Open concluded with 36 holes on Saturday, meaning it was almost as much of an endurance contest as it was a match of shot-making skills. Playing inspired golf, Palmer attacked the Oakmont layout during the third round that final morning. With the Army cheering wildly every time he hitched up his pants—something he did a dozen or so times every hole—Palmer hit one of the par 5 holes with his second shot and drove his tee shot onto the green of the par 4 seventeenth hole, a prodigious blast. He hit 16 greens in all, but he couldn't put the field away for keeps because he needed 38 putts to get around the Oakmont greens. He finished with a 1-over-par 73, and Nicklaus, shooting

a 72, pulled to within two strokes of the lead, which Palmer now shared with Bobby Nichols. If Palmer had made just half the putts that were practically gimmes for a player of his stature, the Open would have been closed. Instead, it was wide open.

At lunch between rounds Palmer seemed surprisingly nervous as he munched on a ham and cheese sandwich and downed a peculiar elixir—coke mixed with milk. Nicklaus, on the other hand, was surprisingly at ease; he had won the Ohio Open championship at the age of 16, beating a large field of outstanding professionals, and the word was that the kid was nerveless; nothing bothered him.

Maybe not, but after eight holes of the final round that afternoon—and with just ten holes to play—Palmer seemed to have things completely under control, leading Nichols and Phil Rodgers by two strokes and Nicklaus by four. Then the wheels began to come undone. On the par 5, 480-yard, uphill ninth—a hole that he had reached in 2 in the morning but had then 3-putted—Palmer powered his second shot into the light rough alongside the green, some 20 yards from the pin. Obviously trying to put too much finesse into the shot, Palmer chili-dipped his recovery—plopping it about 10 feet—and then made a poor chip, after which he needed two putts to finish the hole with a bogey. Nicklaus, playing just ahead of Palmer, had birdied the ninth, so Palmer's lead over him was down to two strokes. Then, Nicklaus birdied the par 4 eleventh hole,

LEFT: *Arnold Palmer blasts out of a sand trap in the first round of the 1979 PGA Championship.* RIGHT: *22-year-old Jack Nicklaus chips onto the 18th green, on his way to a playoff victory over Arnold Palmer for the 1962 U.S. Open.* OPPOSITE: *Nicklaus, steady in the playoff, putts on the 13th green.*

and when Palmer bogeyed the par 3 thirteenth after hitting his tee shot into a bunker and making a poor recovery, Nicklaus and Palmer suddenly were tied for the lead with five holes to play. In five holes Nicklaus had picked up four shots on Palmer, and suddenly the Army was quiet. For a change.

Nicklaus and Palmer both had good chances to win over the final holes. They both missed makeable birdie putts of less than 10 feet at the fourteenth. On the short, par 4 seventeenth, Nicklaus tried to carry the green with his drive but landed in a greenside bunker; he made a poor recovery but followed with a strong chip and a firm putt for his par. Palmer had eagled the seventeenth in the morning, and he tried to drive the green again. He missed, but a delicate chip left him with a 10-foot putt for a birdie. Victory was staring Palmer in the face as he studied his putt.

Suddenly, he walked away from the ball. Later, Palmer said, "I overheard the TV announcer summarizing my putt up in the booth." Asked if he agreed with the announcer's opinion, Palmer snapped, "No." Sure enough, as he had done so often throughout the Open, Palmer then missed the putt. Palmer and Nicklaus both had good birdie tries at eighteen, but both missed.

Palmer finished that last round with a 71, 1 under par, but Nicklaus shot a 69, 3 under, and they tied for the Open at 283, two strokes better than Nichols and Rodgers. Playoff time.

Those who were in the crowd of 10,000 for Sun-

day's eighteen-hole playoff remember three things about the Palmer-Nicklaus showdown:

1) The gallery, composed mostly of members of Arnie's Army, was incredibly noisy and rude, particularly to Nicklaus, whose shots were greeted by boos and whose every move was accompanied by some snide comment from the gallery. No one could recall a crowd as inhospitable as the fans this day at Oakmont. It was to Nicklaus's credit that he kept himself elevated above the masses, but the taunts, the boos, the boorishness had to bother the young Ohioan.

2) Palmer became upset, and reacted accordingly, when he felt that Nicklaus, one of the slowest players in golf history, took too-too-too much time preparing to hit some shots. "Jack plays too damn slow and I told him so," said an irate Palmer after one hole. On the other hand, Palmer makes everyone appear to play slowly because he plays very speedily, never surveying his shots from 27 different angles, the way the Nicklauses of the world usually do.

3) Nicklaus won mainly because Palmer couldn't sink a putt t-h-i-s long all day, or, for that matter, all tournament. Over 90 holes Palmer had a staggering 10 3-putt greens; Nicklaus, on the other hand, had only one. Nicklaus stunned the Army on the very first tee when he whacked his drive practically out of sight and then took a one-shot lead over Palmer by making a routine par 4 while Arnold, who had hit his six-iron second shot over the green, was struggling to a bogey. Nicklaus extended his lead to two shots with a 4 at the fourth, then he doubled his margin to four strokes by birdieing the par 3 sixth hole while Palmer, who had hit his tee shot into a bunker, was making a bogey. Palmer then began to pick away at the Nicklaus lead, and after birdies at the tenth, eleventh, and twelfth holes he suddenly trailed by only one shot. But then Palmer's putter killed him again. Nicklaus made a routine par 3 at the thirteenth, Palmer 3-putted still one more time—and the Nicklaus lead was two strokes. Jack played smartly down the stretch, as the two players matched par until the home hole, where Nicklaus made a bogey 5 to Palmer's double-bogey 6.

When all the strokes were added up, Nicklaus had a 71, Palmer had a 74 and the Fat Kid from Ohio was the new U.S. Open champion. More importantly, on that day at Oakmont the face of golf took on a whole new look, one that would dominate the sport for the next 20 years. Ohio Fats had come to the palace of the king and had pulled off his coup. Jack Nicklaus was now the king of golf.

THE HEX OF THE MERRY TEX-MEX

When the big names of golf met in a playoff for the
1971 U.S. Open championship, it was the comical hustler named Trevino who beat the king named Nicklaus

For most of his life, a place like the Merion Golf Club in Ardmore, Pennsylvania—just off Philadelphia's Main Line—was off limits to Lee Trevino. Merion has always been one of the reigning bastions of blue blood, old wealth, tartan blazers, and posh clubbiness in America. Merion members still like to tell the story of their chairman of the greens committee who one year took it upon himself to remove a honeysuckle vine from a fence along the back nine. The chairman was told that he had overstepped his authority in snipping the honeysuckle and was forced to resign from the club.

Trevino never had to worry about such things when he was growing up. He is a red-blooded Tex-Mex who never had more than a dime in his pocket when he was a kid, who grew up on the other side of the tracks, as they might say around Merion. There were no Trevinos to be seen around Merion, or, for that matter, around any other country club. No, sir. No Tex-Mex hustlers from Muni courses allowed. Trespassers will be prosecuted. Keep off the grass, especially the Merion Blue. Hey, boy, yes you, the service entrance is around to the rear.

No one has ever accused Jack Nicklaus of being a "clubbie," but it is a fact that he grew up in a "club" environment. While the Scioto Club in Columbus, Ohio, may well lack—by design, mind you—some of the pomp, the circumstance, and the airs of Merion, it is a private place, for members only, and you don't belong there if you have to ask what the initiation fee is. Nicklaus was always able to show up at the club at, say, 10 A.M. and find himself a game, and that was a lot better than getting to the Muni at 4:30 A.M. so you could get an 11:43 A.M. teeoff time, which is what the hustling young Trevino always had to do.

Whatever the differences in their backgrounds, here now were Trevino and Nicklaus meeting at fabled old Merion in an 18-hole playoff for the 1971 U.S. Open championship. It was a dream match, as the headline writers all labeled it. Nicklaus—20 pounds slimmer now than he had been two years earlier—had the world of golf all to himself throughout most of the 1960s. Then suddenly this hotshot young Tex-Mex with a red shirt, black pants, red socks, black shoes, a baseball-style cap, and a bandage across his forearm—To cover up the tat-

tooed name of a lady who's not his wife, friends explained, adding that Trevino had picked up the tattoo during his military days overseas—showed up at Oak Hill in Rochester and won the 1968 U.S. Open. And instead of going away, he stayed around and began to make life miserable for all the golf pros—and particularly for Nicklaus.

Indeed, between that 1968 Open and the 1971 Open, Nicklaus had to share center stage with Trevino; Nicklaus won nine tournaments, Trevino eight. Also, a large segment of the golfing public—namely, Muni golfers—suddenly had someone with whom they could identify, someone who knew what it was to play golf the hard way. The name Trevino began to bring big bucks from advertisers; they quickly bought up the successful Tex-Mex, who now even had his own corporate logo: a sombrero, which he displayed on all his clothes, luggage, golf equipment.

For all his success, though, Trevino also managed to have plenty of fun. He usually was the first one to arrive at, and the last one to leave, a party, and on the golf course he always seemed to spend more time cracking jokes to the gallery than concentrating on his shots. Trevino's behavior perplexed Nicklaus, who never has been called the life of a party and never has had a funny way with words. Several months before the 1971 Open Nicklaus took Trevino aside for a little chat. The gist of Nicklaus's advice to Trevino was this: "Lee, I hope you never find out how good you really are." In other words, if Trevino ever really applied himself to golf, there'd be no stopping him.

Trevino took Nicklaus's words to heart. "What Jack said just filled me with confidence," Trevino said before the first round of the Open. "I've worked hard on my game, I've played well—very well—in six straight tournaments, and I think I can win here at Merion." As for Merion, Trevino described it as "a course that has 16 birdie holes but 18 bogey holes. I'll eat all the cactus around El Paso if anybody breaks 280 for four rounds."

Trevino started the Open with a round of 70, even par, but Nicklaus shot a 69. They both scored 72 in the second round, then the next day Nicklaus shot a 68 to edge Trevino by still another shot. So, for three rounds, Nicklaus was one under par and Trevino was one over,

and Nicklaus trailed leader Jim Simons, a young amateur from western Pennsylvania and Wake Forest, by two shots, with Trevino four shots off the lead.

On Sunday Nicklaus caught the faltering Simon with a birdie at the fourth hole, but Jack promptly followed that with a double bogey at the fifth. Trevino, meanwhile, was blazing hot, and when he birdied the fourteenth to go two under for the round, he found himself in the lead by a shot. Simons had bowed out, and it was a showdown between the Merry Mex, Trevino, and the Golden Bear, Nicklaus.

Trevino parred fifteen, sixteen, and seventeen, and so did Nicklaus, but Jack had to work overtime, holing putts of from 6 to 12 feet. "You won't see any greater clutch putting than the show Nicklaus put on over those three holes," Trevino said later. Still, Trevino needed only a par on the eighteenth—a monster hole that calls for a well-placed drive out of a shoot and a long-iron approach to a small, slick green—to win the Open. Trevino likes to fade the ball, but this time he faded his drive too much to the right, and then hit his three-wood approach shot over the green. His chip rolled to within eight feet of the cup. Trevino studied his putt—the Open championship was at stake—from every angle, but as he prepared to strike the ball his concentration was broken when a young boy fell off a nearby tree. When Trevino finally putted, he made a poor effort— and then tapped in for his bogey.

Now it was up to Nicklaus, and you cannot play the demanding eighteenth much better than Jack did. He drilled his tee shot down the middle, spanked an approach to within 15 feet—and now *he* had a putt to win the Open. Nicklaus had made three putts of similar length in succession, and he put a good stroke on this putt, too, but the ball just slipped past the edge of the cup. Playoff.

Having grown up among golf hustlers, Trevino is a masterful player when the competition is *mano-a-mano*—one against one. The pressure never bothers him. Not that Nicklaus has ever been one to buckle when the going gets tough, but when they were waiting to start their eighteen-hole shootout on Monday afternoon, Nicklaus appeared to be unusually tense as he sat under a tree while Trevino was chattering away a-mile-a-minute. Then, suddenly, Trevino reached into his golf bag and pulled out a snake and tossed it at Nicklaus. Actually, it was a rubber snake, but Trevino's message was clear: "Golden Bear, I'm gonna have some fun today."

Once the laughter subsided, they played away, and

TOP: *Lee Trevino, the irrepressible "Super Mex," watches his iron shot head toward the green as a polite gallery looks on.* ABOVE: *Trevino sinks a putt for par on 18, forcing a sudden death playoff with Art Wall at the 1971 Canadian Open, which Trevino won. The previous month, Trevino won the U.S. Open.*

77

Nicklaus jumped into the lead by making a par 4 at the first hole while Trevino was taking a bogey. Then the fun started for Trevino. On the par 5 second hole Nicklaus hit his long approach shot into a bunker near the green. Nicklaus has never been noted for his sand play; in fact, it has long been the weakest part of his game. Inexplicably, he failed to get the ball out of the trap with his first explosion, and he ended up with a bogey 6 on the hole. Trevino made his par and was now even.

On the par 3 third hole, Nicklaus encountered disaster once again. Trevino and Nicklaus both hit their tee shots into the same bunker. Trevino blasted out to three feet and made the putt for his par, but Nicklaus once again left his first shot in the bunker and eventually made a double-bogey 5. So Trevino led by two strokes after three holes. Nicklaus closed that margin to a single stroke with a birdie putt of six feet at the fifth hole, and after they both made par 4 at the sixth, a rainstorm delayed play for 20 minutes. Trevino later regained his two-shot lead with a tap-in birdie at the eighth. On the short ninth Trevino made a routine par, but Nicklaus almost had a hole-in-one as his tee shot checked out the cup before stopping three feet away. Jack made the putt for his birdie, and at the end of nine

Trevino led by a shot.

The tenth hole at Merion is ridiculously short, just slightly longer than 300 yards, and there was speculation before the Open that the longer-hitting pros, including Nicklaus, might well drive the green by airmailing their tee shots over the rough and the bunkers. Trevino and Nicklaus both opted for the safe route, however, and their tee shots left them with simple wedge-shot pitches to the pin. Trevino didn't distinguish himself with his effort as he ended up 40 feet from the pin. Nicklaus, only 40 yards from the flag, was in excellent position to tie the match. But then Jack hit the type of shot that millions of hackers hit every weekend: he chili-dipped his pitch, fluffed it, puffed it—and the ball traveled no more than 20 yards. The look on Nicklaus's face was one of anguish, of disbelief. For his next shot, Jack made another poor pitch, and he needed two putts to get the ball into the hole. Trevino, stunned by Nicklaus's generosity, got his ball down safely in two putts, and extended his lead to two strokes once again.

Remarkably, Nicklaus regained his composure immediately and made a birdie 3 at the testy eleventh, a hole on which he had taken triple-bogey 7 in an earlier round. This brought him back to within one stroke of Trevino—again. But Nicklaus would get no closer. Trevino replied to Nicklaus's birdie with a birdie of his own at the par 4 twelfth, sinking a 25-foot putt, and after they matched pars at the short thirteenth, Trevino canned a 10-foot slider to save par at the fourteenth and preserve his two-shot lead.

It really ended at the fifteenth. Nicklaus was less than 8 feet from the cup with his approach, while Trevino was at least 25 feet away. But as Nicklaus continued to study his putt, believing that he could make it and thus shave Trevino's lead in half, Trevino curled his putt into the center of the cup for a birdie. Nicklaus made his putt, too, but his hopes were fading fast. They ended at the seventeenth green. Nicklaus and Trevino both hit their tee shots into a bunker, with Nicklaus's ball ending up in a fried-egg lie. Trevino extricated himself skillfully, blasting to three feet and making the putt. Nicklaus did well to get the ball out of the bunker, but needed two putts and took a bogey. On the eighteenth hole, leading by three shots, Trevino made a routine par to finish the round at 68, and Nicklaus made par to finish with a 71.

Yes, just what Nicklaus had done to Arnold Palmer nine years earlier at Oakmont, Lee Trevino had done to Nicklaus at Merion. Being the king of golf can be an occupational hazard.

Lee Trevino blasts out of a sand trap on the first hole of an 18-hole playoff with Jack Nicklaus for the 1971 U.S. Open Championship. Trevino bogied the hole to go one stroke down, but finished with a 68 and the championship while Nicklaus got a 72.

THE SHOOTOUT AT TURNBERRY

For two days the greatest shotmakers playing the game—
Tom Watson and Jack Nicklaus—waged a private war for the 1977 British Open championship,
and when the battle was over, Watson's 65–65 finish beat Nicklaus's 65–66 by a shot

In sports parlance, there is one word whose meaning is grossly distorted on almost every occasion an author or a speaker employs it. The word: GREATEST.

But in the game of golf, the word "greatest" can be applied to one particular moment—or, as it really was, two rounds that contributed to one moment—that occurred in July of 1977 without fear of debate. The place was the Turnberry Hotel's Ailsa Course, or just plain Turnberry, which is located hard by the Firth of Clyde and overlooks the island bird sanctuary known as the Ailsa Craig. The occasion was the 1977 British Open championship, or more specifically, the final two rounds of the 1977 British Open. For on those two days over the famous Turnberry links, Jack Nicklaus, the greatest golfer of the 1960s and the 1970s, and Tom Watson, the scrub-faced Stanford product from Kansas City, who at the time was generally regarded as Nicklaus's heir apparent, staged the greatest head-to-head shootout ever seen on any golf course anywhere.

One of them won the Open title, of course, but no one who was there, or who saw it on television, or who read about it, can ever say there was a loser. Even runner-up is not the proper word.

Before we get to the events of July 8 and July 9 that created this "greatest" moment in golf history, bar none, a few words of introduction. Watson, then 27, was indeed the emerging star; he had won the British Open in 1975, dominated the American tour for almost two years, and won the 1977 Masters by outgunning Nicklaus, of all people, down the stretch. His game was solid through the bag; the only comment all those TV doctors of the swing ever made about Watson's swing pattern was something to the effect that they thought it occasionally became too mechanical, too programmed. Maybe it was then, and maybe it still is today, but as one player said, "Go tell it to Tom's bankers." Behind Watson's back, though, there were whispers that he was not mentally tough enough under pressure. Watson had indeed seemed to throw away a couple of big tournaments, including a U.S. Open, just when he should have been practicing his victory speech. Maybe that Masters win over the mighty Nicklaus would put all those whispers to rest.

As for Nicklaus, then 37, he had ruled the sport, with only the briefest of interruptions, for 15 years. He had conquered Arnold Palmer, and he had turned back all the Lee Trevinos, Tony Jacklins, Johnny Millers, Tom Weiskopfs, etc., who were supposed to force him into a premature retirement. Nicklaus was spending more time designing golf courses than playing them, and he was working harder perfecting his free throw technique (so he could beat his kids at basketball) than his sand shots, but when it came time for the majors, Jack was always ready. And the British Open is a major.

Clearly, Watson and Nicklaus were in peak form when they arrived at Turnberry, and the Ailsa was waiting for them. Turnberry had long been considered of championship quality, but it was the site of the Open for the first time. During World War II Turnberry had been converted into an R.A.F. base, and even today one can chance upon scraps of an old bomber that didn't quite make it to the runway. The Ailsa and the contiguous Arran layouts sit on linksland below the splendid Turnberry Hotel, which is perched atop a hill, just above a nine-hole par 3 course, and majestically takes in what seems to be a view of the whole world. Turnberry is about 30 miles below Prestwick, on Scotland's west coast, and there is only one road in and one road out. Also, there are not many places nearby where one can

Tom Watson (left) and Jack Nicklaus, between rounds at the 1977 British Open held at Turnberry, Scotland. The two were tied at 203 after the third round. In the final, brilliant 18 holes, Watson shot a 65 while Nicklaus finished with a 66.

79

bed down for an evening—except, of course, for the Turnberry Hotel itself. For these reasons, the ruling Royal and Ancient was always reluctant to schedule its Open for Turnberry, but it finally relented for 1977. Now the British Open, Turnberry, Watson, and Nicklaus share a large place in golf's history books.

Watson and Nicklaus warmed up with 68s the first round and 70s the second round. Nicklaus closed with a back nine of 31 that first round; the next day his 70 would have been no higher than a 67 if he had holed any of the rather makeable putts he continually rolled past the cup. And so it was that Watson and Nicklaus were paired together for the third round at Turnberry on Friday, July 8. At the start of play that day they were both one shot behind the leader, Roger Maltbie of the United States. But it was only a matter of holes before Watson and Nicklaus turned the Open into a private war.

Nicklaus started the match—by definition, it was not a match, because Watson and Nicklaus were competing at medal play, not stroke play—by holing a four-foot putt for a birdie on the first hole. Watson, in turn, birdied the par 4 third hole. Then, on the par 3 fourth, where the green sits in a precarious position atop a cliff, with a shoulder-high mound on the right side and disaster everywhere else, Nicklaus made a birdie two—and so did Watson. Suddenly, it seemed that the entire gallery had descended on the Nicklaus–Watson match. Or as another competitor said, "I was almost run over by the crowd. No one wanted to watch the rest of us, and no one did. They all wanted to watch Nicklaus and Watson. And you know, I did, too."

On the short sixth hole, Nicklaus made his third birdie of the round and pulled two strokes ahead of Watson, who bunkered his tee shot and made a bogey. Then, at the long seventh, Watson rifled his second shot onto the green and two-putted for a birdie, while Nicklaus holed a seven-foot putt for his birdie. Jack now had four birdies in seven holes, and at the turn his 4-under-par 31 led Watson by two strokes. The birdie barrage resumed on the tenth, where the tee overlooks a lighthouse: Nicklaus and Watson both canned their putts for 3s. Nicklaus made his first real mistake of the day at the fourteenth, taking three putts to get down. Watson made a par the hard way, getting up and down in two, and pulled to within a shot of Nicklaus. Watson then wiped out Nicklaus's margin at the short fifteenth as he made a birdie while Jack was taking a routine 3. Watson made still another birdie at the par 5 seventeenth, which played unexpectedly short all week because of favorable weather conditions, and Nicklaus made a

birdie, too, after missing a five-foot putt for an eagle. They both parred the eighteenth hole to finish the round with 65s. They both were atop the leader board at 213—seven under par. No one else was even close.

It seemed unlikely that Watson and Nicklaus could match the level of Friday's play during Saturday's final 18 holes, but as it turned out, they not only matched it, they exceeded it. As on Friday, Nicklaus and Watson had the gallery practically all to themselves, and they treated the spectators to a demonstration of total shot-making, starting right at the first hole. For the second straight day, Nicklaus began with a birdie, and when he followed with a par 4 at the second while Watson was stumbling to a bogey 5, Jack found himself with a two-stroke lead. But as Watson had shown the day before,

Tom Watson, moments after he sank his last putt to win the 1977 British Open. Both Watson and Jack Nicklaus had shot identical 68s in the first round, 70s in the second, and 65s in the third. Watson's final round of 65 beat Nicklaus by one stroke.

two-stroke leads in a match like this aren't worth the scorecard they're written on. Then Nicklaus made still another birdie at the short fourth hole to extend his lead to three strokes.

Aye, the crowd was saying. This Jack, he is getting even with Tom for the Masters. Three shots. Nobody spots Nicklaus three shots and survives. Nobody.

Well, just when people were beginning to wonder if Watson might do a complete fold, Tom rattled off birdies at the fifth, seventh, and eighth holes—and the match was even. But then Tom bogeyed the ninth, and Jack negotiated a safe par 4 to regain the lead by a stroke—33 for Nicklaus, 34 for Watson.

Moving to the final nine, Watson and Nicklaus had matching pars at the tenth, then at the short eleventh Nicklaus seemed ready to double his lead to two strokes when he hit his tee shot onto the putting surface while Watson landed in a bunker. But Watson made a marvelous bunker recovery and dropped his putt for par. Nicklaus had only a 13-foot putt for his birdie, but he missed the cup. On the next hole, though, Nicklaus extended his lead to two strokes by dropping a 25-foot putt for his birdie. So Jack led by two shots with six holes to play.

Watson may have been down, but he definitely was not out. He promptly birdied the thirteenth hole, sinking a 15-foot putt, to reduce Nicklaus's lead to a single shot. Watson and Nicklaus made their pars at the fourteenth; then came the fateful fifteenth, a long par 3 of 210 yards. Watson's tee shot stopped off the green on some hardpan, some 75 feet from the cup. Nicklaus, meanwhile, was on the green safely. To all the world, Nicklaus appeared to have a sure 3 while Watson appeared on the verge of making a bogey. As Watson surveyed his putt, a British TV commentator observed, "He'll do well to get it down in two." Watson finally stroked his putt—banged the putt, that is—and the ball rolled up and down the slopes, went left and went right, and suddenly it crashed against the flagstick, popped up into the air and dropped into the cup for a birdie 2—a miracle birdie 2, to be exact. Lee Trevino had done much the same thing—chipping or putting into the cup from off the green for miracle birdies—to Nicklaus in the 1972 Open at Muirfield, and Jack no doubt felt that he was watching a bad rerun on videotape. Nicklaus failed to make his birdie putt, and now the match was even.

As they walked together to the sixteenth tee, Watson said to Nicklaus, "Jack, this is what it's all about, isn't it." Nicklaus said, "You bet it is." Then they halved the sixteenth with pars.

At seventeen, the par 5 that was still playing short, both Watson and Nicklaus hit strong tee shots. Watson was away, and he struck a pure three iron to within 20 feet of the cup; he was looking at an eagle. Nicklaus then took out a four iron but hit the ball "fat," as he said; his shot landed short and to the right of the green. However, Nicklaus made a fine pitch shot to about four feet of the cup. Watson missed his eagle putt but tapped in for the birdie. Now the pressure was on Jack. He read the putt to break just a hair from left to right, but he either pulled the putt or misread the break; whatever, the ball rolled over the lip on the left. Watson led by a shot.

Playing safely, Watson struck a one-iron off the eighteenth tee and ended up in the middle of the fairway, 150 yards from the pin. Nicklaus, for some reason, went with his driver and blasted the ball into the rough, ending up in a thicket of rough. Most players would have played their recovery the safe way, chipping out onto the short grass. Not Nicklaus. Summoning all his strength, he mightily chopped at the ball with his eight iron and, incredibly, powered it onto the green, although almost 50 feet from the pin. Watson then lofted a perfect seven-iron shot to within two feet of the hole. It was over . . . Or was it?

It is never over when Nicklaus is involved. Jack knew that his only hope was to make his long putt and then pray that Watson missed his tap-in. So Jack holed his putt, sending the gasping crowd into a frenzy. Watson later said that he fully expected Nicklaus to sink that putt, but the look on his face as the ball dropped into the cup said otherwise. Watson waited for order, and then he stepped over his ball and calmly rolled it dead into the heart of the cup for a birdie 3—and the Open championship.

Watson had shot another 65 in the last round, while Nicklaus had shot a 66. Watson had come from two shots behind with six holes to play by birdieing four of those six holes; in all, Watson's card for the final 18 holes showed seven birdies and two bogeys, Nicklaus's card revealed four birdies and no bogeys. Watson finished the tournament at 268, 12 under par, while Nicklaus finished at 269, 11 under par. Watson broke the British Open record by eight shots, Nicklaus by seven. As for the third-place finisher, his name was Hubert Green—and he was 10 strokes behind Nicklaus at 279.

Late that night Nicklaus offered a simple explanation for Watson's victory. "Tom," Jack said, "just played better than I did."

A WAKE-UP CALL FOR THE BIG BEAR

*Jack Nicklaus had not been heard from in almost two years,
but just when people were saying that he was over the hill, Nicklaus stormed back onto the scene
by winning the 1980 U.S. Open at Baltusrol*

There comes a time in the life of every athlete, great or not-so-great, when he or she is forced to ask himself or herself, "Am I done? Is my career over? Should I pack it up and go home for good?"

Sadly, too many great athletes over the years have successfully avoided facing up to this question. They enjoy the limelight, the money, the camaraderie, the life-style, so they overstay their welcome and milk their past for an extra year or two. They say they owe it to the fans not to quit. They say they still have a few more home runs in their bats, or a few more goals in their hockey sticks, or a few more birdies left in their golf bag. Then, as Willie Mays can tell you, they suddenly begin to strike out time after time against pitchers they used to own, and they soon become an embarrassment—to the franchise, to the fans, to themselves. Their reputation becomes tarnished; indeed, people remember what they saw last, not what they saw when the athlete was young and vigorous and better than his contemporaries. It is a sad situation.

Certainly, 40-year-old Jack Nicklaus had to be ask-

ing himself all of the above questions as he prepared to play in the 1980 U.S. Open at Baltusrol in New Jersey. Of course, Nicklaus insists that the above questions never entered his mind. Maybe, maybe not, but the big question on the lips of everyone at Baltusrol was: has Jack had it? And there was good reason to believe that Nicklaus's almost-20-years' domination of the golf world was over, finis, kaput.

As he arrived at Baltusrol, the scene of his record-breaking victory over Arnold Palmer in the 1967 U.S. Open, Nicklaus was in the worst slump of his career. He had not won a major championship in 23 months, or since the 1978 British Open at St. Andrews, and he had not won a tournament of any kind since the 1978 Philadelphia Classic, played the week after his triumph at St. Andrews. In 1979 Nicklaus had finished so far down the official tour money list—in seventy-first place—that he barely earned enough money to fill up the gas tanks of his private jet. And 1980 had been just as unprofitable. In nine tournaments Nicklaus had played well only once—at Doral, in Miami, where he lost a playoff to Raymond Floyd. Otherwise, he finished in such positions as thirty-third, forty-third, and fifty-third, and the week before the Open he missed the 36-hole cut at Atlanta.

To say the least, Jack was not in peak form as the Open got under way at Baltusrol.

One obvious reason for Nicklaus's relatively shoddy play was his inactivity. Instead of playing and/or practicing golf, Nicklaus was spending most of his time working on his corporate endeavors as chairman of the board of Golden Bear, Inc. He was designing golf courses, selling automobiles, making eyeglasses, endorsing clothes, hawking credit cards—you name it. And then there were the nocturnal basketball games with his kids in the driveway. Jack had put golf on the back burner. But then Nicklaus began to read and hear all the reports of his demise, and obviously he was bothered by them.

So, suddenly, Jack put his businesses on the back burner and rediscovered the game that had made him a multimillionaire. He played golf before going to the office, and that had not been the case for several years. He imported Phil Rodgers, an old friend from tour days in the 1960s, to help him reshape his short game, and he spent endless days working his swing under the practiced eye of Jack Grout, his first and only teacher, who had been the pro at Scioto when Nicklaus was growing up in Columbus. And while the 1980 tournament results had not been very rewarding, Nicklaus was not at all unhappy with his game on the eve of the Open. "I'm just this far away," said Nicklaus, spreading apart the tips of his right thumb and forefinger about an eighth of an inch.

It was extremely hot and humid all four days at Baltusrol, and the course conditions—there was really no wind any day, and the fairways were unusually fast because of a drought—were very conducive to low scoring. The opening round was more like a battle for the Ohio State Alumni Championship than anything else. A Buckeye named Tom Weiskopf, playing several holes ahead of a Buckeye named Nicklaus, shot the lights out at Baltusrol; he bogeyed the first hole and then made eight birdies over the next seventeen holes to finish with a 63. Now, a 63 should give you a lead of several strokes, but not this day.

There was Nicklaus breathing down Weiskopf's neck, which is usually red. Like Tom, Jack made an early bogey—at the second hole, a short par 4, when he put his one-iron tee shot under a tree. But then Nicklaus made birdies at the third, fifth, and seventh holes to turn in a 32, two under par, and on the back nine he woke up the ghosts of Opens past by birdieing the eleventh, twelfth, and thirteenth holes in succession. Up ahead Weiskopf could not believe all the red numbers that were appearing alongside Nicklaus's name on the leader boards.

"Here I go and shoot an almost perfect round . . . and Jack won't let me enjoy the glory."

Nicklaus also made birdies at the fifteenth and seventeenth holes, and on the eighteenth green he had a three-foot putt for a birdie that would put him in the clubhouse with a 62, 8 under par. But Nicklaus made his only really poor putt of the day, and the ball slid past the cup. Still he had a 63 on the board, and those two numbers told a message.

The next day Weiskopf ballooned to a 75, and another one of Nicklaus's top challengers, Spain's Severiano Ballesteros, was disqualified because he failed to be at the course for his scheduled mid-morning starting time. Nicklaus may not have known it at the time, but the man who would worry him the most over the next three days was his playing partner, Isao Aoki of Japan.

As it turned out, Nicklaus and Aoki played together all four rounds, and they were an odd sight; Nicklaus would outhit Aoki by 30 to 60 yards off the tee, but then Aoki would roll in another putt from some great distance to make a birdie or save a par. Then he would smile politely to the crowd, which didn't quite know what to make of the little man with the funny putting stroke. Golfers are taught to keep their putters flat on the ground; Aoki, though, addressed his putts in such a way that the toe of the putter head was aimed to the sky, and then he hit the ball almost on the hosel of the club.

Unique or not, that style worked unbelievably well for Aoki, who needed only 27 putts while shooting a 68 in the first round and just 23 putts—13 on the front nine, 10 on the back side—while shooting a second-straight 68 in the second round. Nicklaus, meanwhile, shot a 71 that second day and took a two-shot lead into Saturday's third round. He played only two poor holes, the sixth, which he three putted, and the twelfth, where he put his tee shot into the lip of a bunker and ended up making a double bogey. Still, he was happy with his play for the two days, and his total of 134 for 36 holes was an Open record.

On Saturday Aoki shot his third straight 68 and tied Nicklaus, who managed a 70, for the lead; in truth, though, neither Aoki nor Nicklaus played spectacular golf. But they played well enough to lead the field.

And so now it was Open Sunday. Tom Watson was

OPPOSITE: *Jack Nicklaus doesn't seem pleased with this iron shot on a practice round before the 1980 U.S. Open at Baltusrol Country Club in New Jersey.* ABOVE: *Nicklaus showed a master touch during the championship play, however. He finished with a 63 on the first round and won with a 272.*

83

lurking close to the lead, but he started the final round with a bogey and slowly fell back. Lon Hinkle made a brief charge, but he, too, fell back. And Keith Fergus, a young pro from the University of Houston's golf factory, tried to break up the Nicklaus-Aoki monopoly, but in time he fell back, too.

Nicklaus took a one-shot lead after two holes, Aoki having bogeyed the short but nasty second. Then Nicklaus extended his lead to two shots with a birdie at the third, knocking home a six-foot putt. From the sixth through the eighth holes Nicklaus got somewhat lucky. He kept hitting his tee shots into the rough, but except for the seventh, he was able to get his muscled recoveries onto the putting surface. He bogeyed that seventh, made pars at the sixth and the eighth, and lost only one shot of his lead as Aoki, too, encountered difficulties. Then Nicklaus regained his two-stroke lead by parring the ninth while Aoki was bogeying.

Nicklaus was charged up, and he relentlessly con-

ABOVE: *After winning the 1980 U.S. Open, Nicklaus had new confidence in his short game. Here, he hits to the 3rd green during first round action at the 1980 PGA Championship.* OPPO-SITE: *Nicklaus, the Golden Bear, sinks a birdie putt during the 3rd round of the PGA tournament. He won with a 274.*

tinued his attack on Baltusrol. He nursed his two-shot lead from the tenth through the sixteenth holes by playing each and every shot immaculately; he hit his tee shots to the preferred areas, and he landed his approach shots exactly where he wanted to land them. And as Nicklaus stepped on the seventeenth tee, he still led Aoki by two shots.

Baltusrol may well be the only championship-caliber course that finishes with successive par 5 holes. This obviously favored Nicklaus, who hits the ball longer than Aoki. Nicklaus desperately wanted to birdie number seventeen, so he could play the last hole in a safe but direct manner. He hit two booming shots and then delicately flipped a wedge to about 25 feet. Aoki's pitch shot rolled to within five feet of the hole. Nicklaus knew that Aoki would not miss his putt; he had watched in what at times had to be stunned disbelief as the little Japanese holed everything for almost four rounds. No, he would not miss such a putt. Nicklaus worked on his putt for an interminable time, and then he rolled it into the middle of the cup. As the ball plunked into the hole, Nicklaus broke out with a smile that had not been seen in a couple of years.

Sure enough, Aoki made his birdie putt, too, so Nicklaus had not won anything yet. If Aoki eagled the eighteenth hole and Nicklaus parred it, they would tie for the championship. Anything, of course, was possible. Nicklaus played two safe shots to the hill just below the green; Aoki's two shots left him perhaps 100 yards from the flag. Aoki handles his wedge almost as well as he handles his putter, and he scared the wits out of Nicklaus when his pitch shot rolled over the edge of the cup and stopped a few feet away.

Calling on his new-found short game, Nicklaus pitched skillfully to about 10 feet short of the cup. Nicklaus was away. All Jack wanted to do was lag the ball up the slight hill and stop it dead on line for a tap-in par—and victory. What he did was lag the ball into the cup for a birdie. Aoki, naturally, then rolled in his birdie putt, too, but it was too late. Nicklaus had established an Open record with a winning score of 272, two fewer than Aoki. And Jack's score was three strokes lower than his winning total in 1967 on the same course.

Finished? Jack Nicklaus? No way!

The 1980 was the eighteenth major championship triumph in Nicklaus's distinguished career. Two months later this over-the-hill master won number nineteen as he took the P.G.A. title at Oak Hill in Rochester, N.Y.

"We shouldn't have woken the Big Bear up," said Lee Trevino.

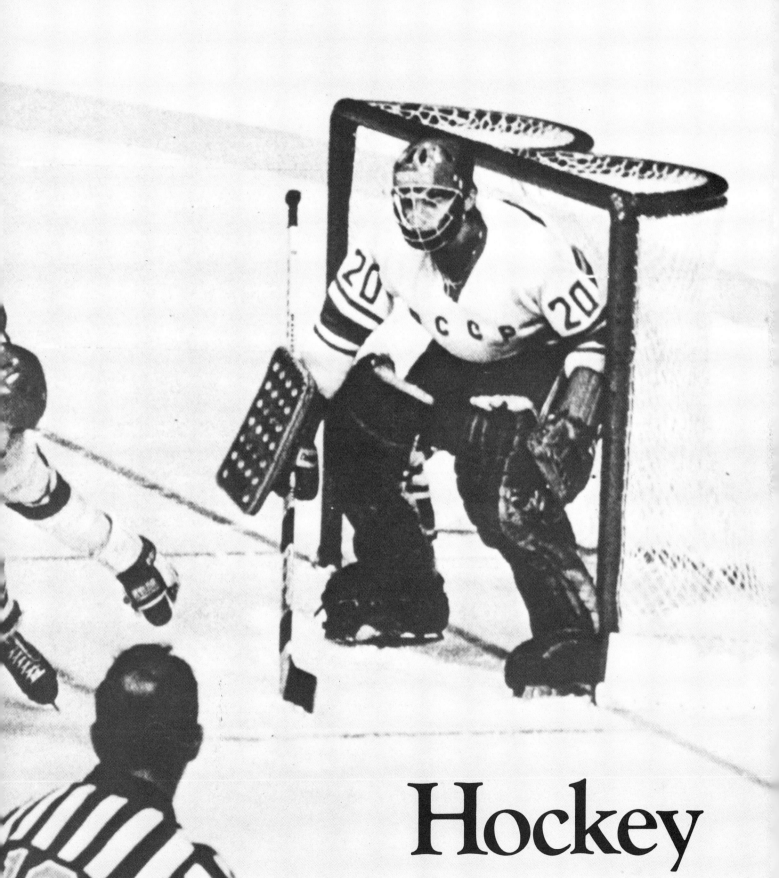

Hockey

HE SAVED HIS COUNTRY

The Soviets were only one game from victory over Canada in
hockey's first Summit Series, but then Paul Henderson became a Canadian hero for life by scoring
the winning goal in three straight games to give Team Canada a thrilling victory

In 1954 the Soviet Union, having studied volumes of Canadian instructional manuals and having analyzed films of Maurice Richard and Gordie Howe in action, invented the game of hockey. Over the next 18 years the Soviets won four Olympic gold medals and 11 world championships, never losing a game to Canada in either competition. But this Soviet supremacy hardly bothered the people of Canada, who, of course, considered hockey to be their national pastime. As they saw it, the best players in the world were the professionals in the National Hockey League. To them, the Soviets had defeated Canadian "amateur" teams—schoolboys, plant workers, minor league castoffs—not the NHL pros. The distinction was very clear.

By 1972 the Soviets had grown tired of winning Olympic and world championships by one-sided scores. They clearly had exhausted the competition at the ama-

teur level and were ready to expand their hockey horizons. Mind you, the Soviet players were hardly amateurs; they played hockey for a living 11 months of the year, spending the other month on an all-expenses-paid vacation at a seaside dacha. By North American standards, the Soviets were as professional as the NHL skaters.

There was another reason, too, why the Soviets wanted to break away from the amateur competitions: cold, hard cash. All the Olympic and world titles never put a single ruble in the hockey federation's coffers, but a series against the NHL pros would, the Soviets knew, realize a profit for them of well over $1 million.

And so it was that in 1972 money talked and, despite the vehement protestations of the Olympic hockey hierarchy, the historic "first" series between the Canadian pros and the Soviet "amateurs" was arranged. Eight games, with the first four in Canada and the last four in Moscow. The winner would get bragging rights to the world.

"If Canada loses even one game," said Team Canada coach Harry Sinden, surveying his lineup of NHL All-Stars, "it will be a national disgrace."

So, it was indeed a national disgrace when the Soviets routed Canada 7–3 in game one before more than 19,000 stunned Canadians in the Montreal Forum on the night of September 2. "This is absolutely Canada's worst day since the price of winter wheat sank below a dollar during the Depression," said one Canada rooter. For a time, though, it had appeared that Canada might well blow the Soviets right back to Moscow; Canada took a 2–0 lead before the game was five minutes old and seemed totally in control. But then the Soviets abruptly took charge and outscored the Canadians 7–1 over the final 55 minutes, embarrassing the NHL pros with their artful puck handling, pinpoint passing, remarkable stamina, and solid goaltending. "They outplayed us everywhere," Sinden conceded.

Two nights later Canada tied the series, winning 4–1 in Toronto, and then the teams played a 4–4 tie in Winnipeg before the Canadian end of the series concluded with a 5–3 Soviet triumph in Vancouver, where

PRECEDING PAGES: *Team Canada vs. the U.S.S.R. team,*
Vancouver, B.C., 1972, Game 4. The Soviets steal
the puck at their end of the ice. They won 5–3.
ABOVE: *Moscow, Sept. 28, Game 8. Canadian fans see*
their team win the game and take the series 4–3–1.

the supposedly patriotic Canadian fans booed their NHL heroes in disgust. Thus, the Soviets took a 2-1-1 series lead back home to Moscow, and left Canadians everywhere in shock.

"After seeing what they did to us at our game, in our rinks, I'm afraid nothing in sport is sacred anymore," said Team Canada forward Frank Mahovlich. "Give those guys a football and they'll beat the Dallas Cowboys in two years."

As the Soviets traveled through Canada, they were read the daily newspaper editorials berating the Team Canada skaters—most press critics contended that Team Canada was losing because its players were spoiled, overpaid, uncoachable fat cats—and found the criticism quite amusing. One night Soviet assistant coach Boris Kulagin was asked how much money the Soviet team's goaltender, Vladislav Tretiak, who had completely outplayed heralded NHL stars Ken Dryden and Tony Esposito in the first four games, earned in his supposedly full-time position as an Army private.

"He makes what all army lieutenants make," Kulagin said.

"But Tretiak's a private, not a lieutenant," Kulagin was reminded.

"Oh, he was a private before this series began, but now he is a lieutenant."

"Well, does he make $200,000 a year, like Team Canada's Brad Park?"

"Is Brad Park an army lieutenant, too?"

Soviet captain Boris Mikhailov, another so-called army lieutenant, joined Kulagin in the laughter. "Brad Park makes $200,000 a year," Mikhailov chuckled, "but I get paid once a month."

As the Soviets headed home to Moscow, Kulagin said, "We came here to learn from the Canadian pros, and now it is obvious that maybe the Canadian pros can learn something from us. These four games have taught us that the Canadian players are ordinary people, just like us."

Two weeks later, on September 22, the series resumed in snowy Moscow. Inexplicably, the Team Canada players had spent a week in Stockholm on their way to Moscow; Canadian officials had figured that Canada would have the series well in hand following the games at home, and what better way to prepare for ten days of Spartan life in Moscow than to relax for a week in friendly, swinging Stockholm. "It was too late for us to change our travel plans," said one Team Canada official, "or else we'd have sent the whole team to Flin Flon, Manitoba, for a week to get in shape."

For a long time in game five, though, it seemed that maybe Canada's bizarre training schedule would pay dividends. With just 11 minutes to play in the game, Canada led the Soviets 4–1. Then, suddenly, the Big Red Machine broke loose and pumped four goals past Tony Esposito quicker than anyone in a Canada uniform could spell Gennadii Tsygankov, the name of one of the Soviet defense stars. It was a shivering display of hockey might, and left Canada trailing the series 3-1-1.

"What we need now, right now, is a hero," said Canada's Bobby Orr, perhaps the best player in the world in those days but confined to a spectator's role for the series because of recent knee surgery. Of all the so-called superstars on Team Canada's roster, only one, Phil Esposito, had played like a superstar against the Soviets. Instead, the best Canadians had been such unheralded performers as Bobby Clarke, Gary Bergman, J.P. Parise, Pat Stapleton, Bill White, Serge Savard, and Paul Henderson.

And it was Henderson, who in nine years in the NHL had given no previous intimations of immortality, who dramatically rose up and almost single-handedly saved Canada and the NHL from a frosty grave in Siberia. In game six Henderson gave Canada a 3–2 victory when he boldly intercepted a pass at the blueline and slapped a hard shot past Tretiak from 35 feet away. Two nights later, in game seven, the score was tied 3–3 with barely two minutes to play when Henderson took a pass from Serge Savard, swung around a Soviet defenseman and beat Tretiak cleanly over the right shoulder. So, suddenly, the series was tied at 3-3-1.

Undeniably, game eight—Thursday night, September 28, 1972—was the greatest ever played. Skating smoothly and passing crisply, the Soviets scored three power-play goals and moved into a 5–3 lead after two periods. If Canadian goaltender Ken Dryden had not been both lucky and good, the Soviets might have led by 8–3, so masterful was their domination over those first 40 minutes. But the Canadians were not dead—not yet, anyway—and as they skated out for the final period, their 1,000 fans inside the Sports Palace made enough noise to be heard in Vancouver.

"We need an early goal," Sinden had informed his beleaguered players between periods. The indomitable Esposito scored that goal, slipping the puck under Tretiak at 2:27 after fanning on his original shot. That goal seemed to inflame the Canadians, and suddenly they owned the puck. With slightly more than seven minutes to play Brad Park, a bust in earlier games but a brilliant performer now, shot the puck in front of Tretiak and

Yvan Cournoyer rapped it past the Soviet goaltender to tie the score at 5–5.

Soviet hockey fans normally sit on their hands throughout a game; indeed, the 1,000 Canadians in the 12,000-seat Sports Palace for each game made more noise than the 11,000 Muscovites. But now the building was in an uproar as the teams raced from one end of the ice to the other and Dryden and Tretiak matched great saves. Everyone knew what was at stake, and the whole world, it seemed, was watching. The television audience in the Soviet Union numbered more than 100 million people, and another 15 million people watched on TV throughout Europe. Some 20 million people in Canada—the entire population of the country—stopped everything they were doing to watch this game, and millions more watched in the United States.

There would be no overtime period, no sudden death, so both teams continued to press furiously in the final moments. Then, suddenly, it was all over. With just 34 seconds to play that man Henderson—the man who had kept Canada's hopes alive with the winning goals in the two previous games—did it again. Esposito and Cournoyer battled for the puck in the corner, and Cournoyer passed it out to Henderson, who was standing all alone in front of Tretiak. Henderson seemed startled when he found the puck on his stick. Tretiak stopped Henderson's first shot, but the rebound came back onto Henderson's stick—and Henderson snapped it into the net.

"When I saw the puck go in," Henderson said, "I went completely bonkers."

So, too, did an entire nation as the party in Canada lasted for days. Henderson had brought Canada from the brink of disaster to a 4-3-1 victory over the Soviets in the first World Series of hockey. "When we get back home," said Harold Ballard, the owner of Henderson's NHL team, the Toronto Maple Leafs, "I'm going to renegotiate Paul's contract and give him at least another $25,000. That's a cheap price to pay for what he did. He saved a country's pride, that's what he did."

Throughout the 1972 series with Team Canada, the Soviets had gotten strong goal tending from Vladislav Tretiak, shown here fending off a Canadian attack during the final game. Canada won the game when Paul Henderson scored with 34 seconds left, giving the series to Canada in a surprisingly tough match.

MIRACLE AT LAKE PLACID

By conservative estimates the vaunted Soviet hockey
machine was supposed to rout the young U.S. Olympians by seven or eight goals . . .
but on a frosty afternoon in Lake Placid the Americans scored the upset
of the 1980 Games—and maybe of all the Games—by beating the Soviets 4–3 en route to the Gold Medal

In February of 1980, the mood of America was, in a word, glum. Domestically, inflation was soaring through the roof, gasoline and fuel oil prices were sky-rocketing, and the country was being hit hard by layoffs, particularly in the automobile industry. Internationally, the hostages were still in Iran, the Soviets were in Afghanistan, and the U.S. had announced a boycott of the impending 1980 Summer Olympic Games to be held in Moscow.

And things weren't going very well in Lake Placid, New York, where the U.S. was hosting the 1980 Winter Olympic Games. The ticket situation was a mess; people from all over the world showed up at various sites to pick up their prepaid tickets and were told there were no tickets for them. Traffic jams kept thousands of people from attending events to which they had purchased tickets (there was only one road into and one road out of Lake Placid, and cars were backed up for miles and miles). Worse, the bus shuttle system was a monument to chaos. Also, many of the athletes were complaining about their living quarters; in fact, the Olympic village had been designed to accommodate prisoners and would become a penal colony following the games.

Clearly, what America desperately needed was a lift.

Not many people at Lake Placid, or anywhere else, for that matter, held out much hope for the medal prospects of the U.S. Olympic hockey team. The Soviet Union, fresh from a chilling romp over the National Hockey League's best players in the 1979 Challenge Cup competition, was undeniably the number one hockey power in the world and was seeded number one at Lake Placid, followed by number two Sweden and number three Czechoslovakia. The U.S. was placed number seven in the eight-nation competition. For the U.S. skaters, a bronze medal represented their wildest dreams, a silver was practically unthinkable, and a gold was flatly out of the question. Nobody, but nobody, beats the Soviets. Not even the NHL pros. Indeed, on the eve of the games, the Soviets had trounced the U.S. team 10–3 at Madison Square Garden; the Soviets toyed with the Americans in the final period, playing keep-

away with the puck and trying not to run up the score. The margin of victory—seven goals—was hardly a clear reflection of Soviet superiority.

The U.S. faced the toughest early draw in the tournament, too; Sweden and Czechoslovakia—the favorites for the silver and the bronze medals, respectively—would provide the opposition in the first two games. Two losses, as expected, and there would be no medal of any sort for the U.S.

In the opening game against Sweden, the U.S. trailed 1–0 after the first period, and in the dressing room tempers were on edge. Rob McClanahan, a forward on the top U.S. line, had injured his leg, and at the urging of the team's trainers he was removing his equipment; there would be no more hockey for him this day. Seeing McClanahan getting undressed, U.S. coach Herb Brooks suddenly exploded in a verbal tirade, questioning McClanahan's courage, his heart, his ancestry. It was an ugly scene, one that had the U.S. players worrying that their coach had perhaps cracked under the strain. Brooks finally was led from the room. Stung by Brooks's outburst, McClanahan put his uniform back on and joined his teammates for the final two periods; when he was not taking his usual shift on the ice, McClanahan—in terrible pain—had to stand behind

Mark Johnson (10) and Robert McClanahan (24) celebrate Johnson's goal that tied the score 3–3 in the U.S.A.-U.S.S.R. Olympic hockey game at Lake Placid, N.Y., 1980. The Soviet goalie is Myshkin who replaced Tretiak after a poor first period.

the bench and do exercises to keep the leg from cramping up. The U.S. tied the score at 1–1 late in the second period on a goal by Dave Silk, but the Swedes took a 2–1 lead in the third period and seemed well in control. As the clock ticked away the final seconds, Brooks removed his goaltender, Jim Craig, in favor of an extra forward, hoping that the U.S. might capitalize on the manpower advantage and steal a tie. Which is exactly what happened. With 27 seconds to play, defenseman Bill Baker blasted a shot into the net to give the U.S. a 2–2 tie.

Millions of Americans watched the game-tying goal on television, and they joined the U.S. players in the wild celebration. But they didn't know of the ugly scene in the locker room between the first and second periods. "You know," said one of the U.S. players, "McClanahan was just an innocent victim of fate. Herbie was looking for something, anything, to use to get us going, get us mad, and when he saw Robbie getting dressed, well, that was it. Herbie's message was that it was us against the world, and everyone had to play—whatever their pain. Robbie understands now that Herbie didn't mean anything against him personally."

Two nights later the U.S. players provided the shocker of the games to that point by routing Czechoslovakia 7–3. Late in that game a Czech player gave a cheap shot to a U.S. skater, ramming him from behind with a stick, and the TV microphones picked up the irate voice of Herb Brooks telling the Czech—and, indeed, all the world—exactly what it was that he could do with his stick. Brooks's words had a strong imprint on Americans everywhere; suddenly, here was someone speaking out for America.

Norway, Romania, and West Germany fell in order to the young Americans, but now it was time for all good things to come to an end. There, looming on the horizon, was the Big Red Machine, the vaunted Soviets, champions of the last five Olympic Games, the best team in the world bar none.

The American players obviously belonged in a lower league. They had been together as a team for only six months; on the other skate, the nucleus of the Soviet squad—about a dozen players, including goaltender Vladislav Tretiak, defenseman Valery Vasiliev, wing Aleksandr Maltsev, and the forward line of Boris Mikhailov, Vladimir Petrov, and Valery Kharlamov—had remained intact since 1970. But the Americans were a cheeky, feisty lot, and they had long forgotten that 10–3 humiliation by the Soviets less than two weeks before.

Who were these Yanks? They were the kids who grew up next door, a collection of college students and recent college grads who had signed six months of their life away to a tough taskmaster named Herb Brooks. Conditioning, Brooks knew, was the ultimate edge of the Soviets on the ice; to beat them, you had to be in shape to skate with them for 60 minutes. Not 40. Not 50. Not 59. 60 minutes. Not even the NHL All Stars had ever been able to do that. So for six months Brooks skated his players each day until their tongues hung out. He made them run to and from practices, and when he was not happy with their performance in a game, he would keep them on the ice and skate them—without sticks—for an hour.

The U.S. team played more than 60 games leading up to Lake Placid, winning more than 50 against a collection of college, minor league pro, and rival Olympic teams. By the time they reached Lake Placid the U.S. players were a united lot; united on the ice and off, and united in their feelings toward the coach. As one Olympian said of Brooks, "He has treated us all the same—rotten. He has played no favorites. We may not like him, but we respect him—we *definitely* respect him—and we know that he is a great coach."

Brooks, who had been an All-America forward at the University of Minnesota in the 1950s and later coached the Gopher varsity to several NCAA championships, never let up on his young charges. Compliments were not part of his modus operandi. Most of the U.S. players would be turning pro after the Olympics, taking the big bucks of the NHL; some would be going to Europe to play hockey in leagues where the competition was about on a level with U.S. college hockey leagues; others would be returning to school; and some would be hanging up their blades for good. Brooks treated them all alike. "You're playing worse every day," Brooks would tell his players, "and right now you're playing like the middle of next month." Or he'd say, "Gentlemen, you don't have enough talent to win on talent alone." Or, "Let's be idealistic, but let's also be practical." Or, "You can't be common because the common man goes nowhere. You have to be uncommon." It was like that day in and day out for six months.

But now that was all behind the U.S. players. Standing there at the other end of the ice were the Soviets. "Gentlemen, you don't have enough talent to win on talent alone . . ." Brooks's words were ringing in the ears of the U.S. players. The arena was packed to the rafters; indeed, $22 tickets commanded as much as $550 apiece. The U.S.A. versus the U.S.S.R. Both were undefeated in Olympic competition, and the gold medal would probably go to the winner.

As expected, the Soviets took command immediately after the opening faceoff and ripped a goal past Jim Craig in the early moments. But then, shockingly, the U.S. tied the score at 1–1 when Buzz Schneider blasted a 50-foot shot past Tretiak. Hardly bothered by Schneider's goal, the Soviets went ahead 2–1, and as the seconds ticked away in the first period they were in total control. Only Craig's brilliant work in the U.S. goal kept the score that close.

Then, as the spectators were heading to the refreshment counters, Dave Christian skated the puck into center ice and slapped a 110-foot shot at Tretiak, hoping against hope that the puck would take a crazy bounce and carom past the goaltender. Tretiak should have casually caught the easy shot, dropped it, and whacked it into the corner. Or caught it and held it until the buzzer sounded, ending the period. Instead, Tretiak stupidly played the puck with his leg pads, and it bounced off his pads and rolled back toward the flow of play—in the direction of the slot between the two faceoff circles.

Seeing Tretiak's blunder, Mark Johnson—the spark of the U.S. team—busted through two Soviet defensemen, took the loose disc, and moved in against Tretiak. Johnson faked a shot by dropping his shoulder. Tretiak bit for the fake and went to his knees. Sorry. Johnson artfully pulled the puck back onto his stick, moved to his left, and snapped a shot into the net. Time of goal: 19:59. Score: U.S.A. 2, U.S.S.R. 2. And there was bedlam in Lake Placid.

When the Soviets returned for the second period,

there was a new masked man in their goal: Vladimir Myshkin, the same Prince Myshkin who had shut out the NHL all stars in the 1979 Challenge Cup. For the first time in his career, Tretiak, 29, considered to be the number-one goaltender in the world, had been removed from a game by his coach; Tretiak sat on the Soviet bench with his head hidden by his gloves, experiencing, he said later, the worst moment of his hockey career.

Myshkin had an easy time in the second period, turning aside the two harmless shots that the U.S. took at him. The Soviets, meanwhile, took 12 shots at Craig and scored on one, a Maltsev production, to take a 3–2 lead into the final period. Throughout the Olympics the U.S. team had saved its best performance for the end of each game; in fact, the U.S. outscored its opponents by a total of 27–6 in the final two periods. But who *ever* outskates the Soviets in the final period? The mood in the arena was electric now, and spurred on by a continuous chant of U.S.A., U.S.A., U.S.A., the Americans tied the score at 8:39. Dave Silk slid a neat pass through two Soviet defensemen to the ubiquitous Mark Johnson, who rifled the puck under Myshkin. Score: 3–3.

Johnson's goal gave the Americans new life, and they charged all over the rink. Suddenly, unbelievably, there was Mike Eruzione, the U.S. captain, skating down the middle inside the Soviet zone, and there was the puck heading directly onto his stick. And just as suddenly, at exactly 10:00 of the third period, there was Eruzione drilling a wrist shot past Myshkin, who never saw the puck until it was in the net and the red light was on. Score: U.S.A. 4, U.S.S.R. 3.

That was it. Oh, the Soviets had chances, plenty of chances, to tie the game in the final 10 minutes, but the U.S. players never lost their cool, their poise, their intensity. And when the countdown ended—5 . . . 4 . . . 3 . . . 2 . . . 1—it was the Soviets whose tongues were hanging out and the U.S. skaters whose heads were held high, who were piling atop one another in celebration, who were skating around the rink waving the Stars and Stripes, who were singing the National Anthem, who were at center stage of the greatest upset in the history of hockey. And two days later they clinched the Gold Medal by defeating Finland 4–2, outscoring the Finns 3–0 in the final period.

"The first Russian I shook hands with after the game had a smile on his face," said Mark Johnson.

Maybe he did. But it was hardly a smile to match the smile that a band of hearty young U.S. hockey players put on the face of Americans everywhere on that Friday afternoon in February, 1980.

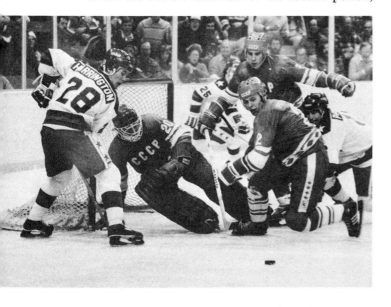

Olympic Games, Lake Placid, New York, Feb. 22, 1980. U.S.S.R. vs. U.S.A. Harrington's shot on goal goes off the pads of Soviet goalie Tretiak. It was a game in which the young Americans kept coming back, finally winning 4–3 on their way to the gold medal.

Horse Racing

THE NAME WAS RIGHT

The greatest horse of all time? Don't bet against Citation,
who won the Triple Crown in 1948 and is the horse against whom all other horses are compared

"Gee, Ben, are you sure I'm on the right horse?" Eddie Arcaro, the jockey, asked Ben Jones, Calumet Farms's trainer, just before the parade to the post for the 1948 Kentucky Derby. Jones was saddling two colts for Calumet that day: Coaltown, a truly beautiful horse who could run like the wind, and a rather ordinary-looking bay named Citation. Arcaro was aboard Citation. "You're on the right one," Jones snapped.

It turns out that Arcaro was on the right horse not only for that day, but for all time. Citation may not have been handsome, and he wasn't particularly big, but there was something special about him nonetheless. He had a look of intelligence in his large, shining eyes the likes of which track people had never before seen. He could eat like, well, a horse. He had a kind and gentle disposition, and he was in such control of himself that after a race he would be relaxing in his stall long before his rivals had cooled off. He ran smoothly, almost effortlessly in low, daisy-cutting strides. One writer described him on the run as "sniffing for moles."

He could win at any distance, under any weight, on any track. In one seven-week period as a three-year-old, Citation won four races at distances of six furlongs, a mile and a quarter, and two miles. Ben Jones once said, "He beat the best of his time at their own game. He beat the best sprinters sprinting, the best mudders in the mud, the best milers at a mile, and the best distance horses going a distance." Arcaro, once he was convinced, said, "He was a Cadillac."

Citation was foaled in April of 1945 at Calumet Farms in Lexington, Kentucky. His bloodlines were French and English, rather than American. His dam, Hydroplane II, never won a race, but she did come by Hyperion, an excellent stallion, out of Toboggan, a fine mare. Citation's poppa was Bull Lea, who was the son of Bull Dog, whose full brother was Sir Galahad III, the sire of Gallant Fox, the Triple Crown winner in 1930 who also produced another Triple Crown winner, Omaha. If all this sounds confusing, suffice to say Citation came from the best of families. The name Citation was suggested by Mrs. Otto Lehmann, a friend of the colt's owner Warren Wright, the baking soda magnate. "It was during the war," said Mrs. Lehmann, "when you were hearing a lot about citations. It seemed like a good name for a good horse."

Because he was born in April, Citation was three months behind most other two-year-olds, but during his first racing season, he still won eight of nine races. The only race he failed to win was the Washington Park Futurity, in which he finished second to his filly stablemate Bewitch (Calumet was loaded with great horses at the time, and both Citation and Bewitch came into the race undefeated.) Citation might have won, but Jimmy Jones, Ben's son, had instructed his jockeys to let whichever horse was ahead at the top of the stretch win the race. Bewitch happened to be leading as they headed for home.

Citation got off to a splendid start as a three-year-old, winning a sprint at Hialeah and then the seven-furlong Seminole Handicap against older horses, including Armed, the Horse of the Year in 1947. After riding him to two more impressive victories in the Everglades Handicap and the Flamingo, Citation's jockey, Albert Snider, decided to take a few days off and go fishing with friends in the Florida Keys. Snider and his party were never seen or heard from again.

Calumet managed to enlist the services of Arcaro to replace Snider. To better acquaint horse and rider, two races were scheduled at Havre de Grace in April. The first was the Chesapeake Trial, and it turned out to be Citation's only defeat of the year. Not only did he have a new jockey to contend with, but mud and interference as well. He might very well have caught the winner, Saggy, but Arcaro wisely decided not to push the colt in an inconsequential race before the Kentucky Derby. A few days later in the Chesapeake Stakes, horse and jockey vindicated themselves.

Citation was also impressive in winning the Derby Trial, but his stablemate Coaltown had just broken the nine-furlong record at Keeneland in the Blue Grass Stakes, a feat that would earn him honors as Champion Sprinter of the Year. So Arcaro still had his doubts as the six horses went to post for the Derby on May 1. As if to confirm his misgivings, Coaltown moved out to a commanding six-length lead in the backstretch. "I knew I had the rest of the field beat at the half-mile pole," said Arcaro. "I looked back and the other horses were too drunk to cause us any trouble. We moved when I

PRECEDING PAGE: *Secretariat (1A), ridden by Ron Turcotte, wins the 1973 Kentucky Derby, the first jewel in the Triple Crown. Sham, with Laffit Pincay aboard, is a close second. Secretariat began the race behind 12 other horses in the 13-horse field, but came on to win in a record time of one minute, 59⅖ seconds.*

clucked to him, and I could see we'd move on out at Coaltown."

Going into the home stretch, Arcaro brought Citation up even with Coaltown. The two horses ran head to head for a few moments, and then Arcaro asked Citation once more. The colt pulled away and finished four lengths in front of Coaltown. Someone described Citation at the finish, "Ears pricked, looking for more horses to run down."

The Preakness was a bag of oats for Citation. Only three horses challenged him—Coaltown was not among them—and he went off at 1-10. On an off track, he took a light gallop and breezed home five and a half lengths ahead of Vulcan's Forge. The only trouble Citation had was in the winner's circle. For some reason, he did not like the blanket of black-eyed Susans they were trying to drape him in.

To keep Citation sharp for the last jewel of the Triple Crown, the Belmont, Jimmy Jones entered him in the Jersey Stakes, which he won by 11 lengths. But some horsemen questioned Jones's wisdom in running Citation in an added race, and consequently seven opponents entered the Belmont. Citation had problems all

right, but they had nothing to do with the Jersey Stakes; Arcaro was concealing a badly injured shoulder, incurred the week before, because he didn't want to be pulled off the horse. The injury necessitated Arcaro whipping with his left hand, something he had never really done before. Then disaster nearly struck at the starting gate when Citation stumbled out of the gate. What had happened was that Arcaro, noticing that Citation's left foreleg was resting on a ledge alongside the gate instead of on the ground, smacked at the leg with his whip just as the gates opened. The startled Citation lost his poise for a moment.

But Arcaro steadied him quickly enough, and Citation went right to the lead. "I just let him run a little, up that turn, then I took him up again because he went so fast, it scared me," said Arcaro. Citation finished eight lengths in front of Better Self, and on that day, June 12, 1948, he became the eighth Triple Crown champion and the last before Secretariat 25 years later. And from that day forward, Arcaro favored a left-hand whip.

Citation remained unbeaten the rest of the year. But in the last race of the season, the Tanforan Handicap at Bay Meadows, near San Francisco, Citation de-

Citation, Calumet Farms' Triple Crown winner in 1948, leads in the home stretch of the Belmont Stakes, Eddie Arcaro up. Trainer Ben Jones said of Citation, "He beat the best sprinters sprinting, the best mudders in the mud, the best milers at a mile, and the best distance horses going a distance."

97

veloped what's known as a "hot spot" on his left forean-kle. That injury led to other ailments, and Citation was forced to sit out his entire four-year-old season, the time when a horse normally reaches his prime. As a five-year-old, "Big Cy" won only two of nine starts, but he never finished worse than second, and he staged some memorable duels with Noor, a great handicap horse. In most of his losses, Citation was giving away unfair weights, and he was simply not as sound as he once was. Ordinarily, he might have been retired, but owner Wright had made a dying wish that Citation become horse racing's first millionaire. Finally, on July 14, 1951, the six-year-old Citation won the $100,000 purse for the Hollywood Gold Cup and pushed his career earnings over the million mark. Ironically, the horse Citation

beat that day was Bewitch, the same filly who had beaten him the first time.

Citation proved to be an unspectacular stallion—he certainly didn't produce another Citation. But then, there never was another Citation. In April of 1968 a computer race was held to determine the greatest horse of all time. Citation overtook Buckpasser in the stretch and withstood a challenge by Man o' War to win the imaginary "Race of the Century." Man o' War's death in 1947 was met with great public sorrow. In contrast Citation died quietly on Saturday night, August 8, 1970, at the age of 25. His epitaph might have been the words of an unnamed groom who, after seeing Citation run, said, "That there horse just ain't human."

—Steve Wulf

Eddie Arcaro atop Citation, after the horse had won the 1948 Belmont Stakes to complete the conquest of horse racing's Triple Crown, Citation was the 8th horse in history to win the Kentucky Derby, the Preakness, and the Belmont Stakes, and 25 years passed before Secretariat achieved the same record.

HEADS YOU WIN, TAILS I WIN

The lady lost the coin toss but still won the great horse Secretariat,
who in 1973 had the type of year that Citation had enjoyed in 1948 . . . a Triple Crown campaign,
the first by any horse in 25 years

The one hundred and fifth running of the Belmont Stakes on June 9, 1973, gave us the greatest performance by a thoroughbred in this century, but it really all began with a coin toss that Penny Tweedy had lost three years before. It seems that Mrs. Tweedy, who had taken over the management of the Meadow Farm in Doswell, Virginia, from her father, Christopher Chenery, had also inherited an arrangement he had with Kentucky's Claiborne Farm and its owner, Ogden Phipps. Claiborne's stallion, Bold Ruler, was bred to two of the Meadow's brood mares every year, and every two years the two farms would flip a coin to determine which would get the first draft choice. The loser would get the first pick the following year. Well, in 1970, Mrs. Tweedy lost the toss, and Phipps chose a filly by Bold Ruler out of Somethingroyal. She turned out to be The Bride, who never finished better than sixth in four races. The next year Mrs. Tweedy took a colt from the same parents. Elizabeth Ham, a long-time aide to Chenery who once worked in the League of Nations, thought Secretariat might be a nice name for the colt, and that's what he was named.

At the time, the Meadow Farm was strained both financially and artistically. Mrs. Tweedy had hired Roger Laurin to be her trainer, but after two years he left to run the Claiborne stable. For his replacement, he recommended his 59-year-old father, Lucien, and Mrs. Tweedy reluctantly accepted him. Never has a son repaid his father so handsomely, and never has a horse owner been so lucky.

Lucien Laurin took charge of this big, fire-red colt with bright eyes, three white stockings, and a star on his nose. The first time Mrs. Tweedy, who kept a book on all her horses, saw the colt run, she wrote, "Wow!" As good as the colt looked, he ate even better, and for a time Laurin found himself with a chubby horse. Consequently, Secretariat was brought along rather slowly. But in the late spring of 1972 Laurin reported to Mrs. Tweedy that he was ready to run. Laurin had only one reservation. "He was so damn good-looking," said Laurin, "that I said to myself he probably won't be worth ten cents as a racer."

Ten cents was about right after the colt's first race.

On July 4 at Aqueduct, Secretariat was entered in a five and a half furlong sprint for two-year-olds. But coming out of the gate another horse bumped him, and Secretariat was nearly knocked off his feet. Said his jockey, Paul Feliciano, "If he wasn't such a strong horse, he would have fallen." He recovered to finish fourth, but from then on Secretariat left the starting gate rather deliberately. After two races, Ron Turcotte, a French-Canadian like Laurin, replaced Feliciano as the colt's jockey; he had just ridden Meadow's Riva Ridge to victories in the Kentucky Derby and Belmont.

The colt quickly made a name for himself, even though the New York *Daily News* referred to him as "Filly Secretariat." He finished first in the Champagne Stakes, although he was taken down for interference. He closed out his two-year-old season with impressive wins at Aqueduct and in the Garden State Stakes, and was named Two Year Old of the Year.

Two things of note happened to Secretariat over that winter. The first was that he grew even larger—over an inch. The second was that Mrs. Tweedy syndicated him for breeding purposes for a record $6 million. Twenty-eight shares—she kept two—were offered to breeders at $190,000 apiece with the stipulation that the horse race until November 15, 1973, with the Meadow keeping all purses.

On St. Patrick's Day, Secretariat made his debut as a three-year-old, winning the Bay Shore at Aqueduct.

Secretariat takes the lead in the first turn of the 1973 Belmont Stakes, Ron Turcotte up. Secretariat never relinquished the lead, and by the end of the race was in front by an astonishing 31 lengths. His time of 2:24 smashed the previous track record.

After a win in the Gotham Mile, Secretariat was entered in the Wood Memorial, a key prep for the Kentucky Derby. The entry of Secretariat and Angle Light went off at 3-10, and although their backers were rewarded, the wrong horse crossed the finish line first. Angle Light had beaten Sham by a head, with Secretariat an inexplicable four lengths behind. The racing press felt betrayed. Gene Ward of the *Daily News* could hardly disguise his disappointment when he wrote, "This was the horse that was going to win the Triple Crown for the first time since Citation . . . this was the syndicated marvel whose backers invested $6,000,000, and Ron Turcotte, his rider, just didn't want to admit . . . he got beat."

On May 5, 1973, 13 horses went off in the ninety-ninth running of the Kentucky Derby. Secretariat, the number ten horse, broke out slowly and cut to the rail, settling comfortably into last place. In the backstretch, he casually began to swallow up other horses, while, ahead of him, Sham moved into second position. On the far turn, Sham took the lead, with Secretariat, now coming wide, in pursuit. They were the only two horses in the final furlong, and at the three-sixteenths pole they established eye contact. Secretariat said goodbye and finished two and a half lengths in front of Sham. It was a remarkable performance by both Secretariat, who shaved $^3/_5$ of a second off the Derby record with a time of 1:59$^2/_5$, and Turcotte, who became the first jockey in 71 years to win back-to-back Derbies. Sham was nearly as impressive, tying the old record of 2:00 flat despite having lost two teeth in a starting gate accident.

Now restored to his pedestal, Secretariat took on five horses in the Preakness on May 19. He got off well and bided his time in fourth place until Turcotte, sensing a slow pace, clucked him after the first quarter. This was much earlier than Secretariat's usual move, and Laurin was chagrined. There was no need to worry. Sham took chase, but he still finished two and a half lengths behind the breezing Secretariat. The clockers for the *Daily Racing Form* had him in 1:53$^2/_5$, which would have been a record, but the electronically timed track clock had him in 1:55. Secretariat was robbed of his record, and Penny Tweedy was robbed of her purse by a pickpocket, but the second jewel of the Triple Crown was ample compensation.

In the week before the Belmont, the press descended upon Barn 5 at Belmont Park in the hopes that the horse might talk. Even his groom, Eddie Sweat, developed into something of a national celebrity. Secretariat became the first horse *or* human to appear on the

covers of *Time, Newsweek,* and *Sports Illustrated* in the same week. But the pressure began to show on Laurin, who sometimes got snappish, and on Mrs. Tweedy, whose charm was beginning to strain. On the Friday before the race, though, the anxiety was punctured by Secretariat's spectacular workout: 1:34$^1/_5$ for the mile, just off the track record. Still, that night Eddie Sweat was so worried that he had a nightmare about his horse building up a big lead, then falling down in the stretch.

Facing Secretariat the next day were four horses,

Pvt. Smiles, My Gallant, Twice A Prince and Sham, the horse who had bravely gone after Secretariat in the Kentucky Derby and Preakness. Saturday dawned bright and clear, and by noontime, the temperature was above 90 degrees. A throng of 70,000 began to file through the gates of Belmont, and with each race that day, the anticipation grew. As Turcotte mounted Secretariat for the eighth race, he looked down at the fretting groom and asked, "What's the matter, Sweat?" Eddie replied, "A little nervous, I guess." Turcotte said, "Me,

Secretariat, majestically alone, flies down the home stretch to win the 1973 Belmont Stakes and the Triple Crown. His 2:24 bettered the previous track record set by Gallant Man in 1957 by 2⅗ seconds or the equivalent of 20 lengths.

too, but it's all in the game, isn't it?"

Secretariat made a majestic entrance onto the track, almost as if he were a king acknowledging his subjects. Indeed, the world would be his kingdom that day. He was the first horse into the gate, and the first one out of it. Sham, under Laffit Pincay, quickly came up to challenge, and the breakneck chase was on. Their fractions—23⅗ seconds for the quarter and 46⅕ seconds for the half—were so swift that Penny Tweedy gasped, "Oh, oh, I'm scared." She had every right to be since such times in a mile and a half race are usually considered suicide. And no horse since 1950 had ever led after a half mile and gone on to win the Belmont.

Finally, Sham broke. But Secretariat was only beginning to roll. After a mile, he was timed in 1:34⅕. Turning for home, he was 20 lengths in front of the second horse, Twice A Prince. "Oh, God," thought Eddie Sweat. "It's just like in my dream. Stay on your feet, Red!" Secretariat did more than just stay on his feet. When Turcotte saw the times he was putting up on the tote board, he asked Secretariat to try for the Belmont record, and the colt was more than happy to oblige. He finished a mind-boggling 31 lengths in front of Twice A Prince and over 45 lengths ahead of poor Sham, who swam home last. Secretariat's time of 2:24 was 2⅗ seconds (the equivalent of 20 lengths) better than the previous mark set by Gallant Man in 1957.

Secretariat and his entourage, owner Mrs. Tweedy, trainer Laurin, jockey Turcotte, groom Sweat, and even Governor Nelson Rockefeller were buffetted by the hundred photographers who swarmed the winner's circle. Horsemen had begun to think that no horse would ever win the Triple Crown again—six since Citation had won the first two legs only to lose the Belmont. But this chestnut did it, and the world beat a path to his stall door. He kept up a full schedule of races after the Belmont, and although he did lose a little of his lustre by failing in the Whitney and the Woodward (all his losses that year were in races beginning with a "W"), he closed out his career by beating his stablemate Riva Ridge in the Marlboro Cup, a race established especially for him, and finally by capturing the Canadian Invitational at Woodbine, near Toronto. At a special parade in his honor on November 6 at Aqueduct, the track on which he had first raced, Secretariat made his last public appearance. Before retiring to stud, Big Red joined the stable of stars at the William Morris Agency, which handled such other sex symbols as Elvis Presley and Sophia Loren.

—S.W.

101

Track and Field

THE MIRACLE MILE

They said that no one would ever break the four-minute mile,
but on a bloody treacherous day in England in the spring of 1954, Roger Bannister did just that by
crossing the finish line in 3:59.4

The weather in Oxford, England, was miserable on Thursday, May 6, 1954. It was the day of the long-standing track meet between the Oxford University Athletic Club and the team from Britain's Amateur Athletic Association. The winds were gusting up to 15 miles an hour, and the leftovers from two days of heavy rain continued to fall. It was a day that anyone might want to forget. In fact, when Roger Bannister first arrived at the Iffley Road track that afternoon, he decided he wasn't going to run.

Roger Gilbert Bannister, born March 23, 1929, had entered Oxford in 1946. He went out for the track team partly because his size—6 feet 1 inch tall, 150 pounds—was ill-suited for crew. His first race was a 5:21 mile on the very same Iffley Road track. But inside of two months, Bannister had improved his time to 4:30.8. Within two years, he had established himself as one of the world's best milers. His training methods, though, were considered rather unusual. He had no coach, probably because he couldn't get along with any of them. He was a medical student and would often use himself in experiments. He would, for instance, run on a treadmill until he reached complete exhaustion to test oxygen intake. Still, he was the great hope of England in the 1952 Olympics. But he finished a disappointing fourth in the 1500 meters.

Perhaps that failure steeled his determination to become the first man to break 4 minutes in the mile. Bannister began listening to Franz Stampfl, an Austrian coach who had moved to England to escape Hitler. Stampfl told Bannister that he had the pace, but needed additional strength. Bannister was not only racing against time, he was racing against two men, as well—Wes Santee of the United States and John Landy of Australia. In 1953 Santee, at the age of 21, had lowered his mile mark to 4:03.1. Landy, who had no one to race against in Australia, was timed in 4:02.4. Bannister himself had a 4:02, but it was disallowed. As the 1954 season approached, the track world was anxious over the possibility of a four-minute mile. In the spring, Landy announced his intention of going to Europe to seek better competition. Bannister and Stampfl then decided that they should try for the magic mark at the earliest possible opportunity. That opportunity was the otherwise routine meet between the AAA and Bannister's former Oxford Club.

Bannister worked his usual morning shift at St. Mary's Hospital in London on May 6. He had not run in four days, and had yet to run a mile in training. He boarded the 1·45 P.M. train from Paddington Station

PRECEDING PAGES: *Jesse Owens wins a 200-meter heat in the 1936 Olympics held in Hitler's Berlin.* ABOVE, OPPOSITE, AND FOLLOWING PAGE: *A sequence showing Roger Bannister kicking into high gear on his way to the first sub-four-minute mile in track history, run on May 6, 1954. Bannister's time of 3:59.4 might have been even faster, except for poor weather.*

with Stampfl. Bannister was chary of the weather, and Stampfl tried to convince him that today was the day, no matter the weather. But when Bannister arrived in Oxford, and saw the conditions, he made up his mind not to run.

Also scheduled to run in the race that day were two friends of Bannister, Chris Chataway and Chris Brasher. Chataway, like Bannister, had run for Oxford, and he would later set the world record in the 5,000 meters. Brasher, from Cambridge, was one of the world's best steeplechasers. He was also an excellent mountain-climber, who was considered by Sir Edmund Hillary for the team that would climb Mount Everest. Brasher missed out on that opportunity, but on this day he would help Bannister climb the Everest of track.

Chataway, Brasher, and Stampfl worked on Bannister and finally talked him into running. Lo and behold, the weather began to clear between 5 P.M. and the start of the race at 6. The winds subsided somewhat, although there were still occasional gusts, and the rain stopped. The three runners finalized their plan for the race.

Only about 400 people were there to see the race, although in later years the number of spectators would mysteriously grow to 100,000. The sporting press, though, was well-represented because the writers had gotten wind of the attempt. To make sure that the historic time would be ratified, three official timers were on hand. One of the race officials that day was Norris McWhirter, a friend of Bannister who later became the editor of the *Guinness Book of World Records*.

As a sign of the tension, one of the seven runners jumped the gun for a false start. When the gun did sound, Brasher took the lead, setting a brisk pace of 57.4 seconds in the first quarter-mile while protecting Bannister from the breeze. Still Bannister was so anxious that he yelled "Faster, faster," to Brasher, who could not hear him. Brasher continued to set the pace and finished the half-mile in 1:58.2—on target for a 3:56.4 mile.

On the third lap Brasher began to weaken, his job done, and Chataway took over the lead. At the three-quarter mark, Chataway was timed in 3:00.4 and Bannister was at his shoulder. Now Bannister took the lead. He was on his own. A year later, in his book *The Four Minute Mile*, Bannister waxed poetic about those last 300 yards:

I had a moment of joy and anguish, when my mind took over. It raced well ahead of my body and drew

my body compellingly forward . . . The only reality was the next two hundred yards of track under my feet. The tape meant finality—extinction perhaps . . . The air I breathed filled me with the spirit of the track where I had run my first race. The noise in my ears was that of the faithful Oxford crowd . . . The faint line of the finishing tape stood ahead as a haven of peace . . . The arms of the world were waiting to receive me if only I reached the tape without slackening . . . I leapt at the tape like a man taking his last spring to save himself from the chasm that threatened to engulf him.

What actually happened was that in the last three hundred yards, Bannister began to lengthen his stride. He passed the 1,500 meter mark in 3:43, which equaled the world record for that distance. Going around the last bend, a stiff cross wind struck Bannister full force, but he fought through it and poured it on down the last straightaway as the crowd poured out of the stands, moving to both sides of the track and behind the finish line. Bannister crossed the tape, his face contorted, and collapsed into the arms of Stampfl and Leslie Truelove, an AAA official. All three timers had him in 3:59.4. (It was later surmised that had the wind not been blowing, Bannister would have been two seconds faster.) Just to make sure, the track distance was measured again and found to be one mile, one inch.

McWhirter made the official announcement: "Ladies and gentlemen, here is the result of event No. 9, the one-mile: First, No. 41, R.G. Bannister, Amateur Athletic Association and formerly of Exeter and Merton Colleges, Oxford, with a time which is a new meeting and track record, and which, subject to ratification, will be a new English native, British national, British all-comers, European, British Empire and world's record. The time was three minutes and fifty-nine point four seconds."

One of the first to congratulate Bannister was his mum. "I knew you would do it one day, Roger," she said. Bannister ran over to thank Brasher and Chataway for their roles in his glory. And then he attended to the adoring public.

Less than two months later, Landy would break Bannister's mile record. Nowadays, high school runners break the 4-minute mark, so it may be hard to think of the first 4-minute mile as a great achievement. But on May 6, 1954, on a miserable day in Oxford, England, a young medical student named Roger Bannister conquered time itself.

—S.W.

A HERO FOR THE AGES

Jesse Owens won four Gold Medals at the 1936 Olympics in Berlin,
but best of all, he struck a victory for America by sending Adolf Hitler from the stadium in disgust

In 1936 Adolf Hitler was reaching the height of his horrible power, and the Berlin Olympics were to be his showcase for the theories of Nazi supremacy. He boasted of his Aryan supermen and scorned the United States's reliance on "black auxiliaries." But by the time the Games ended, one of those black auxiliaries had won four gold medals and become not only an Olympic hero, but a hero for all time.

James Cleveland Owens was the grandson of slaves, the son of a sharecropper. He was born on September 12, 1913, in Danville, Alabama. He picked cotton with his family until the Owenses moved to Cleveland in 1922. In junior high school, he accidentally acquired a new first name. When his teacher asked him what his name was, Owens replied, "J.C." She thought he had said, "Jesse." One day, Charley Riley, a coach at Fairmount Junior High, measured out a 100-yard route along a sidewalk and told Jesse to run. Riley's stopwatch timed the kid in 11 seconds, and the coach promptly threw the watch away. The next day, when Owens repeated his performance, Riley knew that he had a future

champion in his hands and he had wasted a stopwatch.

At East Technical High School, Owens soon became a nationally known sprinter. He enrolled at Ohio State, but because he wasn't on athletic scholarship, he had to work his way through school as an elevator operator and then as a page in the Ohio state legislature.

On May 25, 1935, at the Big Ten meet in Ann Arbor, Michigan, Owens, then a sophomore, had perhaps the greatest single day an athlete has ever had. A painful back injury incurred in some fraternity horseplay had kept Jesse from training all week, and his status was in doubt that day. But in the space of 45 minutes, without benefit of a warmup, Owens equaled the world record in the 100-yard dash (9.4 seconds); broke the world record for the broad jump (now the long jump) in his only try with a leap, 26 feet 8¼ inches, that would last for 25 years; set a world record in the 220-yard dash (20.3 seconds), also topping the 200-meter record in the process; and set a new mark for the 220-yard low hurdles (22.6 seconds), bettering the 200-meter low hurdle record as well. Between 3:15 and 4 P.M., Jesse Owens broke five world records and equaled a sixth.

By the Olympic year of 1936, Owens was hailed as the world's fastest human. He qualified for all his Olympic events, and together with the 65 other American team members, he sailed for Europe. On the first day of competition, Hitler heartily congratulated the first three gold medal winners, two of whom were German. But he snubbed the high jump champion, Cornelius Johnson, an American black.

On the second day of competition, Owens flashed to easy triumph in the 100-meter dash. His time of 10.3 seconds was both an Olympic and world record, but because it was wind-aided, it was disallowed. Needless to say, Hitler was not there to congratulate Owens.

The following day was the day of the broad jump, and it was in this event that Owens scored his greatest victory. He was up against the great hope of Germany, Lutz Long, the very model of the "master race." Owens, angered by Hitler's snub, was determined to prove that he was the best—too determined, in fact, because on his first qualifying jump in the trials, his right foot hit almost six inches beyond the edge of the takeoff board for a foul. On his second jump, Owens took a much more

Jesse Owens, hero of the 1936 Olympics, competing in the broad jump. Owens' leap set a new Olympic record. He also won the 100-meter dash, set a world record in the 200-meter dash, and was part of the 400-meter relay team that set a world record.

107

careful approach—too careful, because his jump was not long enough to qualify. Years later, Owens would describe his own thoughts at that point. "What if I don't qualify? What if I've come four thousand miles for nothing, just to shame my country, my race and myself?"

With his legs weak from fear, Owens stood waiting for the officials to call his name one last time. Just then Long came up and tapped him on the shoulder. "Hello, Jesse Owens," he said in a thick German accent. "I'm Lutz Long. I don't think we have met so far." Lutz, it turned out, wanted to help Owens. The German said, "Do not worry about it. You do not have to be best in the trials. You need only to qualify. So why not be sure that you do? Then you will have the chance to be the best in the finals." Long advised Owens to draw an imaginary line a foot in back of the takeoff board and jump from there. In that way, he wouldn't foul and would still qualify with even a routine jump. Owens relaxed and easily made the finals.

The broad jump finals were moved to the other side of the field so that Hitler could get a better view of them. Lutz's second jump set an Olympic record, but then Owens topped that with a leap of 26 feet 5⁵⁄₁₆ inches. Long still had one jump left, but he had hurt his leg on a previous try. Under the outraged gaze of Hitler, Owens rubbed liniment into Long's throbbing leg. Long's final jump was short, and Owens had his second gold medal. It was a triumph of friendship, though. For years the two men kept up a correspondence, until Long was killed in World War II.

The day after the broad jump, Owens became the first athlete since Paavo Nurmi in 1924 to win three gold medals when he easily won the 200-meter dash in a time of 20.3 seconds, another Olympic record. Hitler fled the stadium rather than confront Owens. The feeling was mutual. "The Führer did me a great favor when he left the stadium," said Owens. "It avoided what, for me, would have been a most distasteful situation."

Owens was not scheduled to run in the 400-meter

ABOVE: *Jesse Owens breaks the tape in the 100-meter dash well ahead of his U.S. teammate Ralph Metcalf, at the '36 Olympics.* OPPOSITE: *The 400-meter relay team of Owens, Metcalf, Praper, and Wykoff, winners of the event in the 1936 Olympics in the world-record time of 39.8 seconds.*

relay. But he and Ralph Metcalfe, another black, replaced Marty Glickman and Sam Stoller. Glickman, who later became a sportscaster, and Stoller were Jews, and the American Olympic officials, Avery Brundage chief among them, apparently did not want to offend the Nazis by allowing them to compete. Owens ran the first leg of what proved to be a world record time of 39.8 seconds, and he had his fourth gold medal. Of the 11 medals won by U.S. athletes in the Games, six belonged to blacks. It was a clear refutation of Nazi beliefs.

Owens returned to the United States a hero, but heroes are sometimes quickly forgotten. He tried leading a swing band, dancing with Bill "Bojangles" Robinson, running against horses, dogs, and automobiles, playing a detective in a movie, touring with the Harlem Globetrotters. At one point he had to make do as a playground janitor. "When I came back, after all those stories about Hitler and the snub, I couldn't ride in the front of the bus. Now what's the difference?" Jesse Owens deserved better, and eventually things came to him. For several years he served as a good-will ambassador for the U.S. But he was deeply hurt by the black athletes in the 1968 Olympics who labeled him an "Uncle Tom" because he tried to mediate between them and the U.S. Olympic Committee. It was an unfair smear on someone who had glorified his country, his race, and himself. In his last years, though, Owens became an inspirational public speaker, and he revived the memory of the 1936 Olympics. He died on April 1, 1980, at the age of 66, the greatest hero in the history of track and field.

—S.W.

109

A JUMP INTO THE 21st CENTURY

*With one giant leap, Bob Beamon not only broke the world
long jump record at the Mexico City Olympics in 1968, he fractured, shattered, ruined it with an
effort that was beyond belief*

Ten months before Neil Armstrong took his first step on the moon, someone actually did make a giant leap for mankind. Someone was a skinny 22-year-old named Bob Beamon. At precisely 3:46 P.M. on October 18, 1968, in Mexico City's Olympic Stadium, Beamon, competing in the Olympic long jump finals, launched himself into the air. "It felt like a regular jump," he said.

Beamon landed 29 feet, 2½ inches from the takeoff board. It was no ordinary jump. Beamon had surpassed the world record by an incredible, astounding, impossible—no one word could describe it—21¾ inches, nearly two feet. He had skipped over the 28 foot barrier altogether. As one writer put it, "Beamon took off in 1968 and landed in the next century." It was the greatest single feat in the history of track and field.

Nobody could have had an inkling of what Beamon

was to do, least of all Beamon. He wasn't even the best long jumper in America at the time. Ralph Boston of the U.S. and Igor Ter-Ovanesyan of the Soviet Union were the co-holders of the world record of 27 feet 4¾ inches. Beamon, the son of a shoemaker from Queens, New York, was considered a raw jumper of great ability. His first loves, though, were basketball and the conga drums. His coach at the University of Texas-El Paso, Wayne Vandenburg, had this to say about Beamon: "He does a lot of things very poorly mechanically when he first leaves the board. There has never been a long jumper in the class of Beamon who does things the way he does them." But Beamon was such a natural that when he was in the sixth grade, he was long-jumping over 19 feet, and in the ninth grade he reached 24 feet.

The stadium crowd that day certainly had no way

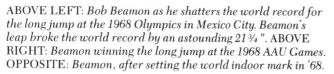

ABOVE LEFT: *Bob Beamon as he shatters the world record for the long jump at the 1968 Olympics in Mexico City. Beamon's leap broke the world record by an astounding 21¾".* ABOVE RIGHT: *Beamon winning the long jump at the 1968 AAU Games.* OPPOSITE: *Beamon, after setting the world indoor mark in '68.*

of knowing they were about to be witnesses to history. Many of the 40,000 people were looking fretfully at the pregnant sky. Still others were paying attention to the finals of the men's 400-meter dash, which was about to start. They missed the track steward calling for the fourth competitor in the long jump, number 254, to take his first try. Number 254 himself was very relaxed. Beamon had come to Mexico City with a lot on his mind—he didn't know where he was going to school that fall, he was having family troubles, he was about to lose his home in El Paso, and he had a huge telephone bill to pay. The day before the finals Beamon had fouled twice and barely qualified on his last jump. That night he went into town to relax and ordered a cognac. The drink worked, and Beamon slept soundly. He woke up feeling great, and the feeling carried through the afternoon. As he stood at his mark, his only worry was fouling again. He lowered and raised his head twice, slowly closing and opening his eyes. Then he took off.

Beamon later said he felt a little slow through the first steps on the approach. But as he accelerated, his stride felt comfortable. He reached the takeoff board in full, perfect stride, and up he went.

Watching his jump together were Boston and Lynn Davies of Great Britain, both former gold medalists. Beamon seemed suspended in the air for a long time. "That's 28 feet," said Boston. "No, it can't be," said Davies, although he knew Boston was right. The great Jesse Owens, working as a commentator, followed Beamon's flight through binoculars and told his listeners, "His body went up five and a half to six feet in the air, and with his speed, that will do it."

When Beamon finally came down, he himself thought he might have the world record, but still he had no idea of how far he'd gone. The long jump was measured with an optical device that slid along a rail running parallel to the landing area. To line up Beamon's imprint in the dirt, the judge kept sliding the sight further and further along until it fell off the end of the rail, just beyond the 28-foot mark. "Fantastic," said the judge to Beamon. "We will have to measure it with a tape."

When the result was announced in meters—8.90—Ter-Ovanesyan said to Davies, "Compared to that jump, we are all children." Boston delivered the news to Beamon. "You went about 29 feet, 2 inches," he said. Suddenly realizing what he had just done, Beamon collapsed to his knees in almost a prayer position. Spectators began beseeching him, the men for autographs, the women for kisses. And the skies opened.

There were some skeptics who said that Beamon had plucked the record, literally, out of thin air. Mexico City is 7,349 feet above sea level, so not only did Beamon have less resistance, but the lighter air enabled him to get a faster approach. But those conditions might account for, at the most, eight or nine inches. Even given that, Beamon's jump would still have been better than a foot longer than any previous attempt. And both Boston and Ter-Ovanesyan, jumping in the same air, couldn't even better the old record.

Long jump records have traditionally been the most enduring. In 1901 Peter O'Connor of Ireland jumped 24 feet 11¾ inches, and that record lasted 20 years. In 1935 Owens leaped 26 feet 8¾ inches, a mark that stood for 25 years. There's no way of knowing how long Beamon's record will last, but it wasn't until the 1980 Moscow Olympics—12 years later—that another jumper reached the 28-foot mark that Beamon skipped altogether—Lutz Dombrowski of East Germany, who won the gold medal with a leap of 28 feet ¼ inch.

Call it what you will, a fluke, an accident, a stroke of luck. On October 18, 1968, Bob Beamon was the right man in the right place at the right time.

—S.W.

Swimming

THERE WAS GOLD IN THE WATER

A bust in the 1968 Olympics, Mark Spitz swam to seven gold medals in the 1972 Games

You've seen the poster of the pin-up boy. Swimmer, good looking; very good looking. Perfect white teeth flashing in a victory smile. Dark features. Omar Sharif mustache and closely cropped mod hairstyle. Stars and stripes bikini suit. And, oh yes, around his neck, and on his chest, the real eye catcher: seven gold medals, arranged so carefully. Brilliant. Oh, yes, you've seen that poster.

The Mark Spitz story begins in 1958, when he was eight years old. That was when he first splashed through a YMCA pool in Sacramento, California. Within a week, he was swimming 75 minutes a day.

It picks up two years later, when swimming practice kept the 10-year-old away from his after-school Hebrew lessons. That's when, so the story goes, his father, Arnold Spitz, explained to the rabbi, "Even God likes a winner." That's also about the time Arnold Spitz taught his son the basic fact of competitive life.

"How many lanes in a pool, Mark?" Arnold would ask.

"Six."

"And how many lanes win, Mark?"

"One."

At the age of 14, Spitz had been in the winning lane often enough to qualify for the national championships. At 15, in the Maccabiah Games in Tel Aviv, against athletes from 30 other countries, he won five gold medals. By the age of 17, he had established five world records in international competition, and had set or tied five American records within a year. In 1968, he went to Mexico City for the Olympics. He predicted six gold medals for himself; he won two—both in relays. In individuals, he got one silver (second place) and one bronze (third). A year later, in the 1969 Maccabiah Games, he won six golds.

Now we cut to 1972. In the four years between the Mexico City trauma—he had been called a choke, and an arrogant one, at that, following those games—he had established himself as the greatest swimmer in collegiate history while at Indiana University. And now, for the 1972 Olympic Games in Munich, he was entered in seven races—four individual, three relay. A number of observers believed he could win seven golds. When he arrived in Munich, swimming officials booked a mass press conference for him. Someone asked him for a pre-

diction. "I'm making no predictions," he said. "I feel fine. I feel great. I'll just swim my best."

The 200-meter butterfly came first, on August 28, 1972. That was just one of the races he had been favored to win four years earlier. He had finished eighth then. This time he placed first, finishing more than two seconds ahead of two teammates. Within an hour, he joined the 400-meter freestyle relay team of Dave Edgar, John Murphy, and Jerry Heidenreich. It won the gold. The following night, Spitz overtook teammate Steve Genter on the final lap to win the 200-meter freestyle. Three for three.

Two nights later, on August 31, he beat his own world record in the 100-meter butterfly for his fourth gold. Later that night, he anchored the victorious 800-meter freestyle relay team of John Kinsella, Fred Tyler, and Genter for number 5, breaking the record of four golds by a swimmer, set previously by Americans Don Schollander and Johnny Weismuller. "I'm thrilled," Spitz said. "I'm proud."

There were still two races to go—the 100-meter freestyle and the 400-meter medley relay, but Spitz, Mr. Perfectionist, indicated he might pass up the 100. "I wanted to break Schollander's record and I've done that," he said. "It's tremendous, the pressure of not losing. It's reached a point where my self-esteem comes into it. I just don't want to lose. And I know the medley

PRECEDING PAGES: *Mark Spitz on his way to a 7th gold medal as he swims the butterfly leg of the 400-meter medley relay at the 1968 Munich Olympics.* RIGHT: *Spitz's take-off for the 400-m medley relay. He broke a world record in each of his seven events.*

is a cinch; six out of six is better than six out of seven." To that, his tutor, Sherman Chavoor said, "If he drops out of one, I'll break his damn neck." We'll never know what Chavoor might have done to Spitz's neck; Spitz won the 100, defeating Australia's defending champion, Mike Wenden, and his U.S. team won the medley. He had raced seven times, and won seven times, and in each race he had entered, he—or his team—had set a world record.

But there was never any time for the champion to celebrate his seven gold medals, the most won by any competitor in 76 years of Olympic history. The day after his final victory, Arab terrorists seized control of the Israeli athletes' living quarters. Spitz learned of the raid at a morning news conference, shortly before he faced reporters. "I don't want to get up to that microphone," he told a U.S. swimming coach. "I'd be a perfect target for someone with a gun." So Spitz remained

seated, between two coaches, and responded to questions for a short while. And when the press conference ended, he was escorted by soldiers to a downtown Munich hotel, and then the airport. "He is too popular to take chances," an Olympic official said. Spitz flew to London, where he announced that the 400-meter relay race had been his last competitive race. Asked about the events in Munich, Spitz said, "They're tragic." Eleven Israelis had been killed in West Germany.

Before the games had commenced, at that press conference where he refused to make predictions, Spitz was asked about his feelings of competing as a Jew in Germany, Hitler's Germany. "I've thought about it, I'll admit," he said. "But I have no qualms about Germany at all. Maybe I should, but I wasn't even born when all that stuff happened. I wasn't affected by it. My parents weren't. I've never even heard of any relatives being involved in it.

"I don't think I've ever been asked how it feels to be a Jew coming back to Germany. I've been asked if I like Germany, and I've answered that I've had some of my best times here. I don't even know if they know if I'm Jewish here. I don't know if they care. I've never felt any antagonism."

But he did feel that antagonism in 1968. In the Colorado Springs training camp before the Olympics, he ran into anti-Semitism ... from his own teammates. "Some of the older guys—the tough guys—on the team gave it to him," Chavoor said four years later. "They tried to run him right off the team. It was 'Jew-boy' this and 'Jew-boy' that. It wasn't a kidding type of thing, either. I heard it with my own ears. I remember one particularly brutal day on a golf course out there when it really got brutal.

"Mark didn't know how to handle it. He tried to get ready for a race and he'd get so wound up he'd come up with all sorts of imaginary sicknesses; sore throat, headache, like that. He was psyched."

But in 1972, he was psyched up. And he raced seven times in Munich. And he won seven times. And then he retired. The glittering pin-up poster made him a natural resource. He traded on his fame for a while, appearing as a spokesman for the dairy industry—drink milk and be a champ—and then he appeared on some variety shows. What he proved, before retiring from acting for dental school, was that as an actor, he was a great swimmer. What he proved in the Munich pool was that he was the greatest Olympic swimmer who ever lived.

—Larry Brooks

Mark Spitz, gold medal winner in the 100- and 200-meter freestyle events, 100- and 200-meter butterfly events, 400- and 800-meter freestyle relays, and the 400-meter medley relay. He retired from competitive swimming after the 1968 Olympics.

Soccer

THE LEGEND OF EDSON ARANTES do NASCIMENTO

*The world knows the man as Pele, the greatest soccer player of all time, and people
everywhere still remember his performance in the 1970 World Cup . . . when he led
Brazil to victory for the third straight time*

Brazil's two greatest exports are coffee and a small man named Edson Arantes do Nascimento. The world knows him as Pelé, and he played soccer so well and with such love that they once stopped a war for him. He played in 1,363 games and scored 1,281 goals, but one game—the final of the 1970 World Cup—endeared him to the globe.

In that game in Mexico City, Brazil had a chance to become the first nation ever to win three World Cups and thus retire the Jules Rimet Trophy. But in order to tell Brazil's story, and Pelé's, let's back up to October 23, 1940, when little Edson was born in the small town of Tres Coracoes, just outside of the port city of Santos. As a child he played with a rag ball—a real ball was too expensive—on the streets and beaches of Bauro, where he grew up. By the time he was 10, he was already marked as someone special. At 13, playing for a small local club, he scored nine goals in an 11–0 game and attracted the attention of the Santos club, which signed him to a contract to take effect on his fifteenth birthday. At 15, he was starting for Santos, and within two years he was chosen to represent Brazil in the 1958 World Cup in Stockholm, Sweden.

The Brazilians had never won a World Cup before this child of 17 led them. In the quarterfinals, the 5 foot 6½ inch marvel scored the winning goal against Wales. Against France in the semifinals, he scored three times. In the finals versus the host country, Sweden, Pelé was spectacular. With Brazil leading 2–1, Pelé lost himself among the taller defenders at Sweden's goalmouth. He waited for a centering pass to float down, caught it on his right thigh, flicked it across to his left, then up onto his head, where he softly tapped the ball once before turning and firing a powerful header past the astonished goaltender. The legend was born. With seconds left in the game, Pelé headed home another goal from an almost impossible angle to ice Brazil's 5–2 victory.

Four years later in Chile, Pelé and Brazil were again on their way to a World Cup victory. But in an early game, Pelé injured his groin and was forced to watch Brazil's triumph. The 1966 World Cup, which took place in Great Britain, was a disappointment for both Pelé and his nation. Brazil failed to reach the quar-

terfinals, and Pelé blamed European officials for losses to Hungary and Portugal.

The 1970 World Cup in Mexico gave Brazil an opportunity for vindication. But the team first had to contend with internal strife, brought about by a change in coaches. The brilliant but volatile João Saldahna had been replaced (after brandishing a gun at an inquiring reporter) by former World Cup winger Mario Lobo Zagalo. But that disadvantage was balanced by the adoption by Mexican fans of Brazil as their second team. The Brazilians had been careful to cultivate their hosts with good will and small gifts. They also had one other advantage—Pelé.

The site of the games was a matter of great controversy because of Mexico's high altitudes and temperatures. To make matters worse, many of the games started at noon, in the worst heat, to accommodate European television. But this was a problem that all teams had to face.

Pelé scored a goal in Brazil's opening 4–1 victory over Czechoslovakia, but it was a missed goal which embellished his legend. He had noticed that the Czech goalkeeper wandered far from the goal when the ball was in Brazil's end of the field. That was the case when Pelé, to the bewilderment of the crowd, let loose a powerful kick toward the Czech goal, 65 yards away. The goalie was helpless to retrieve it in time. Fortunately for the goalie, though, the ball just slid by the corner post.

Brazil next had to face England, the 1966 Cup champion, and most soccer fans agreed that this match was to be the most crucial of the games. It was also a contest of styles, the attacking game of Brazil versus the workmanlike, defensive play of the British. On this day, the heat was intense. Ten minutes into the game, Pelé was given a perfect high pass in front of the net. He jumped and headed the ball toward one corner of the net. So sure was he of his shot that he yelled his characteristic "Goooaaalll!" The English goalie, Gordon Banks, must not have heard him, though, because he threw himself into the air and just tipped the ball enough so that it went over the crossbar. Pelé later said it was the greatest save he had ever seen. "He was like a salmon leaping up a falls," Pelé said of Banks. The first half ended without either team scoring.

It was Pelé who won the game, although he did it without scoring. In the second half, a teammate named Tostao dribbled past three defenders and delivered a perfect pass to Pelé. He could have taken the shot, and indeed Banks played the ball as if he would. But Pelé instead passed to Jairzinho, who fired the ball by the surprised Banks. It was the only goal of the game. Brazil finished group play with a 3–2 victory over Romania as Pelé scored twice, first on a free kick and then from point-blank range.

Pelé was again the dominant player in Brazil's 4–2 win over Peru in the quarterfinals, even though he didn't have a goal. He set up two scores and twice hit the post with the goalie beaten. Brazil's semifinal opponent was Uruguay. Twenty years earlier, the Uruguayans had beaten the host Brazilians 2–1 in the World Cup championship game. Pelé, who was ten at the time, never forgot the disappointment and tears of his nation, and he was determined to wipe them away once and for all. But Uruguay scored first, and it looked as if the humiliation might be repeated. Brazil came back to tie the score just before the half. In the second half Brazil shook off the physical tactics of the Uruguayans. Jairzinho scored for a 2–1 lead, then Pelé insured victory by drawing the defense to him before passing to Rivelino, who made it 3–1, the final score.

The victory put Brazil in the finals against Italy. Over 110,000 fans crowded into Azteca Stadium in Mexico City on June 21, and the television audience around the world was calculated at 900 million people. Italy had reached the finals by beating West Germany 4–3. Seventeen minutes into the game, Pelé leaped high in the air to head a center pass from Rivelino into the net, over the fingertips of the Italian goalie. Pelé soared in celebration, yelling his "Goooaaalll!" as his teammates smothered him. Their celebration, however, was short-lived because Italy tied the score when a Brazilian defender carelessly flicked the ball back to an imagined teammate who turned out to be an Italian forward. Pelé nearly scored just as the half ended, and in fact the ball went cleanly into the net, but the halftime whistle blew just as he put his foot to the ball. Italy wasn't supposed to be tied with Brazil at the half, but the score stood 1–1.

The Italians continued to put up a great struggle until, with 23 minutes left to play, Gerson scored for Brazil. Minutes later, Gerson passed to Pelé, who headed it to Jairzinho, who scored. Three minutes before the end of the game, Pelé grew in the eyes of the world by passing up a chance to score in order to feed a sure goal to the captain of his team, defender Carlos Alberto. It was a magnificent gesture and a wonderful way to end Brazil's 4–1 victory.

And then the celebration started. The crowd poured from the stands, sweeping up the players and ripping off their clothes. Pelé was left only with his undershorts. When he finally reached the sanctum of the locker room, he found reporters waiting under the showers to interview him. When the team came back on the field to accept the trophy, the people were laughing and hugging and throwing confetti. It was a *carnevale,* the likes of which had never been seen.

Pelé is truly a world figure. He has played in 88 countries, visited with two popes, five emperors, 10 kings, and 108 other heads of state. In Nigeria, a two-day truce in the war with Biafra was declared so that both sides could see him play. In 1975 he signed to play with the Cosmos of the North American Soccer League, and he sold America on soccer while leading the Cosmos into two championship games. When he finally retired, on October 2, 1977, after an exhibition game between the Cosmos and his old Santos club, Pelé told the 76,000 who came in the rain to Giants Stadium in East Rutherford, New Jersey, "The children, the little ones, are the most important. For them, please say with me three times: "Love . . . love . . . love."

—S.W.

Playing for the New York Cosmos, Pele maneuvers past Neil Cohen of the Dallas Tornado in a 1976 exhibition match in Dallas. Pele was the star attraction of the Cosmos in the years after he had led his Brazilian team to 3 World Cup victories.

119

Tennis

DON'T CALL ME, I'LL CALL YOU

*Adolf Hitler called Baron Gottfried von Cramm
to impress upon the German tennis whiz just how important it was to the Fatherland for von Cramm to beat
American ace Don Budge in their Davis Cup match . . .
but it was the American who emerged triumphant after a glorious duel*

PRECEDING PAGES: *Wimbledon champion Billy Jean King lowers the net for 55-year-old Bobby Riggs during an informal match at a Manhattan tennis club in 1973.* ABOVE: *Don Budge serves against Germany's von Cramm at Forest Hills in 1937.*

It was a match between the two best players in the game, Don Budge and Baron Gottfried von Cramm, the glorious German ace. More important, it was America against Germany. Not only was the world's number-one tennis position at stake but national pride as well. In July, 1937, America was still politically neutral, but nationalistic emotion ran high in both countries. In this interzone final of the Davis Cup, the winner would certainly win the Challenge Round because defending champion Britain had lost its finest player, Fred Perry, to the professional ranks.

The United States and Germany were tied at two matches each when Budge and von Cramm walked through the majestic portals leading to Wimbledon's Centre Court. Above those portals still hangs an oak plaque with a Rudyard Kipling exhortation to "meet triumph and disaster and treat those two imposters just the same." Von Cramm was a known anti-Nazi and no doubt preferred Kipling to the Führer, who had telephoned the Wimbledon locker room to emphasize to him the significance of winning for the Fatherland. Budge remembered that "Gottfried came out pale and serious and played as if his life depended on every point." There would be no return call if von Cramm lost.

The proud German began the match like a runaway tractor, grinding up Budge's revered backhand drive. Von Cramm snatched the first set, 8–6, and the second, 7–5, by keeping Budge in backcourt with well-placed and well-directed groundstrokes. Both men were playing superior percentage tennis on grass—miraculous considering the irregular bounce on the surface and the extraordinary speed of Wimbledon's slick pitch. At the end, the umpire's chart showed that Budge had scored 115 placements, 19 aces, and only 55 errors while von Cramm had 105 placements, 17 aces, and 65 errors. Most tournament players never score more than 50 percent outright winners in any match. But superior statistics were no help to Budge, who needed to change his tactical approach to survive.

In the third set, he began to smack von Cramm's service on the rise and follow the return to net for the killing volley. Instantly successful, the tactic broke the German's service at 15 in the first game of the set. In the fourth game, Budge was overeager, and von Cramm shot four straight winners from service to tie the score at 2–all. But Budge broke back at love with a backhand rejoinder and rushed through his remaining service games to win the set, 6–4. After the 10-minute rest period, Budge rode momentum's easy wave through the fourth set, 6–2, to even the match at two sets each.

The match had started at 4 o'clock. It was now 7:30 P.M., and London's gray evening descended quickly with the slippery dew. The bounces were now virtual lightning. The extended rallies in the fading light, the ball almost invisible, created the weird effect of two semaphore operators conversing by means of their racquets.

The *weltschmerz* welled in von Cramm, who sensed that only desperate adaptation could thwart Budge's onslaught. No adjustment was an easy one for the German aristocrat, who could not hurry his stroke and who had to be planted in position to fire his flat, backhand bolts. His facilely elegant game was troubled by an opponent on a streak of good fortune, for a certain lack of versatility prevented him from disrupting his foe's patterns. But von Cramm overcame his rigidity to force Budge's vulnerable forehand into two errors and the break, for 3–1. At 4–1 on the strength of a love service game, von Cramm grew impatient to close out the match, and, for the first time, his composure, usually so secure, was shaken, leaving him for an instant with only a nervous second serve. With the late-afternoon grass as slick as ice, only a miracle worker could have broken service at such a critical stage. Here, the Budge legend grew with every shot. His sickly forehand cured itself and ferreted openings as he boldly attacked the serve on four straight points to win the game at love. Then the American leveled at 4–all after surviving a game-point crisis with a forehand finisher that earlier in the match was unknown to him. At 6–all, the lack of variety that the baron had overcome in pressing his foe's once-frail forehand haunted him again. He attacked the forehand, but instead of faltering under pressure, Budge's revitalized forehand forced two errors to break von Cramm's service at 15. Behind, 6–7, the baron braced to save three match points and then charged to break point. Deuce. Break point again. Deuce. Finally, Budge's fourth match point. In the final rally, Don Budge raced full tilt cross-court and hit a forehand thunderbolt down the line. At the end of the stroke, he sprawled ingloriously on the turf, leaving the whole court open for a winning reply. But there was none, so perfectly executed and placed was Budge's blast. It had scattered chalk dust from two lines and climaxed the struggle that has been called "the greatest tennis match of the ages."

The proud baron, without looking back, met Budge at net with unmistakable dignity. In a firm tone that gave no hint of anguish, he pronounced, "Absolutely the finest match I've ever played in my life. I'm happy I could play it against you whom I like so much."

—Eugene L. Scott

Baron Gottfried von Cramm comes to the net against Don Budge in the U.S. Men's Singles Championship match played at Forest Hills in September, 1937. Budge had already beaten von Cramm in their historic match at Wimbledon in July. Budge won again at Forest Hills, taking the match 3 sets to 2.

THE BATTLES OF THE SEXES

Billie Jean King scored a major victory for Women's Lib and
Women's Lob when she vanquished Mr. Bobby Riggs, that haughty male chauvinist,
in a Houston showdown witnessed by more than 35 million people

The supreme spectacles of sport occur in celebrated surroundings; Churchill Downs for the Kentucky Derby, the Augusta National for the Masters and Wimbledon's Centre Court for the British Championships. In fact, it is axiomatic that the test of a champion is not just the ability to win, but the aptitude to triumph in the grandest grandstand of all.

One significant exception to this rule changed the course of tennis forever. Bobby Riggs versus Billie Jean King in the infamous Battle of the Sexes on September 20, 1973, at the Houston Astrodome. The match had no place in the stuffy forums of the international tennis calendar. There was no history, no tradition—no true title at stake. It was strictly a man-made promotion—a one-shot event with no origin and no future.

But Riggs, the 55-year-old former U.S. and Wimbledon titleholder and current champion of male chauvinism, dubbed his match with King as the Greatest Hustle Ever Told. It was. And it was more than a tennis match—moving tennis once and for all past the crusty country club into the public lap of the masses.

With courtside seats at $100, 30,472 fans gathered at the Astrodome—the largest live gate in tennis history. Another 35 million people watched the broadcast on ABC television with Howard Cosell anchoring the commentary team. The fact that the biggest TV audience for any previous tennis happening was 15 million meant that 20 million viewers were exposed to tennis for the first time. Tennis as a spectator sport had come of age. Soon thereafter, the famous heavyweight challenges with Jimmy Connors taking on all comers, contributed to major TV sports programming, all possible because King versus Riggs recruited millions of new spectators for their sport.

The build-up for the King-Riggs extravaganza was extraordinary, and slowly but surely galvanized the attention of the entire sports world. Five months earlier, Riggs had battered Margaret Court 6–2, 6–1 on Mother's Day and simultaneously bruised the psyches of ardent supporters of the women's movement. Riggs had ballyhooed his exhibition with Court as a war of principle and predicted his winning would deliver all women from the boardroom back to the bedroom.

The hustle was not a dance to Riggs. Since childhood, he had fine-tuned his art of the disappearing handicap. Whether it was pitching cards into a hat for small fortunes or betting on raindrops falling down a window pane (always bet on the heavier drop—it moves faster), he always figured the odds. And as one-time World's Professional Champion in tennis, he knew the angles in his own game too. In 1939, his first trip to Wimbledon, he bet heavily on himself to win the singles, doubles, and mixed doubles, a "triple" that had never before been achieved. In horse racing parlance this deed would have longer odds than the Trifecta and Quiniela combined. Of course, he won. And more than the silver goblets which were the only prizes allowed in the snobbish amateur era. He collected close to $100,000 in bets from his longshot.

A month before the Court contest, Riggs was just another duck-footed veteran who had been out of the limelight for 25 years and never was much of a celebrity even in his prime. But like any brilliant competitor, once you see an opening you go for it. The women tennis pros at the time had been screaming for equal prize money with the men and Riggs had publicly scoffed at the women's unrealistic and piggish pleas.

"Hell, I'm a 55-year-old man and I can lick the best woman in the world", he mocked. First he challenged King and she refused. But when he threw down the gauntlet to Margaret Court, who was in the prime of her career and had won more major titles than any other woman in history, he had the perfect pigeon. Thinking the exhibition would be nothing more than a brisk walk down a country lane and a chance to break up the endless tournament grind, she accepted. Riggs goof-balled Court into a helpless helping of jello in less than an hour before a nationwide television audience. The embarrassing mismatch made Riggs an overnight hero to chauvinists everywhere.

But to Billie Jean King, the leader of women's rights in sports and beyond, Riggs's triumph was an affront to her accomplishments. In 1971, she became the first woman athlete to earn $100,000 in a season. She had pioneered women's pro tennis and propelled it past penny-ante prize money. Singlehandedly she had won

the war with the governing fathers of tennis for equal purses with the men.

Three months after the Mother's Day Massacre, King announced she would play Riggs for a $100,000 winner-take-all plus $50,000 each in television rights money. "Margaret Court opened the door for Riggs. Now I'm gonna slam it shut."

Thus the battle was joined long before the first ball was hit and the verbal volleying continued unabated for three months. At stake was far more than a quarter million dollars. On line was the pride of man and womankind. Or, as Riggs hyped, "This is the battle of the century—the libber versus the lobber."

Riggs flooded the newspapers with sexist slogans. "A woman's place is in the bedroom and the kitchen—in that order," he jibed. All the while, the Riggs legend grew. The public was reminded of his prowess as a competitor with the story of his winning $50,000 on the golf course in a week of side bets. In truth, he was a six handicapper who negotiated at least eight. And then the story of his playing tennis against a millionaire singer for $10,000. Unfair? "I gave him a handicap," Riggs explained, looking hurt lest anyone think he ever took unfair advantage of a foe. "I played Steve Lawrence with eight chairs on my side of the net, carrying a suitcase in one hand, a poodle on a leash with the other, and received serve sitting down."

It is doubtful if Riggs ever handicapped himself so

poorly. No one doubts he carried a suitcase and a poodle—but not in the same match. But Riggs's reputation as a master trickster and huckster made each episode come true.

Riggs criss-crossed the country to appear on television. He added new dimension to the word "talk" on talk shows. He once outgabbed Don Rickles, the substitute host on Johnny Carson's Tonight show. Overnight he became a hot commercial property, endorsing everything from hotels to racquets to vitamins—he popped 415 daily as part of his regular diet.

Mickey Rooney, a pint-sized lookalike of the pint-sized Riggs, wanted to play him in the movies. The World Woman Rodeo Champion extended the mixed-sex theme by challenging Riggs to a goat-roping contest—$10,000 winner-take-all. Amarillo Slim, the world's poker champion, tried to train a woman to take Riggs on in poker. All the while, Riggs believed his own material and thought the fantasy he had created could continue forever. He was already planning his next match after King. Chris Evert. The duel would be billed as "the Beauty and the Beast." And afterwards the next women's champion. And so on.

In the opposite corner of this intersex polemic, fidgeted Billie Jean King whose motto, "Bobby's just fighting for money—I'm fighting for a cause," recruited a solid, if solemn, corps of women supporters. But their battle cry was muted by Riggs's overbearing chauvinist trumpet. After all, hadn't he put women in their place by humbling Margaret Court? Hadn't she choked under the pressure—just like a woman? Bobby's blabbermouthing suggested that his rout of Court forever settled the issue for the women who thought they could equal men.

What really happened in households across America was that people were choosing up sides on the basis of gender alone. "Husbands made wagers with wives over who would do the dishes for a week if Bobby or Billie Jean got beaten" wrote Grace Lichtenstein, a former *New York Times* reporter and an expert on the women's tour. But clearly on the strength of Bobby's mouth, which seemed to be driven by transistors packed under his tongue and backed up by Court's falling apart, Riggs had won the prematch warfare. Las Vegas quoted odds as 8–5 on Riggs with no money being taken on King the last 24 hours. The writers' poll in the Astrodome tallied 22 for Riggs, 10 for King.

Ten days before the match, King had gone into virtual seclusion. Amid reports that she was suffering from hypoglycemia, hepatitis, and nerves, King avoided in-

Bobby Riggs flexes for Billy Jean King as they scrimmage before their "Battle of the Sexes" match held Sept. 20, 1973 in the Houston Astrodome. Riggs, the consummate hustler, beat Margaret Court on Mother's Day in a similar match, but Billy Jean was tougher.

TOP: *Billy Jean King's great concentration and ability to position herself are seen in this photo from a match just before the Riggs confrontation.* ABOVE: *King and Riggs in the Astrodome. King won easily, 6–4, 6–3, 6–3.* OPPOSITE: *Billy Jean makes a difficult shot in a 1980 Wimbledon match.*

terviews except the mandatory prematch press conference where she reassured her world, "I wasn't on my deathbed. You people invented that."

Riggs, on the other hand, for a month beforehand was wagging his tongue nonstop promoting the match and his new book—not necessarily in that order—and had been so confident he forgot the essence of his mission. He rarely practiced. It was understandable really, because he had found fame for the first time in 25 years, and serious training would hinder the enjoyment of his new notoriety. Babes, bucks, and babbling were Rigg's exclusive preoccupations, but never before had they been possible. By the night of the match, it was time to pay the Piper of Pleasure. He looked drawn and wan, his eyes glazed like two doughnuts as if he had confused "uppers" with his vitamins.

The Astrodome motif was the Christian versus the Lions in art deco. Billie Jean King was carried out to Centre Court in a red feathered throne hoisted by four thick-muscled slaves. She was wearing a green sweater over a rhinestone-covered green dress that would have made Cleopatra blush. Riggs waited for a trumpet blast and promptly pulled out on a Chinese rickshaw aided by six sexy babes known as Bobby's Bosom Buddies. Inside, sat the premier pig nestling a giant Sugar Daddy lollipop to his breast.

Billie Jean won the toss—and everything else too. Riggs kept the score close until four all in the first set. But even his most ardent supporters suspected something was wrong. His backhand passing shot floated like tumbleweed and King was swatting volleys all over the court. He was hitting too softly and he was too slow. His serve was pathetic—a slow lob that King was able to chip and cruise the net without worry of counterattack. Riggs was too weak. It wasn't that King was doing anything extraordinarily well, but she didn't have to. She had a wider variety of shots all around and could vary her strategy to suit Riggs's meager response.

King could attack or be patient in the backcourt. She won the first set easily 6–4. As if to show she was in total command, she began to hit drop shots at the beginning of the second. The match had been in progress just under an hour and Riggs was exhausted. His backers believed he was sandbagging, holding back to raise the drama—one last theatric thrill.

No, the Riggs cast in the first scene was the real Riggs. He had nothing more to give. Second set to King 6–3. Bobby tried coming to net behind puff balls, but King simply lobbed over his head, tiring him further and making the result inevitable. Riggs never gave up.

Even the swift Sportface surface did not accelerate Riggs's shots enough to allow him an offensive stance. His role was the puppet on King's string, which ran him in circles all night—exactly like Riggs's victims in his handicap hustles. Set and match to King, 6–4, 6–3, 6–3 in under two hours.

Dozens of theories instantly surfaced as to how the upset had happened. Was it, indeed, an upset? One sinister story was immediately offered by oldtimers (men naturally). King had refused the challenge entirely—until Riggs said she wouldn't lose. Another was that Riggs tanked the match so he could continue his cha-rade for years against new rivals, but this defied logic. Certainly he had more to gain by winning. It was difficult for men to admit what they saw. King had forced Riggs to play her game. She outvolleyed and out-groundstroked him. She wrong-footed him. She had hit 64 percent outright winners. But Riggs was far from humiliated. His mouth revved up right away and talked about a rematch. He was sporting in his praise of how well King had played. He had lost, but yet the Astro-tennis Circus had assured there were no real losers, and the biggest winner of all was not Billie Jean King nor the women's movement but tennis itself.

—E.L.S.

A MATCH FOR THE AGES

Bjorn Borg beats John McEnroe in a magnificent
five-set final for his fifth—and toughest—Wimbledon championship in a row

It was tennis of a lifetime.

It was July 5, 1980, Centre Court at Wimbledon, the finals, and Bjorn Borg and John McEnroe were conducting a string symphony of excellence. Two remarkable players at the peak of their games, they clawed, punched and jabbed, attacked and counterattacked at one another with cunning and power for 3 hours and 53 minutes. They had played five sets . . . and the fourth had included a 22-minute, 34-point tiebreaker that will stand alone as a dramatic and artistic standard as long as tennis exists, as long as championship matches are contested.

And when it was over, the world was left breathless. And when it was over, Borg sank to his knees in triumph, racquet raised in a victory tableau he may now claim as his own. The second-seeded McEnroe had pushed the top-seeded Borg to the limit, and then some, and still—and again—the 24-year-old had conquered the All-England Lawn Tennis and Croquet Club's grass courts. When Borg hit a backhand passing shot on match point, his eighth match point, no less, he had become the first player in modern times to win the most prestigious championship in the sport five straight years. History tells us that Lawrie Doherty won the title five straight years from 1902 through 1906, and that William Renshaw took six straight crowns from 1881 to 1886. But those were the years when the challenge round was in effect, and the champion was required only to defend his crown in the final. Borg's victory over McEnroe was his record thirty-fifth straight Wimbledon triumph . . . seven matches for each of five years. Borg, thy name is synonymous with immortality.

"They should send him to another planet," said Ilie Nastase, whom Borg had beaten in straight sets for his 1976—and first—championship. "The rest of us play tennis. Borg plays something else."

On this day, both Borg and McEnroe had played something beyond the ordinary, and had left the masses gasping in disbelief. The final score was 1–6, 7–5, 6–3, 6–7 (16–18), 8–6, but defining the match in numbers, even numbers so sparkling as those, do not do the players justice. The numbers don't tell us about the seven match points the valiant McEnroe had saved before finally succumbing. And the numbers only hint at the

majesty of play in that fourth set tiebreaker. You can go 18–16, routinely; this was not routine. No way, no time was it ever routine.

The match was a battle of will and personality as much as one of ability. It pitted Borg, the stolid, silent Swede, who grew a beard for each Wimbledon, against the apple-cheeked, fuzzy-haired McEnroe, the brash 21-year-old American. It was Borg's steady ground strokes against McEnroe's serve-and-volley approach. Borg had moved implacably through the field toward his rendezvous with destiny. McEnroe's march through the tournament had been accompanied by one tantrum after another, with players and officials alike the target for his abuse; indeed, McEnroe and Jimmy Connors nearly came to blows in their four-set semifinal match.

But McEnroe was cool for this final, and the left-hander allowed his talent to speak for him throughout the match. His relentless attack, his twisting serves and volleys, pinned Borg deep and kept the champion off balance for most of the first three sets. It was not until the twelfth game of the second set that Borg gained the upper hand in the match, blasting a brilliant backhand service return winner that gave him double set point. It was the kind of scintillating point that often breaks an opponent.

It was also the kind of shot that Borg, uncharacteristically, had had so much trouble with throughout the tournament. Wimbledon had been disrupted by a steady downpour through two weeks of play, and the rain had softened the courts, thus yielding low bounces. For a two-handed player such as Borg, who must scoop and lift, the low bounce is as welcome a visitor as the plague. But the weather had turned sunny the days prior to the final, and the turf had hardened. "I started to play that shot well in the semifinal," Borg said, referring to his four-set triumph over Brian Gottfried.

That shot behind him, Borg seemed to take control. He raced to 2–0 and 5–2 leads in the third set, after holding service in a 20-point game in which McEnroe had held five break points. And after he closed the set on his next service game, and went ahead 5–4, 40–15 in the fourth set, it seemed as though McEnroe was as done as Thanksgiving turkey. The generally reserved Wimbledon crowd was on its feet, cheering, awaiting the moment that Borg would walk through history's gates. They didn't know the fight had just begun.

McEnroe chewed his way back into the match, and won the game by breaking Borg with a backhand service return cross-court winner. McEnroe held. Borg held. And there then followed the 22 minutes and 34 points that captured and held the sports world's attention. Borg had his third match point with McEnroe serving at 5–6, but the Douglaston, New York, native fought it off with a sizzling forehand volley that died on the grass, after Borg had hit a monstrous return of the second serve. Thereafter, every other point of the tie-breaker was match or set point. Both men dived and lunged and sprawled on the grass, doing the seemingly impossible before an audience that had reached the heights of frenzy.

McEnroe finally got his first set-point at 8–7, but this time it was Borg who saved himself, driving a forehand service return down the line past McEnroe's diving attempt at a return. Somehow, the pace quickened. At 16–all, Borg went wide on a service return. And then, in what seemed an anticlimax, he netted a simple forehand volley. Set, McEnroe. Two sets apiece.

Borg, the man of ice, slumped in disbelief. "I couldn't believe it," he said. "I was thinking maybe I'd end up losing the match. It was a strange feeling. I felt terrible, very disappointed. I tried to say to myself, 'You have to forget and go forward,' but it was difficult, very difficult. Always when I had an important point, he played a great shot."

McEnroe, meanwhile, was feeling no pain. "I didn't think he'd get tired, but I thought he might get down mentally," he said. "I was looking forward to the fifth set."

But the fifth set was Borg's. A lesser man—a less-great talent—could never have come back against a player as great and as tough as McEnroe that day. But it is the fifth set that separates the great from the immortal. After losing the first two points of that set, Borg did not lose another service point until the set's tenth game . . . a remarkable string of 19 consecutive winning service points. McEnroe was breathing hard, and he did come back from 0–40 to tie at 4–all. But that was his last gasp. The end finally came when Borg's backhand crosscourt passed a lunging McEnroe at 40–15. The crowd cheered lustily, and Borg sank to his knees.

"Right then, I don't know if I even realized I had won it again," Borg said. "And until the last point, I was never sure I would win. For sure, it is the best match I have ever played at Wimbledon."

Once the match was over, the rush was on to fit it, and the champion, with the proper superlatives. "Electrifying," said former Australian great Fred Stolle. Of Borg, the former British player Roger Taylor said, "He's gone through every kind of testing. If there were any chinks, you would have found them today."

It is not for Borg to place himself in history. He will not say that he believes himself a better player than Rod Laver or Bill Tilden, the two men generally acknowledged as his only peers. "My ambition is to win so much, so many times that people could look and say, 'There could not have been a better man than this'," he said, after his eighty-second win in his last 84 singles matches. "Next year, I think I can win again."

For McEnroe, the defeat left him with honor . . . and a growing hunger to win Wimbledon in 1981. "This was a wonderful final, and Borg played great tennis," said McEnroe, "but I will beat the bearded wonder yet."

To the question, is Borg the best ever, McEnroe's response was this, "He won this thing five times. That should be a hint."

—L.B.

Bjorn Borg prepares his two-handed backhand shot in his epic Men's Singles match with John McEnroe at Wimbledon, 1980. The match went on for 3 hours and 53 minutes with the momentum shifting regularly from one player to the other. Borg finally triumphed.

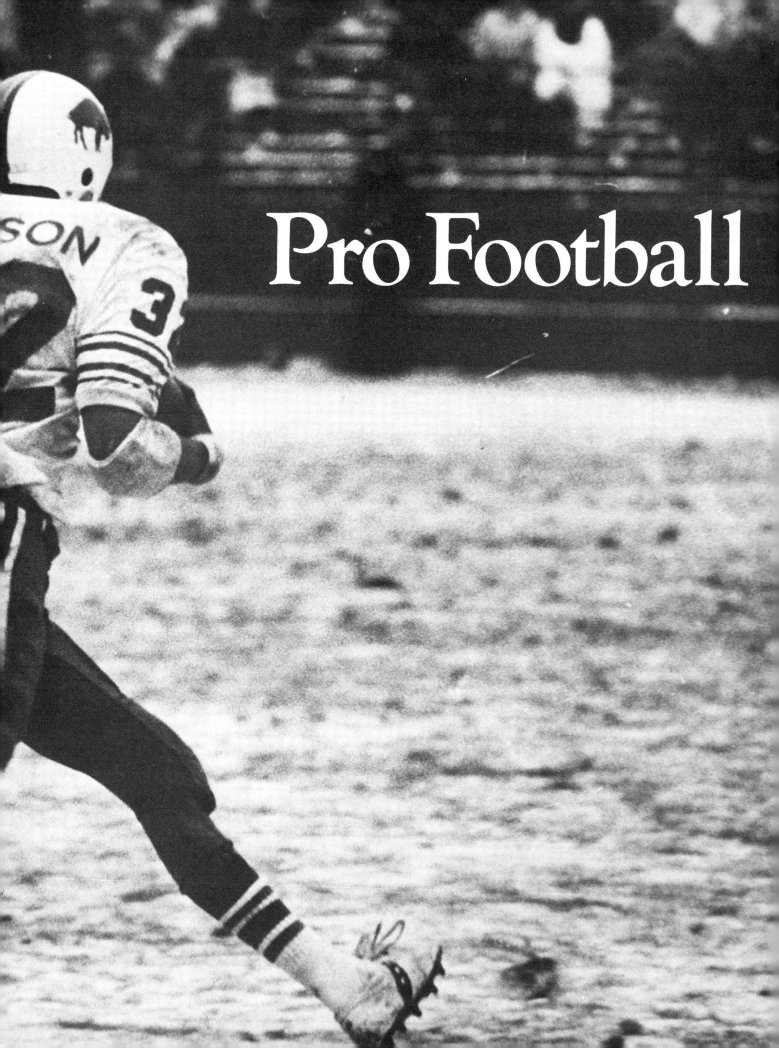

Pro Football

THEY WERE RUNNING OUT OF FOOTBALLS

The Chicago Bears gained sweet revenge against the
Washington Redskins by routing them 73–0 in the 1940 championship game

If we are all united in a common pursuit of perfection, we are also united in the knowledge that we will never quite attain our goal. Perfection ... what an awesome concept. Well, on a Sunday afternoon some four decades ago, the Chicago Bears were awesome. And their effort defined the infinite heights of perfection. On December 8, 1940, the Bears and Redskins met at Washington's Griffith Stadium for the championship of the National Football League.

The Bears won 73–0.

The Bears scored 11 touchdowns, by 10 players. They scored their first on the game's second play from scrimmage, when fullback Bill Osmanski raced around left end for 68 yards and went in when George Wilson's block devastated the two Washington defenders between him and the end zone. They scored their final touchdown with less than three minutes to play when Harry Clark went over right tackle from one yard out. It was 21–0 after the first quarter ... 28–0 at the half ... 54–0 after three quarters. And it was so bad, the score did not completely mirror the destruction the Chicago team had wrought that afternoon; it was left to statistics to fill in the gory details. The Bears gained 382 yards rushing, the Redskins, 22. The Bears' Sid Luckman completed 7 of 10 passes; the Redskins' Sammy Baugh, Frank Filchock, and Roy Zimmerman completed 20 of 51 for 223 yards, and had eight passes intercepted, returned for 117 yards. It was so bad that after the Bears' tenth touchdown made the score 66–0, referee Red Friesell asked Chicago coach George Halas if his team wouldn't please pass or run for any further extra points ... because the officials "were running out of footballs." The Bears passed for their sixty-seventh point, and failed on a pass attempt for their seventy-fourth.

No team in pro football history has ever scored that many points in a single game—26 years later, the Redskins themselves would come the closest, defeating the New York Giants 72–41 in a regular season match—and the impact of Chicago's smashing triumph that winter afternoon had a far-reaching effect on the future of the sport. For the 1940 championship game, the first ever to be broadcast on national radio, had matched Halas's Bears and their modern T formation against Baugh's and the Redskins' traditional single-wing. And 73–0

forced people to stand up and take notice.

"The lopsidedness of the score focused national attention on the T formation," Halas said. "And when Stanford ran over Nebraska a few week later in the Rose Bowl using the same formation, the stampede to copy our offense was on."

A stampede defined by the numbers 73–0 can never be explained, but this one defies logic even more than normally. Because the Redskins and Bears had met at Griffith Stadium just three weeks earlier ... and the Redskins had won 7–3. The Bears had finished their season as Western champions with an 8–3 record; the Redskins, behind the great Baugh's arm, had run up a league-leading 245 points in compiling a 9–2 record. On defense, they had permitted only two teams to score three touchdowns against them in a game.

And so it was that Washington owner George Preston Marshall expressed his outrage upon learning that the odds-makers had made the western visitors a slight favorite for the title match. "That's ridiculous," he said. "We already beat them ... we only lost two games all year ... the bookmakers must be crazy."

PRECEDING PAGES: *Buffalo's O.J. Simpson makes football history by rushing over 2,000 yards in the 1973 season.* ABOVE: *Dec. 8, 1940. The Bears' Bill Osmanski (11) goes for the first touchdown in a game the Bears won against the Redskins 73–0.*

But those words, so silly in the context of history, aren't the ones that really haunted Marshall that day. It seems that after his team's 7–3 win over the Bears three weeks earlier, Marshall couldn't contain himself when a number of Chicago players—and Halas—claimed that an official's call had cost the Bears a victory. "They're frontrunners, quitters," Marshall said. "They're not a second-half team. They fold up when the going gets tough."

Halas fumed when he read Marshall's comments . . . but quietly. And he filed the remarks for future reference. On the day of the championship game, he brought out the newspaper clippings, and read them to his players. "Gentlemen, this is what George Preston Marshall thinks of you," he said. "I think you're a great football team, the greatest ever assembled. Go out on the field and prove it."

And so the Bears did. Before a standing-room-only crowd of 36,000 fans that included scores of Washington dignitaries, they scaled the heights of perfection, and destroyed a very talented team. The Bears that day started a team that included five future Hall of Famers—quarterback Luckman; guard Dan Fortmann; tackle Joe Stydahar; halfback George McAfee; and center Bulldog Turner—and a team has never been better. Or as perfect.

It was a contest for two series of downs. After Osmanski's 68-yard jaunt, Max Krause returned the ensuing kickoff 62 yards to the Chicago 32. Baugh was in business. On second-and-four, Slinging Sammy, the sidearm tosser, spotted end Charley Maloney all alone at the two-yard line—a sure touchdown! And the pass was perfect . . . but Maloney was blinded by a bright sun as he turned back toward the play, and the ball bounced off his fingers. A third-down pass was incomplete, and the Redskins were forced to settle for a field goal. They should have been so fortunate. Bat Masterson's kick was blocked. The contest was over.

The Bears then marched 80 yards on 17 rushing plays, and Luckman's one-yard plunge upped the score to 14–0. Joe Maniaci, Osmanski's replacement at fullback, went 42 yards to make it 21–0 at the end of the quarter. When the Redskins reached the Chicago 18, the Bears batted down four successive Baugh passes. And by the half it was 28–0. And once more Marshall's words came back to haunt him. "They said you were a first-half club, front-runners," Halas told his team. "Show them you're a second-half team, too."

The Bears made it 34–0 two plays into the second half, when Hampton Pool raced 15 yards with a Baugh

interception. The score mounted to 54–0 . . . and 60–0. It was then that the Griffith Stadium public address announcer committed one of the great faux pas in sports history. "Your attention is directed to a very important announcement regarding the sale of seats for the 1941 season," he said. The shocked fans booed thunderously. Marshall remained silent.

After the game, Marshall was a grumpy man. "We needed a 50-man line against their power," he said. "That's all there was to it. And we had the greatest crowd in Washington history and played our poorest game. I'm mortified to think what we did to that crowd."

The Bears were at a loss to explain the final tally. So were the Redskins. So were the reporters at the game. Searching for some possible explanation, a number of observers latched onto Charlie Maloney's first quarter drop of the Baugh pass that might have allowed the Skins to tie the game. "If Charlie hung onto that pass, wouldn't it have been a different story?" Baugh was asked. The quarterback smiled and then delivered one of the great quotes in sports history. "Yeah," he said. "It would have been 73–6."

—L.B.

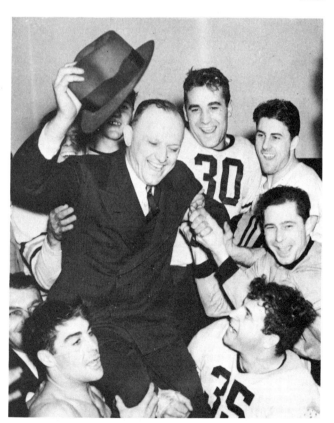

The jubilant Chicago Bears hold their owner-coach George Halas aloft after the Bears blew out the Redskins 73–0 in Washington, D.C. to win the NFL Championship on December 8, 1940. No pro football team has ever scored as many points before or since.

133

THE DAY THE NFL GREW UP

*Professional football became a national institution on
that frosty Sunday in 1958 when Johnny Unitas led the Baltimore Colts to a sudden-death victory over
the New York Giants in the NFL title game*

The arm belonged to Johnny Unitas. The hands belonged to Raymond Berry. The legs belonged to Alan Ameche. But on December 28, 1958, the glory belonged to the National Football League. For it was on that day that the NFL became more than just another league, and professional football more than just another sport. The Baltimore Colts and New York Giants played a championship game of such high drama and excellence that it captured the imagination of the country. When it was over, when the Colts had defeated the Giants 23–17 in the first overtime title game in history, the showdown immediately became known as The Greatest Game Ever Played.

The Colts and Giants played 68 minutes and 15 seconds of football at Yankee Stadium that day, and each minute and each second has its place in American folklore. But it is the final two minutes of regulation time, and all 8:15 of overtime, that is etched indelibly in the history books. It was the time when the improbable became routine . . . and the impossible so possible, indeed.

The Giants had come into the championship match

after defeating the Cleveland Browns 10–0 a week earlier in a special Eastern Division playoff match. The New Yorkers had won their last four games of the regular season to catch Cleveland, and that included a 13–10 win over the Browns on the last scheduled Sunday of the season to force the playoff. The Giants won that playoff-to-force-a-playoff in the final seconds when Pat Summerall's 49-yard field goal through a blizzard snapped a 10–10 tie. (Some observers insist that Summerall's kick traveled at least 55 yards, the yard-markers having been obscured by the snowfall.) A week before that, the Giants had rallied in the fourth quarter to defeat the Detroit Lions 19–17. They certainly seemed a team of destiny.

And it appeared their destiny would carry them to their second NFL championship in three years when they rallied from a 14–3 halftime deficit to grab a 17–14 fourth-quarter lead over Baltimore. The magnificent Giant defense, led by Dick Modzelewski, Andy Robustelli, Rosey Grier, and Sam Huff, had been nearly perfect in the second half, and it was their goal-line stand in the third quarter that had twisted the game New York's

way. The Colts had the ball, first down on the three. Four plays later, the Giants had the ball on the five—four running plays had lost two yards. And from there, old Chuckin' Charlie Conerly, New York's 34-year-old quarterback, led the way. The margin was sliced to 14–10 before the third period had ended, and the Giants had the lead when Conerly hit Frank Gifford in the end zone early in the final period.

And so it was 17–14, Giants, with less than five minutes to play. And the Giants had the ball. "We just had to run out the clock and they'd never get another chance," said fullback Alex Webster. "We were so hot . . . everything was working so well . . . it sure looked like our game." There were two minutes to play when the Giants faced a third-and-four from their own 40. A first down would lock up the game. The Giants would be champions. But that third-down play provided for one of the most debated official's calls in NFL history. Gifford swept right, and collided viciously with the Colts' star end, Gino Marchetti, near the 44. Gifford powered forward, and both men went down . . . with Marchetti's ankle shattered. To this day, Gifford believes that he made the first down. But referee Ronnie Gibbs did not mark the ball until after Marchetti had been taken off the field, and he signaled that Gifford had come up some six inches short. "Without question, I know that I had the first down made," said Gifford, whose two first-half fumbles had helped the Colts construct their lead. "But in all the confusion, with Marchetti screaming and thrashing and all, the ball got

OPPOSITE: *Johnny Unitas carries the ball for short yardage in the NFL title game between the Baltimore Colts and the N.Y. Giants, December 28, 1958, Yankee Stadium.* ABOVE: *A Unitas fumble is about to be recovered by the Giants' Jim Patton (20). Roosevelt Grier (76) also heads for the ball.*

135

kicked around. But listen, we had Don Chandler to punt, and he was the best in the league."

A number of Giants begged coach Jim Lee Howell to run the football on fourth down. "We only needed four inches," said guard Jack Stroud, "and we would have run through a brick wall at that point. We would have gotten it."

But Howell went with Chandler, who had averaged 44 yards a kick throughout the season. And when Chandler hung a booming punt that Carl Taseff could only receive as a fair catch on his own 14, it seemed as if Howell had made the proper decision. The Colts would have to travel at least 70 yards to get into field goal range in fewer than 90 seconds to escape defeat, and against a frenzied defense in front of a frenzied sellout crowd. Impossible! But not for the Colts, who had won their first Western title ever. Not for Johnny U., the 25-year-old QB with the golden arm who had been cut by the Pittsburgh Steelers three years earlier and had languished in a semi-pro league until the Colts picked him up in 1956. He would use the remainder of the game to carve himself a legend.

"Two things were important then," Unitas said. "We had to concentrate on getting the ball upfield, which meant we had to pass. But we knew the Giants would be playing the pass, so we had to pass in a way they wouldn't expect."

The Giants were expecting Unitas to throw to the sidelines, so his receivers would be in position to step out of bounds and stop the clock after a reception. So he threw over the middle. But when his first two passes were incomplete, the Colts faced a third-and-10 with 1:16 to play. On third down, he found Lenny Moore for 11 yards and a first down. An incompletion followed, but then Unitas found the great Berry isolated on Carl Karilivacz, and hit him for 25 yards, moving the ball to midfield, with less than a minute to play. On the next play, he found Berry again, this time for 15 yards. First down on the Giants' 35. The next play—again Berry beat Karilivacz, this time deep down the middle for 22 yards. Three straight passes to Berry had gained 62 yards. The clock was running . . . 20 seconds to play . . . the Colts had no timeouts. Steve Myrha, a reserve linebacker who had kicked just four field goals in 10 tries during the season, and who had had a first-quarter try blocked by Huff, rushed onto the field. There were seven seconds remaining in regulation time when Myrha connected from the 20-yard line to tie the score.

On the sidelines, the Giants sagged. "I remember sitting on the bench next to Charlie (Conerly) that last drive," said Gifford. "We were beat . . . exhausted. When we went into overtime, we didn't have any life left. When they tied us, they had the game won. I knew it. Charlie knew it. Deep down, I think we all knew it."

The Giants won the toss of the coin for football's first fifth quarter. They kept the ball for three plays, and gained nine yards. On fourth and one from the 29, it was time once again for Chandler, and this time his kick traveled 55 yards, before Taseff returned it four yards to the 20. It was time again for Unitas. Time for the impossible. A quick first down moved the Colts to the 31, but suddenly Unitas was facing a third-and-eight. No problem; a flare to fullback Ameche coming out of the backfield got those eight. First down on the 41.

But here again, the proud and battered Giant defense rose up, and two plays later the Colts were facing a third-and-15. Again Unitas. Again Berry. This time for 21 yards and a first down on the New York 43. The Giants were reeling. Ameche cracked through the mid-dle for 23 yards on the next play. And now, once again, it was a matter of time; only this time, the question was how much time it would take Baltimore to win, not how much time the Colts had left to avoid defeat. Quickly, Unitas hit Berry for 12 yards and a first down on the eight. On the last two drives, Unitas had thrown five passes to Berry, and had completed all five, for 95 yards. For the day, Berry caught 12 passes for 178 yards, championship game records. Two plays later, the ball was resting on the one. And then it was the Horse, Ameche, galloping through a gaping hole for the winning touchdown on the drive's thirteenth play. Before he had even hit dirt, Baltimore fans had careened onto the field to celebrate and tear down the goalposts.

So the Colts had won. Unitas and Berry had cemented their legend. And football became more than a game. On December 28, 1958, professional football became an institution.

—L.B.

Mel Triplett (33) of the Giants powers his way to a touchdown, taking most of the Redskin line with him into the goalpost. But, with seven seconds left in regulation play, the Redskins kicked a field goal to tie the score at 17–17. The Redskins then scored a TD in overtime to win the game.

NO. 32 vs. NO. 70

When the irresistible force, Jimmy Brown, No. 32, Cleveland Browns,
met the immovable object, Sam Huff, No. 70, New York Giants, it was hold on for dear life

They met in 15 games of fury. One was a running back, the best of his time, perhaps the best who had ever played football. The other was a middle linebacker, probably not the best of his time, but certainly the most glamorous. Jim Brown, number 32, fullback, Cleveland Browns; Sam Huff, number 70, middle linebacker, New York Giants. Their teams dominated the National Football League's Eastern Division in the 1950s and early 1960s, and when their teams met, each man saw the other as his personal enemy, and himself as the key to victory. If Huff could stop Brown, the Giants would probably win; if Brown had his way, Cleveland would probably emerge with victory. This went on for seven years, from Brown's rookie season in 1957 through Huff's final season as a Giant in 1963. Fifteen games. Small wars within larger ones. And, oh, what lovely wars they were.

Huff had come to the Giants in 1956 out of West Virginia, and the team went 8–3–1 to win the Eastern Division and end Cleveland's six-year string of division titles. And they capped their first year in Yankee Stadium after having moved from the Polo Grounds with a stunning 47–7 victory over the Western Division champion Chicago Bears. Huff's crunching tackles had gained him immediate hero status among the team's fans, as the New York defense captured the city's hearts and minds. The front four consisted of Andy Robustelli and Jim Katcavage at the ends, and Rosey Grier and Dick Modzelewski at the tackles; the unit would remain together for the next half-decade, for four more division titles. Cliff Livingston and Harland Svare flanked Huff at linebacker, while Em Tunnel, Jimmy Patton, Dick Nolan, and Ed Hughes formed the team's thirsty secondary. For the first time, defensive players became glamorous players.

Meanwhile, Paul Brown was anxious to rebuild after his team's 5–7 thud in 1956. It had been the first time in the Browns' 10-year existence—the Browns played four seasons in the All-America Conference before moving to the NFL in 1950—that they had not captured at least a division crown. It had also been the first year that the team had not had the luxury of Otto Graham at the controls as quarterback; the immortal passer had finally retired at 36 following Cleveland's

38–14 championship game triumph over the Rams a year earlier. The trio of Tom O'Connell, George Ratterman, and Babe Parilli couldn't compensate for Graham's absence.

And so it was that Paul Brown eagerly awaited the 1957 college draft, and a shot at Purdue's All-America quarterback Len Dawson. But Brown's wish was not fulfilled; the Steelers plucked Dawson. And so Brown's

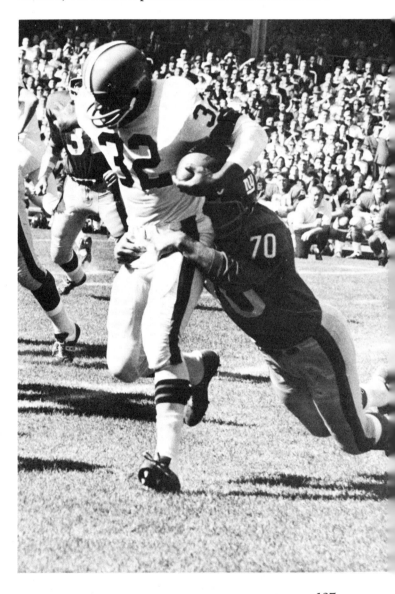

Jimmy Brown is about to break loose from Sam Huff of the N.Y. Giants and ramble for big yardage.
In this 1963 game between the Giants and the Cleveland Browns, Brown scored three touchdowns as his team rolled to a 35–24 win at Yankee Stadium.

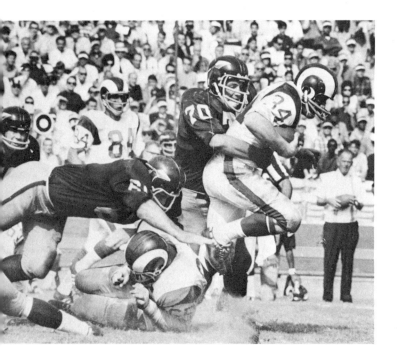

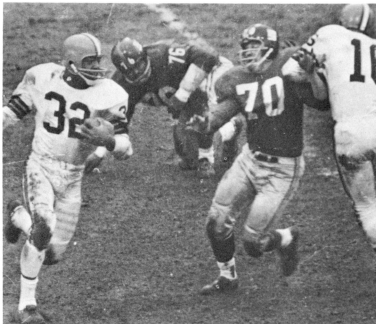

Browns were forced to settle for Syracuse's Jim Brown. Imagine if the Steelers had not chosen Dawson; maybe then they would have kept another quarterback they then owned, fellow by the name of Unitas . . . Imagine the Browns with Dawson, and without Brown. "I have imagined that," Paul Brown said later. "But from the first day of training camp, I knew we had something special."

Jim Brown was 6 feet 2 inches tall, 228 pounds, the prototype fullback, who would run over the opposition. But he also had the agility to elude tacklers; his was a manner that blended power and finesse never before seen in pro ball. He was heavily muscled, so that a single tackler could not bring him down—tackled high, his legs continued to churn, tackled low, his legs punished you—yet he was quick enough to outrun even speedy defensive backs. And he was a smart man. "He had a tremendous ability to do things on his own," his coach said. "Get him in the open past the line of scrimmage and he's liable to run away without anybody in front of him to knock people down."

He led the league in rushing with 942 yards his rookie season, the first of five consecutive rushing titles; he won eight in his nine-year career. "I would not be surprised no matter what Jim accomplishes in this game," Paul Brown said. A year later, the running back set a pro record when he gained 1,527 yards in 12 games, and broke it in 1963, when he picked up 1,863 in

14 games. That latter record stood for a decade, until O. J. Simpson's 2,003-yard season in 1973 eclipsed it. In nine years, Brown would gain a record 12,312 yards, and score 106 touchdowns on the ground, averaging 5.22 yards a carry.

The Browns defeated Huff's Giants twice in 1957 en route to reclaiming the Eastern crown, but the Detroit Lions held Brown to 69 yards on 20 carries as they demolished Cleveland 59–14 for the NFL title. It was a year later, though, that the real Huff-Brown rivalry took hold. By that time, Huff had been glamorized in a network television special, "The Violent World of Sam Huff," in which he had been hooked up to a microphone during an exhibition game. Suddenly, he was Mr. Defense, and his meetings with Mr. Offense, Brown, became billed as hand-to-hand combat situations. Macho against macho.

In 1958 the Giants and Browns would meet three times, including once in a special playoff game. The Giants won all three times: 21–17 in the season's sixth game when the Giants were 3–2 and the Browns 5–0; 13–10 in the twelfth game when the Browns needed only a tie to take the division; and then 10–0 a week later in the Eastern Conference playoff match. And in that playoff victory, the Giants held Brown to eight yards. Eight, as in one, two, three, four, five, six, seven . . . And it was during this season that the Huff legend grew large.

LEFT: *Sam Huff (70), the New York Giants' celebrated linebacker, puts the clamps on Ram running back Les Josephson (34).*
RIGHT: *A classic match-up, Jim Brown (32) vs. Sam Huff (70).*
OPPOSITE: *Brown (32) hangs onto the ball as Packer defender Dave Robinson makes a grab for it in a 1965 NFL title match.*

Tom Landry was the Giants' defensive coach, and it was widely believed that he had assigned Huff the sole responsibility of stopping Brown. That was not so, though Huff's responsibility for taking care of Brown was a large one, indeed. "Our defense was not designed specifically for Sam Huff to follow Jim Brown," said Landry, now the Dallas coach. "Our defense was designed to stop the offense we were working against. Our defense was based on coordination; you know, people. And Sam was one of 11 people. But he got great recognition, which he deserved, because in this particular defense he was stopping Jimmy Brown—who was almost unstoppable. And therefore Sam Huff was the one person everyone could identify with. He'd be at the point of attack much more than Grier, or Robustelli, or Modzelewski."

And so it became Huff against Brown. Shattering collisions. It was widely reported that Huff stepped to the Cleveland sidelines during the 1958 playoff wipeout and told the Browns coaches to remove Brown from the game. "You want to get him killed?" Huff was supposed to have demanded. And as the legends grew, so did reports of bad blood between the men; that Huff would go for Brown's eyes and Brown would kick at Huff from the bottom of a pile. But both men insisted their rivalry was business, pure and simple.

"We didn't get paid to look too fancy," said Huff. "The idea was to stop the runner the best way you could. Sometimes I twisted their heads a little, but most of them didn't seem to mind. Football is a man's game, and any guy who doesn't want to hit hard doesn't belong in it. The football field is no place for a crybaby."

Rest assured, Brown was no crybaby. He would carry the ball 25 times a game, take vicious hits, and slowly rise after each one, appearing exhausted. But by the time he set for the next carry from scrimmage, he was rushing with the power of a locomotive. And Brown respected Huff. "If I were a middle linebacker playing against a back who received the ballyhoo I did, I'd make the same special effort (Huff does)," he said. "Huff played hard, but not dirty."

The Giants defeated the Browns two more times while winning their second straight Eastern title in 1959, and once again, they contained Brown. They extended their winning streak to six before Cleveland trounced the New Yorkers 48–34 in the final game of the 1960 season, one in which the Philadelphia Eagles finally broke the Cleveland–New York domination of the division. That game, Brown thundered for 110 yards on 14 carries. "That fellow's the greatest runner of all time," said New York coach Jim Lee Howell. "You can't stop him forever."

The Giants took the Eastern Division title the next three years, from 1961 through 1963, and in doing so went 3–2–1 against the Browns. In their 15 meetings as Giant and Brown, Huff's team won nine times, Brown's team won five times, and the teams played to one draw. The Giants won five divisions, the Browns, one. And while Huff may have been an overpublicized player, and certainly not as good a middle linebacker as the Bears' Bill George, or the Lions' Joe Schmidt, two greats of the era, it is a fact that the Giants have not won a division title since Huff was unceremoniously traded to the Redskins following the 1963 season, booted out at age 28. "It took the heart out of me," Huff said.

Brown played two more seasons after the Huff trade, and the Browns whipped the Giants four straight times while capturing two more Eastern Conference crowns. He retired at age 29, after a 1,544-yard season in which he scored 17 touchdowns, in order to pursue a career as an actor.

"I always wanted to be able to leave the game as a matter of choice, and at a time when I had the greatest opportunity for the future," Brown said. "This is the time."

Said Huff, "Jim Brown was a phenomenal running back, the greatest who ever played. I am proud to have played on the same field with him. No matter how hard you hit him, he never said a harsh word. If you tackled him or gave him a good lick, he'd pat you on the fanny and say, 'Nice tackle, big Sam.' Pretty soon, you'd think, 'Boy, what a great guy!' He'd lull you to sleep that way. The next thing you'd know, he'd come running through like a freight train. When you hit him, it was like hitting an oak tree."

—L.B.

O.J. TURNED ON THE JUICE

Throughout the 1973 season O. J. Simpson ran and ran
and ran some more, and when he finished running through a snowstorm on the last day of the season,
he had gained a record 2003 yards in 14 games

Records, they tell us, are made to be broken. But some not quite so readily as others. And so it was that when Cleveland immortal Jim Brown rushed for the staggering figure of 1,863 yards in 1963, some 336 yards more than the standard he had established five years earlier (and over 400 yards more than any other man had ever gained in a single season), his coach, Blanton Collier, declared, "A record for the next century, not this one."

It was a fast century. The record lasted a decade.

The Shea Stadium field was covered with snow December 16, 1973, and though neither team had qualified for the National Football League playoffs, both the home New York Jets and visiting Buffalo Bills had emotional incentives motivating them for the final game of the regular season. The Jets, 4–9, wanted desperately to win the game for their coach, Weeb Ewbank, who was retiring after 20 years of pro ball. The Bills, 8–5, wanted to get O. J. Simpson 61 yards . . . 61 yards for 1,864, one more than Jimmy Brown's record.

Simpson had burst into prominence six years earlier as a junior tailback for the University of Southern California. In two years at USC he set 13 school rushing records, led the NCAA in rushing twice—with a two-year total of 3,423 yards—was named All-America twice, and captured the Heisman Trophy as a senior. Indeed, he was so brilliant an athlete—he was a member of USC's record-setting 1967 440-yard relay team—that he was named College Athlete of the Decade (1960s). It was no surprise that the Bills, having "won" the first draft choice for 1969 after finishing 1–10–1, chose the Juice.

But it was a surprise how the Bills used him. John Rauch, in his first year as Buffalo coach, built his offense around quarterback Jack Kemp's arm. And though Simpson, who had expressed reluctance to come to Buffalo after making his life in California, gained 697 yards, he was never given the freedom to exhibit his brilliance. A ball-carrier needs the ball; Simpson carried the ball

only 181 times that season. It got worse. The next season, rookie Dennis Shaw replaced Kemp at quarterback, dominated the offense, and Simpson, who suffered a damaged knee at mid-season, carried the ball just 120 times for 488 yards. Rauch was fired after his second successive 10-loss season, but things deteriorated under Harvey Johnson in 1971. The Bills went 1–13, with Simpson gaining 742 yards on 183 carries. At the age of 24, Simpson was demoralized.

"At that time I was pretty depressed," said Simpson, who was born Orenthal James, in San Francisco July 9, 1947. "The love between me and the city wasn't that great. The possibility of me being traded was excellent. Things had always been my way, then all of a sudden I got booed. I got negative press. . . ."

And then, in 1972, he got a new head coach. Lou Saban returned to Buffalo after a six-year hiatus, and grasped immediately that one doesn't put Van Gogh to work to paint the outside of a barn. "Lou Saban salvaged my career," Simpson said. "He told me he would give me the football and he told me he would get me an offensive line. And he kept his word. I've played with horrible lines. It's been proven that a back is only as good as his line."

So Saban went to work immediately. He drafted All-America guard Reggie McKenzie from Michigan on the second round of the 1972 draft and picked up Jet castoff Dave Foley, a former number one draft choice from Ohio State, and installed him at left tackle. In New York, Foley had been knocked as a poor pass-blocker, but nobody ever said he couldn't block for the run; Saban wanted him to block for the run. Tackle Donnie Green and center Bruce Jarvis also helped immeasurably in 1972. And though the Bills were a 4–9–1 team that year, Simpson exploded into professional stardom. With a line to block for him, and with a coach who commanded that he get the ball, the Juice led the NFL with 1,251 yards, on 292 carries. He was all hips and feints, with the blinding breakaway speed, but at 6 feet 1 inch tall, 212 pounds, he could run over people, too, if necessary. "He's dangerous," said Joe Greene, the Steelers' all-pro defensive tackle. "He scares the hell out of me. I can't put it any better."

But 1972 was only the beginning. Saban's first 1973 draft choice was Paul Seymour, a unanimous All-America offensive tackle at Michigan, whom the Bills moved to tight end. At 6 feet 5 inches tall, 250 pounds, he was the perfect fellow to bury linebackers and allow Simpson to get outside on sweeps. The number two draft was Michigan State's All-America guard, Joe De-

Lamielleure. Veteran Mike Montler moved from tackle to center. And so there the line was constructed—the great wall. Foley, McKenzie, Montler, DeLamielleure, Green, Seymour. They first called Simpson "Juice" as a takeoff on the O.J. bit, but soon they began calling him "Juice" as in voltage. And so O.J. began to refer to the offensive line as "the Electric Company."

The first week of the 1973 season, Simpson carried the ball 29 times against the New England Patriots and gained 250 yards, tying an NFL record set in 1947 by the old New York Yankees' Spec Sanders. He gained better than 100 yards in each of the season's next four games. After five games, he had gained 813 yards.

Now opposing teams aligned themselves solely to stop the run, to stop Simpson. Rookie quarterback Joe Ferguson averaged just 12 passes a game for the Bills. After 12 weeks, and four more 100-yard games, Simpson had gained 1,584 yards. With two weeks to play, he needed 280 yards to break the record; imagine, after eight games of better than 100 yards and another of 250 yards, with a per-game average of 132 yards, Simpson still needed 280 yards in two games to eclipse Brown's record. No wonder Collier had been able to call it a record for "the next century."

But in game thirteen, in a swirling snowstorm in Buffalo, Simpson once more devastated the Patriots. With Ferguson throwing just seven times (and complet-

OPPOSITE: *O.J. Simpson drives through the snow and the Jets' secondary as he heads for the goal line in Shea Stadium, Dec. 16, 1973.* ABOVE: *O.J. gathers the Buffalo offensive unit around him at the press conference held after his record-breaking game. He credited his 2,003 yards to his teammates.*

141

ing just two), Simpson gained 219 yards on 22 carries . . . 10 per try. And so, with one week to play, he had a shot. He had, in fact, far more than that.

"He's so close," Jets' linebacker Ralph Baker said the week of the game. "If he needed 100 yards it would be different, but I think New England opened the door. Now, if they (the Bills) have to, they'll run him 61 times. The best chance you have to stop him is if he gets injured before he gets to 61.

"The guy's a super runner. The biggest problem is getting him to the ground. You can't give him any room to operate. It seems he will put five moves on you in three yards."

Simpson defined his electrifying style this way, "I angle 'em and fly by 'em [defensive linemen and linebackers]. I never challenge 'em head on. I don't take a beating every week. I'm getting hit by defensive backs. The guys in front of me are moving out the linemen, the linebackers. Football is violent for borderline players, the guys on the special teams. Not for me."

As badly as the Jets wanted to win one for the Gipper, er, Weeb, they were also pulling for Simpson. "I just like to watch him," said Joe Namath. "I want to win the game, but I'm pulling for him. I want to see him get what he deserves and I think he deserves the record." Even Ewbank took time to wish Simpson well. "I love O.J.," the coach said. "Let him get his 61 yards, but spread them out." Still, said Baker, "We're not going to make it easy for him. We're going to do our best to stop him. It would be super for the team to stop him."

The Jets could not stop him. Not at all. O.J. gained 57 yards on Buffalo's first drive, slashing through holes his line had opened for him. And then, on the first play after the Bills got the ball for the second time, he got the record. It was a simple power play right, and when De-Lamielleure knocked down end Mark Lomas, Simpson tore through for six yards before being taken down from behind by John Little. There was 10:24 gone in the first quarter when the next century arrived. The record was his: 1,865 yards. Play was stopped, the other offensive players pounded O.J. on the back, and an official handed the ball to Simpson, who was mobbed by his teammates when he took it to the bench. "We were saying, 'Let's get it in the first quarter,'" Simpson said.

Later, the Bills' players were dedicating themselves to lifting Simpson to the unthinkable plateau of 2,000 yards. He came into the game 197 shy of that . . . He had gone over 100 yards by the half, and was at 150 early in the fourth quarter. "Ferguson came into the huddle early in the fourth quarter and said I was 50 yards away," Simpson said. "We broke 20 off on the next play, and were going for it from then on."

There were 6 minutes and 28 seconds remaining when Simpson finally got it, smashing through left guard for seven yards. It was his thirty-fourth carry of the day, brought him to 200 yards, even, and raised him to 2,003 yards for the season. After the play, he was hoisted upon his teammates' shoulders, and left the game.

After the game, a 34–14 Buffalo victory, Charlie Winner, the Jets' defensive coordinator, the man who would succeed Ewbank, said he was "embarrassed that O.J. got so much yardage against us. We couldn't contain him."

And after the game, Simpson brought all of his offensive linemen into the interview room that had been set up for him. He introduced each one, and requested that photographers capture the complete moment on film. "It's their record," Simpson said. He did not say their record was one "for the century."

—L.B.

The Shea Stadium crowd stands to honor O.J. Simpson as the Buffalo Bills hoist him in the air after he became the first 2,000 yard, single-season rusher in pro football history.

BABY, IT'S COLD OUTSIDE

It was a frrrrrigid 13-degrees below zero and the field was frozen—
not to mention fingers, toes, noses, and eyelids—
but the Green Bay Packers somehow stayed warm enough to beat Dallas for the NFL championship
on the most memorable quarterback sneak in history

In 1967, the wind-chill factor had not yet been invented, but the folks in Green Bay, Wisconsin, didn't need a meteorologist's number to tell them it was cold outside the final day of that year. How cold was it? Do the figures 13-below-zero temperature and 15-mile-per-hour winds send a shiver up your spine?

The Packers and Dallas Cowboys had a date with destiny that frigid afternoon. For the second successive year, they were meeting for the National Football League's championship and the right to advance to the Super Bowl. A year earlier, in Dallas, the Packers had prevailed in a classic, 34–27, cementing the title with an end-zone interception in the game's final seconds after the Cowboys had reached the two-yard line. From there, Green Bay rolled to a 35–10 victory over the Kansas City Chiefs in Super Bowl I.

But on this day, in spite of the unbearable weather conditions that had made the playing field slick as a hockey rink—the intense cold had put a grid of heating wires six inches below the sod out of commission—the two teams scaled even greater heights. In fact, the weather conditions added to the drama and legend of this game: the football player as warrior, mind over matter. More than 50,000 spectators hadn't minded spending their New Year's Eve day in the outdoor refrigerator, and had come to the game bedecked in colorful winter clothing, layered and masked like invaders from a planet far, far away. As their reward, they bore witness to the most memorable single play in NFL history, the most played and replayed television football play in history.

Once again, the NFL championship teetered between the teams in the game's final seconds. But this time, it was Green Bay with the ball. This time, it was Green Bay, going for an unprecedented third straight NFL title, that was trailing. Behind 17–14, the Packers had managed to piece together a frantic, slippery, 68-yard drive in the game's final 4:50. They were still a yard shy, but there was still a minute to play. No problem.

But the Packers had driven into the shadows, and the temperature had dropped five degrees from kickoff

time—to 18° below. The Packers were suddenly running on glass. On first down, halfback Donny Anderson slipped while taking quarterback Bart Starr's handoff and was touched down for no gain. Second down produced the same result; a slip, and no gain. And now there were 20 seconds to play, and Starr spent his final time out. A field goal, a chippie for Don Chandler, would tie the score, and send the game into overtime. But Vince Lombardi was having none of that. Later he joked that he had eschewed the field goal "so that the fans wouldn't have to suffer anymore," but the fact was that Lombardi believed games were played to be won

Green Bay, Wisconsin, Dec. 31, 1967, the Packers vs. the Dallas Cowboys for the NFL championship. Here, Dallas defender Mel Renfro (20) is too late to stop Packer end Boyd Dowler from scoring in the second quarter. During the game, the temperature plunged to 18 below zero with a 15 mile-per-hour wind.

. . . not tied. "If they couldn't get the ball in from the one-yard line on three plays, they didn't deserve to be NFL champions," he said. Lombardi was staking his team's title on one play. One play, because there wouldn't be enough time for a fourth-down play if the third-down play failed. One play on a sheet of ice.

The play was a quarterback sneak—"thirty-one wedge" in the Green Bay playbook, Starr diving right for the hole between right guard Jerry Kramer and center Ken Bowman. Starr brought his team to the line. Kramer and Bowman dug in; across from Kramer, so did Dallas tackle Jethro Pugh. Later, Cowboy tackle Bob Lilly had this thought, "We should have gone to the bench during that time out, gotten a screwdriver and gouged out some cleat holes in that ice," he said.

Starr took the snap and Kramer and Bowman exploded off the line, Kramer moving Pugh outside. "It was the fastest I've ever come off the ball in my life, Kramer said. "All Jethro could do was raise his left arm." Starr followed, cradling the football, and fell through the narrow hole his offensive linemen had carved, coming to rest in the end zone. There were 13 seconds to play. And Green Bay had the lead. Chandler kicked the extra point, and when two Don Meredith passes fell incomplete after the following kickoff, the Packers had won 21–17. Kramer was a hero. The diary he had been writing of the Packers' season was published the following year; it was called *Instant Replay*, because his block had become the most famous instant replay of television sports history.

That it should have come down to that final play was surprising enough; after all, it was most un-Packer-like for Green Bay to have found itself in that desperate position after having a 14–0 lead. But it was almost as surprising that the Packers had reached the championship game that year. With expansion to New Orleans bringing the NFL membership to 16 clubs, the league revamped its postseason playoff system by dividing the

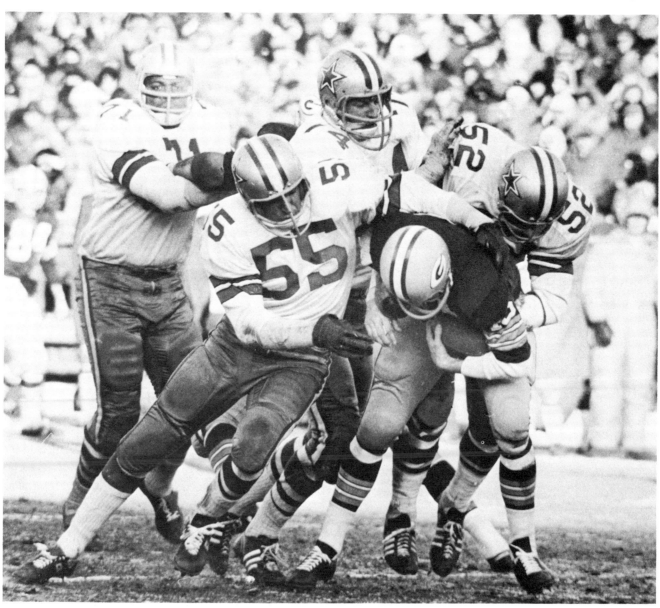

Eastern and Western Conferences into two divisions apiece. The Coastal and Central division champions would meet in a playoff for the Western title, while the winners of the Capitol and Century divisions would meet for the Eastern crown; the two winners would then meet for the NFL championship.

The Packers won the Central Division, finishing 9–4–1, but they were not the best team in the Western Conference. The Coastal Division Los Angeles Rams and Baltimore Colts had each finished 11–1–2. Any previous season the Packers would have been home for the holidays. But the playoff format gave them a second chance. On December 23, they traveled to L.A. to meet the Rams (who had been declared Coastal winners on a tiebreak format) for the second time in three weeks; the Rams had won the first game, 27–24, and were favored to advance to the title game. Though Starr had enjoyed an excellent season, injuries had cost the team both its star running backs, Jim Taylor and Paul Hornung, as well as ball carriers Elijah Pitts and Jim Grabowski. With only Anderson healthy among the regulars, Lombardi added journeymen Ben Wilson and Chuck Mercein to the roster and began using rookie Travis Williams, a kickoff return specialist, in the backfield. The Rams, who had been carried through the season by a ferocious defense and Roman Gabriel's ball-control offense, were healthy for the playoff game.

It was no contest. The veteran Packers destroyed L.A. 28–7; Starr riddled the L.A. secondary, completing 17 of 23 passes for 222 yards, while Williams picked up 88 yards on 18 carries. "I didn't think they could be that awesome," said L.A. defensive end Deacon Jones.

The Capitol champion Cowboys, meanwhile, had clearly been the class of the East, even though their 9–5 record had been equalled by the Century Division

champion Browns. Coach Tom Landry had constructed an explosive, big play offense, behind Meredith and receivers Bob Hayes and Lance Rentzel. Dallas humiliated Cleveland 52–14 in their playoff match.

So it was that Dallas, aching to avenge the previous season's heartbreak, went to Green Bay on December 31, 1967. And when the Cowboys realized the weather conditions, they fretted. Their pregame locker room was dominated by talk of the weather and field conditions, not of the Packers. Meredith saw his receivers dropping balls in pregame drills, noticed that Starr was changing the pace of his throws, and so he tried to do the same once the game commenced. It was no surprise that the poised Packers, who were, after all, more used to those kinds of weather conditions (if anyone can be used to those kinds of weather conditions), took a quick 14–0 lead. It seemed at that point as if the game would deteriorate into a rout.

But instead, the Packers wavered. "We lost our concentration," said Starr. "Maybe we started to think more about the cold and conditions than we thought about our own concentration." So the Packers were human, after all. George Andrie picked up a Starr fumble and scored from seven yards to cut Green Bay's lead to 14–7 in the second quarter. And when the usually sure-handed Willie Wood muffed a punt at his 17, Danny Villanueva's 21-yard field goal cut the margin to 14–10 at intermission.

The game remained 14–10 into the fourth quarter, but it was here that Dallas came up with the big play. A 50-yard option pass from Rentzel to halfback Dan Reeves for a touchdown gave Dallas the lead for the first time in eight championship quarters against Green Bay. And the Cowboys held the lead. And held it. And it was still 17–14 when the Packers took the ball on their own 31 with 4:50 to play. Starr had been sacked eight times already. "I began to think maybe this was the end of it," Kramer recalled. "Maybe this would be the year we wouldn't make it."

But there was time for one more drive. And then there was time for one more play. And then, there was time for one more game. The Super Bowl. And Green Bay dominated the Oakland Raiders 33–14. When it was over, Lombardi was carried from the field by his team. A few weeks later, he announced his retirement as head coach. In nine seasons, his Green Bay teams had won six conference championships, five NFL titles, two Super Bowls. His final NFL title may have been the team's toughest. It was certainly its coldest.

—L.B.

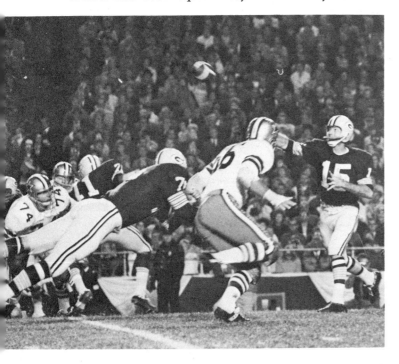

OPPOSITE: *The Dallas defense forces Bart Starr, Green Bay Packer quarterback, to eat the ball and take a 7 yard loss during the 1967 NFL Championship game.* LEFT: *Starr (15) gets a pass away before Cowboy defender George Andrie (66) arrives.*

BROADWAY JOE GUARANTEED IT

When Joe Willie Namath said the New York Jets were going to
upset the 17-point-favorite Baltimore Colts in Super Bowl III, the whole world laughed at him . . .
but Namath, as it turned out, had the last laugh on the whole world

This was January 9, 1969, three days before Super Bowl III in Miami. At the time, you could have filled the 80,000-seat Orange Bowl a dozen times over with people who believed that a Super Bowl IV should never be held. After all, hadn't the National Football League's Green Bay Packers routed the American Football League's Kansas City Chiefs and Oakland Raiders, 35–10 and 33–14, respectively, in Super Bowls I and II? And wasn't it a sure thing that the NFL's 1969 representative, the Baltimore Colts, would wreak even worse havoc upon the AFL's New York Jets three days hence? It was the NFL's ball, so why let the AFL play with it?

Goodness, the Colts had stampeded through a 15–1 season in which they had surrendered just 158 points, an average of less than 10 points per game, and their defense was even better than that. They had four shutouts, two other games in which they didn't give up a touchdown, and five games in which they didn't give up more than one touchdown. In 14 regular-season games, they had permitted only 144 points, a record for stinginess. On offense, 34-year-old journeyman quarterback Earl Morrall, whom the Colts acquired just prior to the season from the Giants upon learning that Johnny Unitas's sore elbow would keep him sidelined most of the year, enjoyed the year of his life, and was named the NFL's player of the year, so skillfully did he guide his team. The Colts were a veteran team, poised. In the NFL championship game in Cleveland on December 29, the Colts had humiliated the Browns 34–0.

Meanwhile, on that same December 29, 1968, the Eastern Division champion Jets had captured their first AFL title, coming from behind in the fourth quarter to defeat the Western champion Raiders 27–23 at Shea Stadium. The youthful Jets, it seemed, were a team of so much style and so little substance—compared to Baltimore, that is—even with a championship season behind them. Joe Namath, at age 24, had reached football maturity, and he did have an explosive passing arm and talented receivers in Don Maynard, George Sauer, and Pete Lammons. But, recited believers of the football gospel, Namath's arm had only carved up the AFL; wait until he got a look at a real defense—maybe the best defense in NFL history.

The day after the league championship games, the Colts were installed as 17-point favorites, an unheard of spread for a championship match of any sort. And in the two-week hiatus between the league championship games and the Super Bowl, AFL executives declared the league would institute a playoff system involving four teams the following year, so fearful were they that the Jets would be beaten so badly as to embarrass the AFL and endanger the future of the Super Bowl.

Most Jets merely listened to the insults, enduring them quietly. Namath did a bit more than that. He told people that "there were at least four quarterbacks in the AFL better than Morrall." A week before the game he and Baltimore defensive end and placekicker Lou Michaels nearly came to blows in a local night club. "His first remarks were that the Jets were going to kick the blankety-blank out of our team," Michaels said. "We're going to beat you and pick you apart," Namath continued. The conversation escalated in intensity and then Michaels invited Namath to "step outside." Matters were settled more amicably when Namath picked up the tab for Michaels and some of his Baltimore teammates.

But Namath wasn't through telling people what the Jets were going to do to the Colts. Namath was a child of his era. He had always spoken his mind, and gone his own way off the field; he wasn't about to change his approach for the biggest game of his life. He wore white shoes at a time when everyone in the league wore black, and he had grown a Fu Manchu mustache when everyone in the league was clean-shaven (Namath finally shaved for a $10,000 commercial fee). The long-haired, free-spirited quarterback who had saved the AFL in 1964 when he signed with the Jets out of Alabama for a record $400,000, thus generating a sum of publicity that guaranteed the then four-year-old league a profitable national TV contract, was turning the Super Bowl into his own crusade. The week before the Super Bowl belonged to him.

And so here it was, January 9, when Namath found himself at an awards dinner in Miami. Someone asked him what the Jets, now 17½ point underdogs, would do Sunday. Namath smiled. "I think we'll win it," he said.

"In fact, I'll guarantee it."

Namath had guaranteed turning the football world upside down. Publicly. Three days later, the football world had been turned upside down. Positively. The final score was 16–7, Jets, and it wasn't that close. Namath had picked the Colts apart, and the Jet defense had forced Morrall into one of the most miserable days of his 14-year career, finally forcing him to the bench. "Joe is so downright honest," said New York tackle Dave Herman. "He said we were going to win for sure. We won. He didn't lie. He never does."

The game itself was strangely muted . . . but shocking for the drama of the event. Namath's Jets were an explosive team, but coach Weeb Ewbank had constructed a conservative game plan. The Colts employed a zone and expected that their blitzing rushers would hurry Namath into errors. They figured to take his long passing game away. They did take his long game away, but they were never able to hurry Namath; indeed, he picked the Baltimore blitz apart with quick hook and flare patterns, and the Jets' running game ate up three and four yards a play with simple power thrusts. "For the Super Bowl," Ewbank said, "we stressed execution." And thus did the Jets execute the Colts. Namath completed 17 of 28 passes for 226 yards, his longest for 39 yards, and no interceptions. With the Colts double-covering his favorite target, Maynard, Namath hit Sauer eight times for 133 yards. Namath was flawless. There was little wrong with the team's offensive line: they protected the QB so well that the Colts were able to

Super Bowl III. The New York Jets vs. the Baltimore Colts, January 12, 1969, the Orange Bowl, Miami. Jet Quarterback Joe Namath hands off to Emerson Boozer. Namath guaranteed three days before the game that the Jets would win it. And, at the finish, the Jets had the first AFC Super Bowl win.

record only two sacks all afternoon, and they controlled the line of scrimmage so well that fullback Matt Snell gained 121 yards on 30 carries.

Still . . . still, the Colts might have fulfilled what the NFL folks believed their manifest destiny if they hadn't tightened up and committed the most crucial and inexplicable errors in the first half. They rolled to the Jet 19 yard line on their first series, but came away scoreless when wide receiver Willie Richardson, wide open, dropped a pass and Michaels blew a 27-yard field goal. Then, after recovering a Jet fumble on the New York 12, Morrall's end-zone pass bounced off tight end Tom Mitchell's shoulder and was intercepted by Randy Beverly. The Colts' great tight end, John Mackey, dropped a sure touchdown pass, alone at the 10. Michaels missed another field goal attempt. Morrall was intercepted again, this time by Johnny Sample, after Tom Matte had roared 58 yards deep into New York territory.

The Jets scored their first—and only—touchdown six minutes into the second quarter, going 80 yards on 12 plays, a classic NFL-Green Bay drive. Seven plays by land, five by air. Straight stuff that ended with Snell going over from the nine on two shots—five off the right side, and then four slanting left. Jim Turner's point-after made it 7–0. Down 7–0, it was the Colts who turned to Mickey Mouse (skeptics had called the AFL a Mickey Mouse league) stuff as the half ended, calling a flea-flicker. Morrall lateralled to Matte, who turned and flung the ball back to the quarterback. The play stunned the Jets and wide receiver Jimmy Orr was alone, 30 yards alone, in the end zone, waving his hands frantically, jumping up and down. But Morrall, incredibly, didn't throw to Orr, as the play had been designed. Instead, he forced a pass over the middle, and it was intercepted. The half ended 7–0. "If we had scored then, we could have been in control," Baltimore coach Don Shula said. "Instead, they had control. And confidence."

The Jets ate up the clock most of the second half, putting together three lengthy and time-consuming drives that culminated in Turner field goals. And the defense had shut the Colts and Morrall off completely. It was 16–0 after 90 seconds of the fourth quarter. And it was here that the Colts, in desperation, turned to Unitas to rally the team, to perform the same kind of miracle he had accomplished in 1958, when he brought the Colts from behind on the final drive in their 23–17 overtime championship victory over the New York Giants. The purists and traditionalists, many of whom were near tears, were pleading for Unitas to do it again,

to come to their defense. They needed the guy in the high-top shoes, the guy with the crewcut, to shut up the upstart.

But Unitas was now 35 years old, had a sore arm, and had thrown only 32 passes all season. And even though he led Baltimore to one touchdown, and brought the Colts into position to threaten twice—throwing on virtually every play he completed 11 of 24 passes with one interception—he could not achieve the greatest miracle of all. He could not stop the advancement of time. He could not transform reality into illusion. On January 12, 1969, the world of football belonged to the young, to Joe Namath, to the New York Jets.

And so it was that an hour after the game, after Namath and his teammates had raced off the field in jubilation, their index fingers thrust into the air to tell the world which team was "Number One," this was the one question everyone was asking, "How long would it take for the NFL to catch up to the AFL?" Johnny Sample, the safety, said two years. Nobody bothered to ask him for a guarantee.

—L.B.

TOP: *The Colts' John Mackey (88) looks for some running room as the Jet defense cuts off the angle.* OPPOSITE BOTTOM: *Johnny Unitas (19), called on late in the game, fakes a handoff. He passed for 11 of 24.* RIGHT: *Jet cornerback Johnny Sample (24) breaks up a pass intended for flanker Willie Richardson (87).*

149

THE LONGEST CHRISTMAS

*The Miami Dolphins and the Kansas City Chiefs played on and
on and on and on in their 1971 AFC playoff game, and then a tie-maker named Garo
Yepremian gave the Dolphins the best Christmas present of all when
he booted a long field goal for victory in the second overtime session*

The Miami Dolphins and the Kansas City Chiefs were playing in the first round of the American Football Conference playoffs, and a nation of football fans sat transfixed in front of their television screens. The Dolphins and Chiefs played. And they played. And they played. The fans sat. And they sat. And they sat. And on Christmas Day, 1971, a country's holiday dinners also sat . . . in ovens. And they sat. And they sat. There had never before been anything quite like it.

Before it ended in the Kansas City twilight, the Dolphins and Chiefs had played more than five periods of football—82 minutes and 40 seconds of drama. The Dolphins had come from behind three times . . . A K.C. workhorse named Ed Podolak had gained 350 yards all by himself . . . The conference's all-star kicker had missed a chippie with seconds left in regulation that would have won it. When this epic was finally over, and Miami had won this longest game in football history 27–24, it was enough so that one man turned to another and said, "I didn't know they made Santa into a tackling dummy."

Both the Chiefs and Dolphins had looked at their holiday meeting as a crossroads for their respective franchises. The old against the new. Establishment versus expansion. The six-year-old Dolphins were young, still barely wet behind the ears, having won their first AFC Eastern Division championship with a 10–3–1 record; two years later they would go 17–0. They had taken the title on the season's final weekend, finishing a half-game in front of the Baltimore Colts. The Chiefs had won the AFC Western Division championship with a 10–3–1 record, but they were in command throughout the season. And if the Dolphins would be appearing in just their second playoff game ever—they had lost to the Oakland Raiders 21–14 a year earlier as the AFC's wild-card—postseason games were old headdress to the Chiefs. This would be their eighth playoff game in 10 years, including the 23–7 victory over the Minnesota Vikings two years earlier in Super Bowl IV.

"Last year we didn't know what the playoffs were about, Miami middle linebacker Nick Buoniconti said the day before the game. "During the week before the

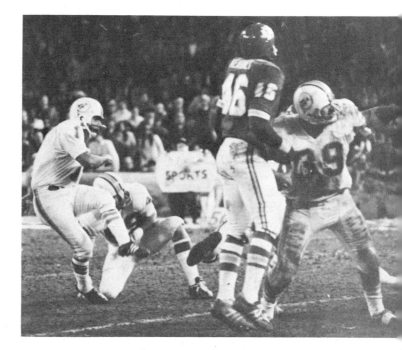

150

game I'd hear a guy talking about the girl he was dating, or a guy talking about which restaurant he'd be going to. We were taking it lightly. But this week, all anybody talks about are coverages, assignments, the game. That tells me one thing—that we're ready."

Each team featured a stingy defense and a ball-control rushing attack with an added feature—the ability to blow away the opposition with the big pass play.

The Dolphins' ground game was dominated by Larry Csonka and Jim Kiick, and the air route by the connection between quarterback Bob Griese and wide receiver Paul Warfield. The Chiefs relied on all-purpose back Ed Podolak and fullback Jim Otis to chew up the yardage, but for dramatics, it was Len Dawson to split end Otis Taylor. "Give Otis room," said Buoniconti, "and it's sayonara."

OPPOSITE: *This sequence shows Miami's Garo Yepremian ending pro football's longest game with a double-overtime field goal against K.C. ABOVE: Jan Stenerud (3) kicking, Len Dawson (16) holding, on the field goal attempt that would have given the K.C. Chiefs a 1971 AFC playoff win. The kick was wide.*

151

There was another similarity between the teams—each had a side-winding placekicker who could claim to be the league's best. Miami's Garo Yepremian had led the AFC in scoring with 117 points, having connected on 28 of 40 field goal attempts and 33 conversions; KC's Jan Stenerud had finished second in the scoring race with 110 points, with 26 of 44 FGA and 32 extra points. The night before the meeting, Yepremian had been informed that Stenerud had been selected over him by the conference coaches as the AFC's placekicker for the Pro Bowl. That had angered him. "I decided right then to prove to everyone the next day they had made the wrong choice," he said later. "I decided I would show the coaches and Stenerud there was a mistake . . . that I would kick better than he did all day." He did. And in the end, that was the difference. After more than 82 minutes, it came down to a couple of feet. Imagine, for want of a Pro Bowl selection, Christmas may have been twisted Miami's way in 1971.

But at the outset, it didn't seem as though Yepremian's toes would prove so important. Nor, for that matter, Stenerud's. Because for the first 15 minutes of that balmy, 60-degree Saturday afternoon, the veteran Chiefs gave the young Dolphins a football lesson, on offense and defense. It was 10–0 for KC at the end of the first quarter.

But the Dolphins rallied immediately. Griese hooked up with Warfield for a 21-yard gain after a Kansas City third-down penalty had given the Dolphins a first down in their own territory, and he followed that with a 16-yard completion to tight end Marv Fleming. One play later, Csonka went over from the one and the Dolphins were back in the game. "That series was probably the key to the game," said K.C. Coach Hank Stram. "Just when it looked like we had firm control of the game and were about to take over the ball again, they broke a couple of big plays, and then they scored. That had to give them confidence."

It didn't hurt when Podolak's fumble on his 12 set up the Yepremian 14-yard field goal that tied the score 10–10 at the half. But the second half commenced just as had the first—with the Chiefs in command, going 75 yards in 15 plays, eating up nearly 10 minutes. When Otis went over from the one-yard line and Stenerud converted, it was 17–10. But the Dolphins came right back, and with a minute to play in the third quarter, Kiick's one-yard plunge and Yepremian's conversion tied it 17–17.

The Chiefs took the lead once more—and for the final time. Dawson's 63-yard bomb to Elmo Wright brought K.C. to the Miami three, and from there, Podolak carried over with six and a half minutes to play. It was 24–17 when Stenerud kicked the extra point. "Our defense had played so well," said Podolak, who carried the ball 17 times for 85 yards, caught eight passes for 110 yards, and returned punts and kickoffs 155 yards, "that we felt secure. We thought it was over." As it turned out, things hadn't even begun. Bob Griese, who completed 20 of 35 passes for 263 yards, riddled the Kansas City secondary, and his five-yard toss to Marv Fleming with 96 seconds to play brought Miami back within a point. Yepremian's conversion tied things. It was at that point that they hauled out the record books. Sudden death. Until that time, there had been just three such games in NFL playoff history—the 1958 NFL Colts-Giants championship, the 1965 NFL Western Division Packers-Colts playoff, and the 1962 Dallas Texans–Houston Oilers AFL Championship. But in a flash, those historical precedents seemed to have been rendered irrelevant. Because Podolak, who was enjoying the day of a lifetime, returned Yepremian's kickoff 78 yards to the Miami 22. Only Curtis Johnson's tackle from behind saved a touchdown, but that hardly mattered—Stenerud was within range. Thirty-five seconds remained when Dawson knelt on the right hashmark, Stenerud's favorite position, 31 yards from victory. "The snap was perfect," the kicker said. The kick was not—he had hooked it wide left. And so into a fifth quarter.

The Chiefs won the coin flip, and Podolak's return set them up at their own 46. Five plays later, Stenerud's 42-yard field goal attempt was blocked by Buoniconti. "I felt like hiding," Stenerud said later that week. "It was unbearable. I never again wanted to play football."

But the Dolphins and Chiefs had football still to play. A Yepremian 45-yard field goal attempt fell short, and so the game rolled into a sixth quarter. And once they went past the 2:54 mark—the Texans had beaten the Oilers 20–17 on Tommy Brooker's 25-yard field goal nine years earlier at 2:54 of the sixth quarter—they had played the longest game in pro football history. But now, the Chiefs had nothing left. And the Dolphins finally ground their way to the Kansas City 30 following a 29-yard burst from Csonka, who was held to 86 yards on 24 carries all day. It was fourth down when Yepremian and holder Karl Noonan trotted onto the field for the final time, and the kicker nicked a spot for himself on the 37. "As soon as I kicked it, I knew it was good," Yepremian said. "I jumped up and didn't even look at the goal posts. Then I realized this was the most important

field goal of my life, so I thought, 'Turn around and see what happens.' "

What happened was that at 7:40 of the second overtime period, referee John McDonough raised both hands to signal success. And the end of the longest game ever played. And for Yepremian, who had come to the United States from Cyprus as a tie-maker, it earned him a new title: the tie-breaker. Of course.

—L.B.

A short gain in a long game. Kansas City's Ed Podolak (14) is brought down by Miami's Vern Den Herder (86) and Lloyd Mumphord (26) during the epic AFC playoff game held Christmas Day, 1971. Miami's win came only after 82 minutes and 40 seconds of play.

Boxing

THE LONGEST COUNT

Gene Tunney was stretched out on the canvas for what seemed
like hours, but the referee got a late start on the count . . . and Jack Dempsey became a big loser

A crowd of 140,000 jammed Soldier Field in Chicago the night of September 22, 1927, to witness the rematch between Jack Dempsey and Gene Tunney for the heavyweight championship of the world. But this was more than just a title fight. It was a global obsession, and millions upon millions of fans, from Manassa, Colorado to Mangalore India, sat transfixed before radios. Ten people in the United States died as the direct result of the fight—five of those deaths alone came in the seventh round, the round of "the long count."

One year before, almost to the day, Tunney, "the Fighting Marine" from New York City, had taken the title away from Dempsey, "the Manassa Mauler," in a 10-round decision in Sesquicentennial Stadium in Philadelphia. Tunney, who was a student of the manly art and of Shakespeare, as well, sent Dempsey reeling at the very start with a surprise right hand—it surprised not only Dempsey, but also the public which had made the champion a 5–2 betting choice. From the first round on, Tunney controlled the fight, and he left Dempsey a beaten and bleeding man. When Dempsey's wife, the former movie star Estelle Taylor, asked him what happened, Dempsey replied, "Honey, I just forgot to duck."

Ironically, defeat endeared Dempsey to the masses much more than victory ever had. William Harrison Dempsey had come out of the copper pits of Colorado and done his earliest fighting in saloons. His official ring debut, for a grand purse of $2.50, came at the age of 19 in Salt Lake City. Dempsey, then called "Kid Blackie," was matched against One-Punch Hancock, and sure enough, he knocked Hancock out with one punch. Later, adopting the name of an earlier fighter known as Jack Dempsey, the Nonpareil, he began a long road to the top. In 1919 in Toledo, Ohio, he was given a shot at heavyweight champion Jess Willard, the man who had beaten Jack Johnson. It was the first $1,000,000 fight—a long way from $2.50—and it was supposed to be no contest for Willard. Well, it was no contest. Dempsey broke Willard's jaw in seven places in the first round and beat him into submission by the third.

Dempsey defended his title only five times in seven years, but two of those fights were memorable. On July 2, 1921, in Jersey City, Dempsey met Georges Carpentier. A French war hero, Carpentier had Dempsey in trouble in the second round to the great approval of the crowd. But Dempsey was a brutal puncher and he fought hardest when hit hardest. He pummeled the Frenchman in the third and put him down for good in the fourth. Studying the fight closely was a young light heavyweight who had won his first fight on the preliminary card that night, James Joseph Tunney.

In 1923 in Yankee Stadium Dempsey again defended his title, this time against Luis Firpo, "the wild bull of the Pampas." In the most savage first round ever fought, there were nine knockdowns, the first and last by Firpo, the middle seven by Dempsey. The champion was hit so hard at the end of round one that he fell through the ring ropes. Dempsey knocked out Firpo, though, in the second. Because Dempsey stood over Firpo and knocked him down every time he got up, a new rule was instituted to force the fighter who scores a knockdown to go to a neutral corner while his opponent is down. The rule would come back to haunt Dempsey.

PRECEDING PAGES: *Heavyweight champ Muhammad Ali has Joe Frazier in trouble in the 13th round of the Oct. 1, 1975 fight in Manila.* RIGHT: *Jack Dempsey (Left) heads toward Gene Tunney as the referee reaches nine in the "Long Count," round 7, September 22, 1927.*

While Dempsey's training regimen and matchups deteriorated, Tunney was boxing his way through the ranks. He, too, fought Carpentier, but it took him 15 rounds to knock him out. Tunney had the greatest respect for Dempsey, but he always knew he would have to beat him some day. When that day came on September 23, 1926, Tunney said he had never known a more gracious loser. The new champion followed in Dempsey's footsteps and went to Hollywood, making a movie called *The Fighting Marine*. He lectured at Yale on Shakespeare, toured Europe and chatted at length with George Bernard Shaw. The public began to think that Tunney thought himself too good to associate with boxing, and his popularity waned. In the meantime, Dempsey trained to become the first fighter ever to win back the heavyweight title. But he was clearly not the mauler he once was. In the fight to see who would meet Tunney, Dempsey was losing to Jack Sharkey when he knocked him out in the seventh round. The knockout punch came while Sharkey was busy arguing with the referee over a low blow.

But the stage was set for the rematch, and what a stage it was. The luminaries at Soldier Field included Rudolph Valentino, Al Capone, Bernard Baruch, Buster Keaton, Jack Johnson, Jim Corbett, Mary Pickford,

Rockefellers, Roosevelts, six governors, and assorted royalty. And there was a new dimension to the rematch—the two men no longer liked each other. Dempsey had written a highly publicized letter accusing Tunney's manager and local officials of conspiring to take the title away from him the year before in Philadelphia. Tunney called the charges "trash" and asked, "Do you think this is sportsmanship?" Still, when the two men, both in superb shape, met in the ring that night, they were talking. Dempsey, deeply tanned and in black trunks, said, "How are you, Gene?" Tunney, in white trunks to match his rather pale body, said, "Quite well, Jack—and you?"

At 10:07 P.M. the fighters were called to the center of the ring where referee Dave Barry explained the rules. "I want to get this one point clear," said Barry. "In the event of a knockdown the man scoring the knockdown will go to the farthest neutral corner. Unless he goes to that corner, I will not begin the count. Is that clear?" Both men nodded to say yes.

Dempsey and Tunney started cautiously, feeling each other out. Tunney quickly saw that he would not have as easy a night as he had a year before. But in the second, the new champion scored heavily with jabs to the face. In the third Dempsey rocked Tunney with a

hard right, but Tunney stole the thunder back in the fourth, nearly flooring Dempsey with a left hook to the body. In the fifth round, radio announcer Graham McNamee told the world, "Tunney is out-Dempseying Dempsey." In the sixth Dempsey willingly absorbed jabs in exchange for a few ferocious hooks, and McNamee said, "Some of the blows Dempsey hits make this ring tremble."

The bell rang for the fateful seventh. Tunney connected with a right to the chin, then kept sticking his left hand in Dempsey's face. Infuriated, Dempsey suddenly became young again and charged. He hit Tunney a left to the jaw that put him on the ropes. Dempsey came in with a right and then a left hook. Another right, a left, a right, and Tunney went down. "I hit him with all the punches I had been trying to hit him with in the ring and in my sleep for the past year," Dempsey later said. With 140,000 people on their feet, screaming, Dempsey went to the near corner and the timekeeper began the knockdown count. But the referee Barry rushed over to Dempsey and shouted, "Go to a neutral corner, Jack!" Dempsey replied, "I stay here." Barry shoved him until Dempsey began to skate toward the far corner. By the time Barry got back to the prostrate Tunney, the timekeeper was counting, "Five." Barry shouted, "One," and the timekeeper began the count again. When the new count reached nine Tunney was

up, but ringside estimates put the time that Tunney was down at anywhere from 12 to 18 seconds. Tunney later said that he could have gotten up in time even if the old count stood and that he was just using the extra seconds. But the long count clearly helped him regain his senses.

When the fight resumed, rather than clinch or fight back, Tunney elected to retreat out of harm's reach. It was a wise decision, and it so frustrated Dempsey that at one point he motioned for Tunney to come to him and fight. Tunney would have none of that. Toward the end of the round, the champion slipped inside and delivered a right below the heart which Dempsey later called "the hardest blow I have ever received." Dempsey had used up his last chance and now it was all he could do to survive. Tunney sent him to the floor in the eighth and scored at will in the last two rounds. But Dempsey refused to go down and he was still punching at the final bell.

It was the final bell for the Golden Age of Boxing, as well. The fight was, in some ways, the last gasp of the Roaring Twenties. Dempsey retired to fight occasional exhibitions and run a restaurant. Tunney made only one title defense, knocking out Tom Heeney 10 months later in a financial and artistic disappointment, before he retired to the business world. He often went to Dempsey's restaurant. Boxing died a little that night in Chicago, but "the long count" lives on.

—S.W.

ABOVE LEFT: *Round 7. Dempsey glares down at Tunney, knocked down for the first time in his career, as Dave Berry delays the count until Dempsey goes to a neutral corner.* ABOVE RIGHT: *Round 8. Dempsey goes down, rocked by a Tunney punch. Tunney controlled the last two rounds and kept his heavyweight title.*

A SWEET ETERNITY

Max Schmeling stunned millions of Americans when he KOd
the supposedly invincible Joe Louis, but Louis gained a sweet revenge when he destroyed the German
in the first round of their rematch

On the night of June 22, 1938, in Yankee Stadium, Joe Louis, the newly crowned heavyweight champion, touched gloves with former champ Max Schmeling of Germany. Two years before, Schmeling had knocked out "the Brown Bomber" in the twelfth round, and Louis wanted nothing so much as he wanted to avenge the only loss of his professional career. After knocking out James Braddock in June of 1937 to win the heavyweight title, Louis said, "I don't want nobody to call me champ till I beat that Schmeling."

But this was more than a fight between two men; it was a fight between two beliefs. The troops of Nazi Germany were preparing to march through Europe, and if Schmeling won again, Adolf Hitler would use his victory as proof of the superiority of the Aryan race. President Franklin Roosevelt, too, attached great significance to the fight. When Louis came to visit him at the White House, Roosevelt asked to feel his right arm. "Joe," said the President, "we need muscles like yours to beat Germany."

The White House was a long way from the sharecropper's shack in Lexington, Alabama, where Joseph Louis Barrow was born in 1914. His family moved to Detroit when he was still a small boy. His mother wanted him to take violin lessons, but, just like in the movies, Joe snuck out of the house with boxing gloves hidden in his violin case. He came up through the Golden Gloves program, and by the age of 20, he was the U.S. amateur light heavyweight champion with a record of 50–4 with 43 knockouts. In 1934 he turned pro, and in the summer of 1935 Louis fought the giant ex-champion Primo Carnera and knocked him out in six rounds. Another former champ, Max Baer, went down in four. Next on Louis's hit list was a Basque hulk named Paolino Uzcudun. Louis KO'd him in the fourth, and Uzcudun's name might otherwise be forgotten, but for one thing. Sitting in the first row, watching the fight, was Schmeling, who had already signed to fight Louis. After the fight, Schmeling said, "I seez someding."

Schmeling, from Hamburg, had knocked out Jack Sharkey in four rounds in June of 1930 to win the world title left vacant by Gene Tunney. But he made only one successful defense before losing the crown back to Shar-

key two years later in a 15-round decision. Schmeling was 30 and seemingly on the way out when he was matched with the up-and-coming Louis, who owned the quickest hands anybody had ever seen on a heavyweight.

Louis was a 10–1 favorite to win the fight, and he was so confident that Schmeling would fall like the other ex-champs, Carnera and Baer, that he spent much of his training time in Lakewood, New Jersey, courting his new-found love, golf. But Schmeling did indeed "seez someding" in the Uzcudun fight. He had seen Louis dip his left shoulder whenever he jabbed, and that made him susceptible to a right cross—Schmeling's best punch.

On June 19, 1936, in Yankee Stadium, Louis and Schmeling met for the first time. Louis won the first three rounds, but in the fourth, Schmeling put his secret to use. He crossed Louis's left with a right to the chin, and followed with a right to the jaw. Louis went down for the first time as a pro. He was up at the count of three, but suddenly he was no longer invincible. Schmeling continued to ply his right, and finally in the twelfth, Louis was knocked out by a right to the jaw. The day after, one of his trainers asked Louis if he wanted to see movies of the bout. "No," said Louis, "I saw the fight."

Two months later, Louis was back in the ring, knocking out another ex-champion, Jack Sharkey, in the third round. Louis was kept so busy—11 fights in seven months—that he had no time to dwell on his defeat. On June 22 in Comiskey Park in Chicago, Louis fought Braddock for the title. Braddock was 32 and rusty, but

June 22, 1938. Yankee Stadium. Joe Louis (right) lands a devastating left to the head of Max Schmeling in the first round of their heavyweight title bout. Louis threw bombs from the beginning and Schmeling was finished off in 2 minutes, 4 seconds.

he had gone to school on the Schmeling fight. He knocked Louis down with a right in the first round. But Louis came alive after that and beat Braddock so badly that his corner wanted to throw in the towel after the seventh round. "I'll lose it on the deck," said the champ, which he did the very next round.

For two years Schmeling had refused to meet Louis, but now that he was champion, Schmeling had no choice. The fight was booked for Yankee Stadium, the site of their last fight, and the two men trained themselves into superb condition. A crowd of 70,000 jammed into the ballpark the night of June 22.

Louis was the first man in the ring, wearing a red, white, and blue bathrobe. The roar of the crowd was thunderous. Schmeling then arrived, dressed in a gray robe. There were boos—and cheers, for some Americans sympathized with the Nazi cause. The bell rang, and a hush fell over the crowd.

Louis, usually a cautious starter, went right after Schmeling with incredible fury. He hit him with left jabs and then landed a right to the jaw with all his might. Schmeling buckled against the ropes, and when he came off, Louis hit him with such a powerful right to the side that Schmeling yelled in pain and went down. He got up, but Louis pummeled him again, and Schmeling fell for the second time. The radio broadcast back to Germany was cut off. Schmeling somehow got to his feet and was greeted with another flurry. When he hit the floor for a third time, his handlers threw in the towel. But New York rules did not allow that, and as referee Arthur Donovan was counting out Schmeling, he casually kicked the towel with a backwards swipe of his right foot. The towel landed on the middle rope and hung there, just as limp and lifeless as Schmeling. The fight lasted two minutes and four seconds, but it was a sweet eternity for Louis and America.

That night the champion rode through Harlem and basked in the joy of his people. Louis became the busiest titleholder in heavyweight history, and he also held the crown the longest: 11 years, 8 months and 7 days, until September 27, 1950, when Ezzard Charles finally took it away from him.

—S.W.

ABOVE LEFT: *Schmeling hangs onto the ropes as Joe Louis continues his first round attack.* ABOVE RIGHT: *The referee steps in to stop the fight at 2:04 of the first round. In that brief time, Louis, who normally began cautiously, had sent Schmeling to the canvas three times with furious blows.*

SUGAR RAY: A FIGHTIN' MAN

*As England's Randy Turpin and dozens of other fighters
discovered the hard way, Walker Smith Jr.—a/k/a Sugar Ray Robinson—was probably the greatest boxer,
pound for pound, ever to put on the gloves*

As good a fighter as Sugar Ray Leonard is, he still can't climb into the ring of boxing history with the man from whom he took his name. Sugar Ray Robinson, born Walker Smith, Jr., in Detroit in 1920, fought professionally for 25 years, and in that time he held six world championships and failed to go the distance only once in 202 bouts. It's a cliché, but it's true: Sugar Ray Robinson was the greatest fighter, pound for pound, who ever lived.

Robinson's family moved to New York when he was still young, and he came up through the ranks of the Golden Gloves. He turned pro in 1940, and by 1942 he was beating lightweight champion Sammy Angott, former welterweight champ Fritzie Zivic, future welter champ Marty Servo, and a man by the name of Jake LaMotta. In 1943, after 40 straight victories—29 by knockout—Robinson finally lost a fight on a 10-round decision to LaMotta. But barely three weeks later, Sugar Ray decisioned LaMotta. In 1945 he twice more defeated "the Raging Bull."

Robinson won his first championship on December 20, 1946, when he decisioned Tommy Bell in 15 rounds for the vacant welterweight title. For the next four years Sugar Ray beat all challengers, including future champ Kid Gavilan (twice) and future middleweight titleholder Bobo Olson. On February 14, 1951, Robinson added the second title of middleweight champion when he beat LaMotta on a technical knockout in the thirteenth round. It was their sixth fight. "We almost got married," Robinson joked. But seriously, he said, "Jake was the toughest guy I ever fought. I hit him with everything, and he'd just act like you're crazy. I never did knock him off his feet."

Robinson would lose the middleweight title six times and win it back five, but his first comeback was the most memorable. In 1951, shortly after taking the crown from LaMotta, Robinson embarked on a European tour, fighting in Paris, Zurich, Antwerp, Liège, Berlin, and Turin. The last stop was London and an easy payday with the British champion Randy Turpin. Robinson was such a heavy favorite that betting was off the board. The only trouble was that nobody told Turpin how good Robinson was. After 15 rounds there was a

Sugar Ray Robinson, holder of six world championship titles. He turned pro in 1940 and continued fighting until 1965. He went the distance in all but one of his 202 fights and is considered, pound for pound, the greatest fighter of all time.

new middleweight champion. As one observer put it, "Robinson fought in London, but he left his legs in Paris."

Turpin was Britain's first middleweight champion since the legendary Bob Fitzsimmons. Turpin came from Leamington, England, and he had a rather unorthodox style that baffled Robinson. The great boxing writer A. J. Liebling wrote, "His jab was like a man running for the pole vault." And Turpin possessed surprising power. "He's a heavyweight in a 160-pound body," said Robinson.

The rematch was scheduled for September 12, 1951, in the Polo Grounds. The day before the fight, Robinson was lying on the sofa in his mother's house. His feet were resting in her lap. "Mom," he said, "you always predict my fights, but you ain't said a word about this one yet." Mom replied, "Ray, you're gonna knock out Turpin in the tenth round, but he's gonna butt you, like he did before."

The next night 61,730 fans, one of the largest crowds ever to see a nonheavyweight fight, jammed the Polo Grounds in New York. Among those in attendance were Joe DiMaggio, Walter Winchell, and General Douglas MacArthur. "Having MacArthur there was like having an order to win," said Robinson. In the first round Sugar Ray began working the body while Turpin preferred the head. No longer baffled by the Briton's style, Robinson found an opening in the second and scored solidly with a right to the chin. But Turpin soon proved, if nothing else, that he could take a punch. The fight began to turn Turpin's way in the sixth. He tagged Robinson with a right-left combination to the head. In the eighth, Turpin's jab landed repeatedly and his legs seemed much the better for wear. In the ninth, Turpin was in such command that Robinson had to resort to clinching. The working press started to write their leads on Robinson's obit.

Seconds after the bell for the tenth round rang, the two fighters banged heads. It was just as Sugar Ray's mom had predicted, and the butt left her son bleeding from a gash over the left eye. Turpin went in for the kill then, but it was a mistake. The 31-year-old Robinson was far from through. He found the same opening he had in the second round, and his right hand found Turpin's jaw. Turpin's knees buckled. A left, a right, and a right put him on his back. Turpin was on his feet at the count of seven, but Robinson was a man possessed. Films later showed that in the next flurry, Sugar Ray threw 31 punches in 25 seconds. Turpin somehow stayed up, but with eight seconds left in the round, Referee Ruby Goldstein stopped the fight. A battered, bleeding Robinson waved to the crowd as his mother climbed into the ring and shouted, "Baby, I told you the tenth round."

In 1952 Robinson defended his title against Olson and Rocky Graziano, knocking the former champ out in three rounds. Sugar Ray decided to take aim at the light heavyweight title owned by Joey Maxim. Try to imagine Sugar Ray Leonard one day challenging for the light heavyweight crown. On the night of June 25, with temperatures above 100 degrees, Robinson met Maxim in Yankee Stadium. The first to go down was the referee, Ruby Goldstein, who collapsed from heat prostration after 10 rounds. Robinson was clearly ahead on all the official scorecards when he too ran out of gas after 13 rounds. He could not answer the bell for the 14th, and Maxim was the winner. Sugar Ray retired for two years after that fight.

After a less-than-successful career as a song-and-dance man, Robinson climbed back into the ring in 1954. Tiger Jones, a journeyman with five straight losses to his debit, put a crimp in Robinson's comeback when he won a decision, but before long Sugar Ray took his old middleweight title away from Olson. In 1957 he lost it to Gene Fullmer in a 15-round decision, then won it right back five months later on a fifth-round knockout. Carmen Basilio then beat Robinson, but, sure enough, in March of 1958, Sugar Ray recaptured the title. He reigned as champion for two more years, until January 22, 1960, when he was beaten by Paul Pender in 15 rounds. Amazingly, Robinson went on fighting for five more years, finally calling it quits in 1965 at the age of 45. He truly was the greatest fighter, pound for pound, who ever lived.

—S.W.

Sugar Ray Robinson keeps his guard up as he shoots a left at oncoming Johnny Lombardo during a ten-round bout in Cincinnati in 1955. Robinson won a split decision. He was so quick that he once threw 31 punches in 25 seconds against Randy Turpin.

THE THRILLA IN MANILA

*Muhammad Ali scored a TKO over Joe Frazier in their third-fight rubber
match in the Philippines, but Ali came away battered and beaten himself and said the bout was "like death"*

Ten forty-five in the morning seems a strange time to hold one of the greatest fights in heavyweight history, but that's when Muhammad Ali, resplendent in a white silk dressing gown with Columbia blue lining, and Joe Frazier, swathed in a simple smoke gray robe, entered the ring of the Philippine Coliseum on October 1, 1975. This was the fight that was dubbed "the thrilla in Manila." It was the third match between these two champions. Ali was colorful, controversial, and a true world figure. Smokin' Joe was dogged, workmanlike, and from Philadelphia. They were like the robes they wore that morning.

Eleven years earlier, a 22-year-old brat from Louisville, Kentucky, named Cassius Clay had stunned the boxing world by taking the heavyweight championship away from Sonny Liston with a seventh-round knockout. In the next five years, Clay changed his name to Muhammad Ali, took on all comers, and inscribed his motto, "Float like a butterfly, sting like a bee," on the American consciousness. But in 1968 he was stripped of his title for refusing to serve in the armed forces because of his Black Muslim convictions. Into the vacuum stepped Frazier, a former Olympic gold medalist like Ali. In 1968 Frazier knocked out Buster Mathis to win

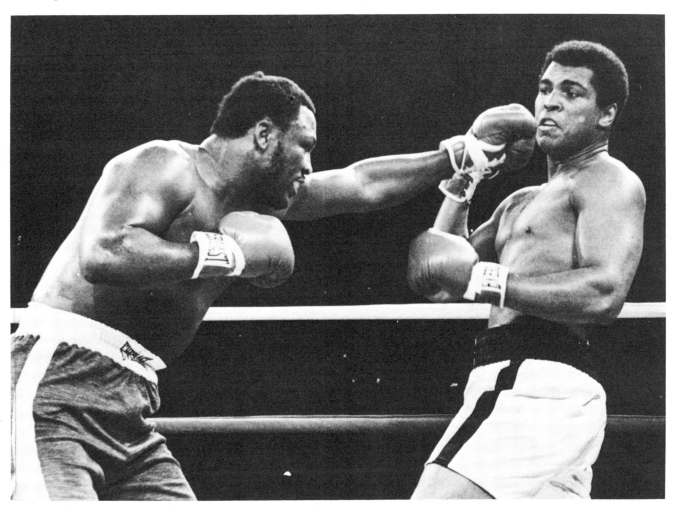

Smokin' Joe Frazier throws a left at heavyweight champ Muhammad Ali in the first round of the "Thrilla in Manila," held October 1, 1975, in the Philippine Coliseum. The battle went back and forth until the 12th round. Ali said of the punishment Frazier gave him, "It was like death."

163

what was called the New York State Heavyweight Title, but which was, in effect, half the world title. In February of 1970 Frazier united both halves by kayoing Jimmy Ellis. In September of that year, Ali announced his return to the ring. He began his second career six weeks later with a third-round knockout of Jerry Quarry. A Frazier-Ali match was soon arranged, to take place on March 8, 1971, in Madison Square Garden in New York. They called it "the Fight of the Century" with some justification. Neither man had ever been beaten professionally. Frazier was the immovable object, Ali the irresistible force. Finally, in the fifteenth round, the irresistible Ali went down, the victim of Frazier's trademark left hook. It was only for a count of three, but it was enough to sway the judges into giving Frazier the decision. However, if the postfight condition was taken into account, Ali would have been the winner because Frazier spent three days in the hospital under observation. Some people said he would never be the same again. Indeed, two years later, Frazier went down six times in two rounds against George Foreman and lost his title.

Ali, too, lost a great deal of luster when Ken Norton broke his jaw and took a 12-round decision from him in March of 1973. In September, Ali barely beat Norton in the rematch. On January 28, 1974, Frazier and Ali, no longer champions, fought for the second time, again in New York. This time Ali won by decision, although the fight was hardly an artistic success. Ali started 114 clinches, and Frazier fought without smoke. But in October of 1974 the amazing Ali regained his title in Kinshasa, Zaire, by making a "rope-a-dope" out of Foreman, knocking him out in the eighth round. A year later came "the thrilla in Manila."

Ali was never very kind to his opponents, but his remarks about Frazier before their third fight seemed unusually cruel. He talked of him as an ignorant and ugly man and called him "the gorilla in Manila." Frazier, who still insisted on calling Ali Clay, whispered to the champ at a prefight reception, "I'm gonna whup your half-breed ass." Ali was having marital difficulties at the time—his second wife Belinda arrived in the Philippines only to find her husband with his soon-to-be-third wife Veronica—and Frazier said, "I'm the better man, physically and morally."

The 10:45 A.M. starting time for the fight was more for the benefit of the millions of closed-circuit TV viewers in the U.S. than for the 27,000 fans in the Philippine Coliseum. President Ferdinand Marcos and his wife Imelda were at ringside, ensconced in elaborate red and gold chairs. Ali, 33 and 224½ pounds, did some mild clowning, picking up the winner's trophy on display in midring and carrying it to his corner. Frazier, 31 and 215½ pounds, jumped up and down, occasionally staring at the champion.

At the bell, Ali, no longer the slender dancer of his youth, stood flatfooted and measured Frazier for the early knockout he had predicted. The challenger bored in, trying to set up his left hook. Ali won the first round by scoring with a left-right combination and then a left hook that sent Frazier to the ropes. In the second round Ali jabbed and landed a hard right, but Frazier kept coming and landed a left hook just before the bell. Between rounds Ali blew kisses to the president and first lady. In the third he continued to paw at Frazier with his left hand, hitting him almost at will and shaking him up twice. But Frazier was as relentless as a jackhammer, and the two engaged in a toe-to-toe trade that had the crowd on its feet. At the end of the round, Frazier spun Ali's head around with a left hook, but Ali's only reaction was to laugh for the crowd.

The second stage of the fight began in the fourth round, although Ali was still inflicting most of the damage. Now fighting from the ropes, Ali plied his right while Frazier went to work on the body. Ali fought the whole fifth round in his own corner, and as Frazier pounded his kidneys, Ali's longtime trainer, Angelo Dundee, shouted at him, "Get out of the goddamn corner." In the sixth Ali took left hook after vicious left hook. The president and his wife had to look away, and at one point Frazier knocked Ali's mouthpiece out. "Man, I hit him with punches that'd bring down the walls of a city," Frazier would say later.

But Ali proved, if nothing else, that he could receive as well as give, and he actually did a little dancing in the seventh round. He even took time to tell Frazier, "Old Joe Frazier, why I thought you were washed up." Frazier's reply was, "Somebody told you all wrong, pretty boy," and then another left hook. The assault continued in the seventh and eighth, and in the ninth, Ali's right eye began to puff from below. By the end of the tenth round, the fight was all even and sliding away from Ali.

The third stage of the fight began in the eleventh as Ali revived. He found new fury in the twelfth, catching Frazier's face with long right hands. Frazier was out of gas, and in the thirteenth Ali sent Frazier's mouthpiece flying into the press row. Frazier very nearly went down. In the fourteenth Ali hit him with nine straight right hands—Frazier could no longer see out of his left

eye to protect himself. At the end of the fourteenth, Frazier's trainer, Eddie Futch, told him, "Joe, I'm going to stop it." Frazier pleaded, "No, no, Eddie, ya can't do that to me." To which Futch replied, "Sit down, son. It's all over. No one will ever forget what you did here today."

"It was like death," said Ali. "Closest thing to dying that I know of." Frazier would fight once more, losing by a KO to Foreman again, before he retired. Ali kept on, defending his title against six stiffs. The seventh stiff, Leon Spinks, took the title away from him in February of 1978, but Ali grabbed it back—his third title—in September of that year. He stayed retired for two years before his foolish attempt at Larry Holmes's crown in 1980. Both Ali and Frazier should have called it quits after Manila, though. Neither will ever know a finer moment.

—S.W.

Ali glances a right off Joe Frazier in 7th round action in Manila. Ali did some dancing in the 7th round, but absorbed punishing blows until the 11th round when he began to come back. He fought with renewed fury in the 12th and 13th, and finally hurt Frazier enough in the 14th to win by a TKO.

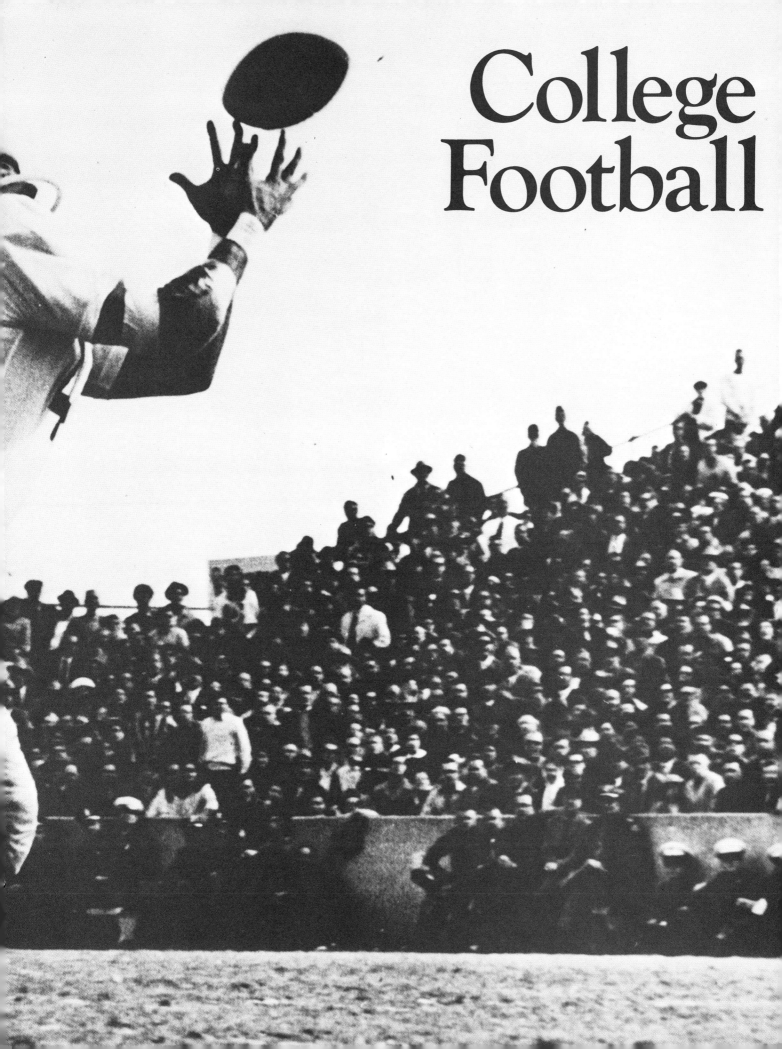

College Football

OKLAHOMA'S NOT O.K.

Oklahoma's 47-game winning streak goes up in smoke
as the Fightin' Irish of Notre Dame score a stunning 7–0 upset victory

In the illustrious annals of Notre Dame football, few characteristics of the Irish teams have warmed the hearts of the faithful as completely as the Gold and Blue's proclivity for putting an end to the winning streaks of others. In 1946 it was the 0–0 tie that broke Army's string of victories at 25. In 1973 the Irish beat Texas 24–11 to snap the Longhorns' string of 30 consecutive triumphs, and in 1953 and 1971 they doled out the defeats to Georgia Tech and Southern California that ended their strings of games without a loss at 23 and 31, respectively.

Oh yes, there *was* one more, and it involved the University of Oklahoma. The Sooners, it seems, had picked up the habit of winning in 1953, and hadn't shaken the habit all the way up until their meeting with Notre Dame in 1957. It wasn't so much that nobody expected *Notre Dame* to beat Oklahoma (Notre Dame, after all, had been the last team to have done so, back in September of 1953). It was just that the numbers had kept piling on top of each other, higher and higher, until even the calmest of football minds had begun to wonder whether Oklahoma would lose to *anyone*, ever again. The boys under Bud Wilkinson had won 47 games in a row (more than any college football team before or since), taken two national championships, and outscored their opponents 1,620 to 276. Only nine of the 47 triumphs had been decided by a touchdown or less, and only twice were the Sooners even given a scare. In 1954, against Texas Christian, Oklahoma needed two fourth-quarter TDs to win 21–16. Against Colorado in 1957, after the Buffaloes had taken the lead on a catch by Boyd Dowler, the Sooners got a touchdown in the last five minutes to win it, 14–13. And while Oklahoma had shut out 22 of its foes during its skein, it had not been held scoreless itself in 123 games.

Oklahoma became the forty-sixth state of the Union on November 16, 1907. For the folks in Norman that meant that the game with Notre Dame on November 16, 1957, was going to be as much a fiftieth birthday party as the Sooners' forty-eighth consecutive win. No betting men fond of their money were taking Notre Dame. Those who brought up the win in 1953 were quickly reminded of the more recent meeting, in 1956, when the Irish corps, led by the flashy quarterback Paul

Hornung, were beaten in South Bend 40–0. While 1956 had been Notre Dame's worst season in history (2–8), in the two games previous to Oklahoma things hadn't been much better. Following losses to Navy (20–6) and Michigan State (34–6), the Fighting Irish were 18-point underdogs going into Norman. Only the foolhardy would have guessed that they would be heroes coming out.

The game was a defensive battle, and as it is with all defensive battles, the intensity is to be found in what *didn't* happen, in the mistakes that defensive teams did not make. On the first Oklahoma drive of the game, it looked as if the game might turn out like the ones that preceded it. Working from his own 42, Sooner quarterback Carl Dodd completed an 11-yard pass to fullback Dennit Morris, ran for 12 yards, and drove his squad to a first down on the Notre Dame 20. In three plays Oklahoma gained only seven yards and elected to try for the first down. Dodd went to the air, and Al Eager, an Irish lineman, broke up the play. Notre Dame, which made only one first down in the opening quarter, made another stand on its own 12 before its 6 foot 2 inch, 205-pound fullback, Nick ("the Greek God") Pietrosante, punted the Irish out of the hole.

The crowd of 62,800 at Owen Field was not accustomed to waiting so long for a score. The audience on national TV began to wonder what it was watching. With six minutes left in the first quarter, Notre Dame made a mistake. Second-team halfback Pat Doyle fumbled as he ran into the Oklahoma line on the Irish 34, and Sooner guard Dick Corbitt recovered. Against the odds, Notre Dame's fired-up defense actually knocked the Sooners back, forcing a punt. The birthday party had become a game.

When Sooner coach Bud Wilkinson was asked for the secret of his team's success, he put it to the good moral character of his players, his program that made every player feel important, and the coaches' meticulous preparation. In South Bend, an assistant coach had been listening. Bernie Crimmins watched three Oklahoma games and enough Oklahoma game film in preparing the strategy for that game to make him look like Peter Lorre. He looked hard for weaknesses in the "big red victory machine," but found only a slight vulnerability to short passes and an even slighter tendency to

Notre Dame vs. Oklahoma, 1957. Oklahoma defender Carl Dodd (22) watches a pass slip through the fingers of Notre Dame receiver James Colosimo. Notre Dame won the game 7–0 and ended a winning streak that Oklahoma began in 1953 and continued for 47 consecutive games until they met the Irish.

Notre Dame vs. Oklahoma, 1956. Two Oklahoma defenders leap high to deflect a Paul Hornung pass. The pass was intercepted by Clendon Thomas and run back for a touchdown. Oklahoma humiliated the Fighting Irish 40–0, setting the stage for the 1957 contest.

react *too* fast. Each day of "Beat Oklahoma Week" a crowd of 400 Notre Dame students showed up at practice to cheer the team as it learned the lessons that Crimmins had to impart. By game time, the team was ready.

Late in the first quarter, the Sooners began a drive from the Notre Dame 41. With some handy running, Dodd made one first down on the 31. Clendon Thomas, the Sooners' All-American halfback, gained seven, but then the Irish closed them down. On the first play of the second quarter Dodd faced a fourth down with one yard to go for a first down on the Notre Dame 21. He fumbled in the backfield, accidentally kicking the ball he was trying to recover. When "the Greek God" recovered for the Irish on their own 48, quarterback Bob Williams went to work. He passed to his right end (Jim Colosimo) for 10, to his left end (Dick Royer) for 9, to Pietrosante for 10, and ran another 10 for himself.

Oklahoma then showed the kind of guts that had kept it from falling in 47 games. Notre Dame had a first down, goal to go, three yards from a touchdown. After Pietrosante hit the line twice, Williams gave the ball to halfback Frank Reynolds. He gained two feet. On fourth down, fullback Jim Just punched into the left tackle hole, and met only Oklahoma. Pushed backwards, he headed around his end, but the Sooner defense dragged him down short of the goal line.

Notre Dame allowed nothing on the Sooners' possession, and halfback Thomas kicked out to the 46. Once again Williams drove his offense, and once again the defense was willing to bend, but not to break. On the Oklahoma 15, Notre Dame faced a fourth down. This time, the offense lined up for a field goal. At the snap Williams rose from his position as holder and threw to Just, who was corralled at the six. First down. The infidels were at the walls, but the Sooners would not panic. Irish halfback Reynolds threw an option pass toward the end zone, but Oklahoma's David Baker made a one-handed interception. Score at halftime: 0–0.

The Irish had squandered opportunities in the first half. A lesser team might have lost all confidence. Said coach Terry Brennan to his troops, "Just slant, gap and blow. Forget the bad breaks and bear down for the next thirty minutes." When they returned to the field, the Irish almost made the mistake that would have given the game away.

A coffin-corner kick by Thomas had nailed Notre Dame back on its own four. On the ensuing series, two Sooners hooked the arms of Williams, who lost the ball. A teammate fell on it, but Oklahoma continued its strategy of giving its foe the opportunity to commit the fatal error. It didn't. The Sooners answered Notre Dame's kick from the end zone with another coffin-corner job, this one by Baker to the three. On the next three exchanges, Thomas kicked to the 4, Baker booted to the seven and—finally—into the end zone for a touchback.

In the fourth quarter the Notre Dame offense was facing the Sooner substitutes, whose fresh faces had spelled doom to weary foes more than once. In this case the Gold and Blue gave Oklahoma—the consummate running machine—a taste of its own medicine. In a

drive that started on the Irish 20 with 12:51 to play, Williams ran a total of 20 plays. All but a jump pass to Royer were runs. On one of them, at the Sooner 12, Williams dropped the ball in the backfield, where it lay for a full five seconds before he crawled over to pick it up. On third down from the Sooner 16, seven yards from a first down, Irish halfback Dick Lynch ran eight yards for a first down. Wilkinson sent his starters back into the game.

On first down, Pietrosante gained four. On second, Lynch went nowhere. On third, Williams ran for one, and on fourth down three yards from the touchdown, Notre Dame chose to go for it.

"They were tight, real tight," said Williams after the game, "just waiting for me to give the ball to Pietrosante." Williams did fake to "the god," and the defense reacted. But the pitch went to Lynch heading around the right end. He scored untouched with 3:50 on the clock. Monte Stickles's point-after made it 7–0.

The battle was far from won. With 1:22 remaining, Oklahoma, with a third-string quarterback at the helm, took over on its own 39. The QB, Bennett Watts, connected with halfback Johnny Pellow twice, for 10 yards

and then, on a deflected pass, for 27. The Irish held on their 24, and on fourth and 14 yet another quarterback, Dale Sherrod, threw a pass into the end zone, where his opposite number and hero of the day, Bob Williams, intercepted.

When the gun sounded, there was mayhem. A crowd of 3,000 met the Notre Dame team at the South Bend airport. Four thousand more awaited the giant-killers on campus. Between verses of the Notre Dame "Victory March," some even heard "Happy Birthday, Oklahoma, Happy Birthday to You." John Cronley of the *Daily Oklahoman* reported the game as follows, "Russia's two sputniks collided in mid-air. The sun set in the east. Hitler was discovered alive in Washington, D.C. And, almost equally incredible, Oklahoma University lost a football game. Father Hesburgh, president of Notre Dame, declared Monday a student holiday. Governor Raymond Gary of Oklahoma, on the other hand, proclaimed it "We're-with-you-all-the-way Day."

The Sooners should have been with Dick Lynch "all the way."

—N. Brooks Clark

Oklahoma Sooner Jakie Sandefer (27) is brought down by Nick Pietrosante (49) in first quarter action of the 1957 meeting between Oklahoma and Notre Dame. Coach Bud Wilkenson's Oklahoma team was unable to get on track because of a dogged Notre Dame defense that neutralized the Sooner offense.

THE GALLOPING GHOST

*Red Grange, ol' Number 77, ruins Michigan by scoring
five touchdowns and throwing for a sixth TD in a stunning Illinois victory*

A bolt of lightning shot from the sky and blew a 50-foot oak into splinters. An old man sitting on his porch didn't even blink. A tornado whirled down the lane, turned up his path, and began to dig a hole in his front yard. The codger was nonplussed. When the hole began to spurt oil, a passer-by had to interrupt.

"Old man!" he said, "doesn't anything make you flinch?"

"Nope," he replied calmly, "not since I saw what

Red Grange, "The Galloping Ghost," played for Illinois and then went on to star with the Chicago Bears. Grange had 9.8 speed in the hundred-yard dash. In 1924 against Michigan he scored four times in the first 12 minutes on runs of 95, 67, 56, and 44 yards.

Red Grange did to Michigan back in 1924."

In the middle of the 1923 football season, the University of Illinois finished construction on its mammoth stadium. The first game played there was a 7–0 victory over mighty Chicago. When the Illini were done that year they had beaten Ohio State 9–0 for an undefeated season and won their first national championship.

The Michigan Wolverines had also gone undefeated in 1923, but didn't play Illinois, so they had to settle for the co-championship of the Big Ten. The last time the teams *had* met, Michigan had triumphed 24–0, and the Wolverines had made it known that they expected the next confrontation—in 1924—to be just as easy. It was not destined to turn out that way.

The showdown was to take place on dedication day for the new stadium, dubbed Memorial Field in honor of the Illini who had died in the Great War. It was also Illini Homecoming Day. The odds were even; the game was a sellout.

Michigan's strong suit was its defense, which had allowed only 32 points in the course of a streak of 20 games without a loss. The Illini were stocked with talent left over from the championship team, but their star without peer was the junior halfback, Harold Grange, known to the world as "Red." He was a unanimous choice for All-America; that is, in the eyes of everyone but the staff of the *Michigan Daily*, which had relegated him to its second team with the explanation, "All Grange can do is run."

The response credited to Illinois Coach Bob Zuppke and printed in the *Daily Illini* ran, "And all Galli-Curci can do is sing." In the public eye, Grange was regarded as the top runner in the nation in that all-triumphant season of 1923. In particular, he gained note after a fantastic runback of an interception against Northwestern had earned him the moniker of "the Galloping Ghost." But even as Harold Grange, he was the perfect hero.

Like most heroes, Grange had come from a modest background. He was born in Forksville, Pennsylvania, in 1903, but moved to Wheaton, Illinois, at the age of five, after the death of his mother. He was diagnosed as having a heart murmur when he was eight, but led an active childhood anyway. He went out for football in high school, he said, because the equipment (except for the helmet and shoes) was free. "The sight of a new uniform for just the asking was too much to resist," he said. He had chosen to attend the university of his home state mainly because, as a resident, it was cheaper for him there than anywhere else.

Grange always conveyed the impression that even though he was an All-American halfback and member of a national championship football team, he was the underdog, too. One of the reasons was a summer job that Grange clearly enjoyed as much as anything. The year he finished grammar school, Grange was among a group of boys to whom the local iceman offered one dollar if he could lift a 75-pound cake of ice on his shoulder. This Red did, and for eight summers thereafter he worked as an iceman on the truck, delivering 200-pound cakes and, he often noted, keeping himself in ideal condition for football.

The job nearly ended Grange's career before it began. When he.was 15, he had fallen into the habit of leaping on the running board of the ice truck while it was moving and depending for support on the handle on the cab. The handle broke off in his hand one day and Grange rolled beneath the truck. The tire of the truck ran over his left leg one inch above the knee. A doctor, first fearing that the joint was crushed, gave Red no better than a 50-50 chance for recovery. Miraculously, the leg healed in time for football and, said Grange, the only ill effect was that his left leg was a little numb for the rest of his life. He became known as "the Wheaton Iceman" after a picture taken after his sophomore year at Illinois (Grange with an ice cake on his shoulder flanked by two models) was printed in papers all over the nation. After Grange turned pro, he worked on the ice truck, business as usual. The only difference was that rather than hitching a ride to work, he drove up each day in a $5,500 Lincoln Phaeton.

Arriving at Illinois, Grange considered himself (166 pounds) too small to play big-time football, and intended to go out for basketball and track. His fraternity brothers had different ideas. They sent Grange out to the freshman field, where he was intimidated by the crew that was, indeed, to go on for the national title. When Grange returned in fright to Zeta Psi, they sent him right back with the threat of a paddling if he did not remain at practice. On the field, he began to gain confidence in his speed (9.8 in the 100-yard dash) and his coordination. And of course, Grange was modest to the

Illinois' Red Grange carries the ball toward the Michigan goal line in the 1924 game. He gained 402 yards in 21 carries, scored 5 touchdowns himself, and threw for a 6th.

end. Scribes wrote that he had uncanny peripheral vision, that he was able to see tacklers coming from all sides. "Peripheral vision," he said, "I didn't even know what it was. I had to look it up."

Grange was not, however, too modest to get himself up for the Michigan game. Zuppke had written him letters all summer describing the Wolverines' intentions of bottling him up. They had successfully stopped Minnesota's Earl Martineau the year before, they reasoned, so why not do the same favor for this iceman from Wheaton?

The temperature at game time was near 80 degrees. The crowd on hand was the largest ever assembled for a game in the Midwest. Zuppke wanted one more edge, one more way of showing the team from Ann Arbor that the Illini were not afraid of them or anyone else. Zuppke thought of the heat. "Anything in the rule book says we can't remove our stockings?" he asked. They looked. There was no such statute, and off came the heavy wool socks. When the team appeared, Michigan indulged the ploy, insisting on a check for grease on the uncovered calves; this only added to the Illini players' pleasure with the innovation.

Grange's action on Memorial Field started early. He accepted Michigan's kickoff on his own five-yard line and ran straight ahead as halfback Wally McIlwain and fullback Earl Britton nailed the first two Wolverines downfield. Grange then cut to the right sideline at the 35 to avoid the oncoming pack. He then reversed his field and cut all the way to the far left sideline on the Michigan 40. It was a footrace to the goal line between Grange and Michigan quarterback Tod Rockwell, and Grange won. Britton made the conversion and Illinois had seven points.

After an unsuccessful Wolverine series, McIlwain hit the right guard for three yards to the 33. Grange then took the ball, cut around left end, cut back to find his blockers, and made it for another score, this one for 67 yards. After an exchange of punts, McIlwain went for a yard over left tackle to the 44. This time Grange went around the right end, luring the secondary to the outside, and then cut back to the center and made a beeline to a touchdown. Britton missed the conversion: Grange 20, Wolverines 0.

Two minutes later, Michigan fumbled a punt, setting up a Grange TD scamper of 44 yards. Time elapsed: 12 minutes. The runs: 95 yards, 67, 56, and 44 yards. Grange leaned up against the goalpost, waited for his team to catch up. In the next series of downs, he told the trainer he was dog-tired, and he left the game. The

Red Grange, playing for the Chicago Bears against the College All-Stars, in the 1925 College All-Star game, carries the ball around the left end.

ovation lasted a full five minutes. In form, Grange said that he "was much too exhausted to fully appreciate the thrill of such a tribute." He also claimed later that "Zuppke's plays were designed to spring me, it had all been a combination of circumstances."

More importantly, Grange felt that this was the game when he developed his trademark of reversing his field, of carving an "S" on the field by starting wide to one side and then veering back to the other. After sitting out the second quarter, he came in to score from 12 yards out in the third quarter, and (as if to show the *Michigan Daily* that he could do more than run) to complete six passes for 64 yards, including an 18-yard touchdown to halfback Marion Leonard. Final score: 39–7. Grange's stats in 41 minutes of playing time: 21 carries for 402 yards (including returns), five TD runs, and one TD pass.

"When I got back to the fraternity house," Grange wrote in his autobiography, "the place was in an uproar. The walls were literally bulging with alums, friends, Zeta Psi's from the Michigan chapter and more newspapermen. Escaping from all this posed a greater problem for me than eluding Michigan tacklers.

"Finally I managed to get up to my room and, after changing clothes, slipped out the kitchen door with one of my more understanding fraternity brothers. We had dinner by ourselves, then took in a movie. Returning about 10:30 that night, and finding conditions somewhat more peaceful, I went straight to bed."

Records are made to be broken, and the accomplishments of one generation always outdo the ones of the generation that preceded it. But as long as running backs are carrying footballs for their alma maters, they will always be measured by Red Grange's lightening strikes against Michigan on October 18, 1924.

—N.B.C.

THE DAY HARVARD WON A TIE

Around the Harvard Yard, they still say that the Crimson
really beat Yale in 1968 even though the final score was an unbelievable 28–28 tie

What follows is the anatomy of a miracle. Yes, miracles *do* happen. And yes, they do so when it's least expected. Just ask someone who was in the crowd for the Harvard-Yale game of 1968. He might be one of those who picked his ticket up from a scalper for $175, but he'll never claim he was gypped. Rather, he'll tell you what he once did not believe, but now knows for sure. That is that there are times when the rules of nature do not apply and arbitrary judgments rain down from heaven as blithely as morning papers are thrown onto doorsteps. If he's a son of Eli, he might once again wonder what degree of hubris warranted such a punishment. If a son of John, he'd probably look upward with a wink. But either one would volunteer—and never doubt—that there was magic at work in Harvard Stadium on November 23, 1968, and that when the day was done, a balding junior named Frank Champi had become a hero.

For the first time since 1909, Harvard and Yale entered their showdown with neither a loss nor a tie on their record, and the demand for tickets had risen accordingly. Harvard could only answer its alumni requests through the Class of 1949. Said one Yale student on Wednesday, "I found *my* turkey for Thanksgiving. He's fat and Old Blue and rich." Many began to wonder out loud how any game could measure up to the billing.

"You see," those same doubters had nodded when Yale took a 22–0 lead midway through the second quarter. Among the 40,280 in Cambridge and in closed circuit showings elsewhere, Crimson alumni began to excuse themselves with dignity. "Yes, terrible pity . . . got to go . . . duty calls . . . very sad . . . must put down childish things and all . . . yes, only a game . . . call me for squash."

It was, after all, so silly to have even *considered* stopping the Yale offense, which included the likes of quarterback Brian ("Mr. Magic") Dowling and halfback Calvin Hill. Even with a Crimson defense (known as "the Destroyers' Club") that had allowed fewer points per game (7.6) than any other in the nation. No surprise, then, that the Elis had scored on a run and two passes by Dowling, one of them to Hill, the other to split end Del Marting. So low were the Harvard hopes that when Hill—the man who had averaged 5.1 yards per carry all

year long—fumbled on the next possession, it made only a slight impression. Harvard took over on its own 36, and interest picked up a bit when John Yovicsin, the Harvard coach, sent in his little-used back-up quarterback. "Number 27," said a squinting fan, flipping through a program. "Let's see . . . 27 . . . Frank Champi . . . QB . . . junior . . . 20 . . . 5 feet 11 inches, 195 pounds . . . Everett, Massachusetts." His stats? Twelve throws, five completions for 46 yards, and one TD. He may have been inexperienced, but he knew how to follow instructions. Directed Yovicsin: "Score!"

The Crimson loyals agreed. If only for appearance's sake, please *do* score.

Champi called five runs, netting 20 yards. With a third down and three yards to go for the first on the Yale 44, Champi threw his first pass. It fell incomplete, but a Bulldog had interfered—first and 10 on the 33. With the aid of an offside penalty, Harvard drove to a third and six on the 15. Champi dropped back for the second time, connected with split end Bruce Freeman at the seven, and Freeman ran in for the TD. The conversion failed, and the score at halftime stood at 22–6.

While the Yale band put forth its obscene halftime show and the Harvard critics chanted "Bore-ing . . . bore-ing," in the Crimson locker room reports differed as to who among the sons of John held out any hope. Said a player, "Yovicsin had given up on us. All he wanted us to do was go out there and get the rest of the afternoon over as quickly as possible." Said Yovicsin, "I knew we could win."

He might have been the only one. Sixteen points was quite a margin to make up against a team with a scoring whiz like Dowling. Now enshrined forever as the character B.D. in the comic strip "Doonesbury," Dowling was then regarded as the living embodiment of Yale's hero, Frank Merriwell. Dowling was a charismatic leader who brought a personal winning streak of 65 games (dating back to seventh grade) to Harvard Stadium. As for Hill, his gridiron career had scarcely begun.

In the second half, the angels began smiling on Harvard early, as linebacker Mike Bouscaren fumbled a punt and Freeman recovered for Harvard on the Eli 25. Champi's third pass of the day went to sophomore end

Pete Varney for 24 yards. Fullback Gus Crim then went over left guard for the touchdown. A game once more: 22–13.

Fair enough, thought the Bulldog loyals. The precious honor of Harvard is preserved. Now some action. The Crimson, however, had two breaks coming. First, Yale fullback Bob Levin fumbled on his own 42, but Champi could not capitalize. Then Hill took matters into his own hands. He went around his left tackle at the Harvard 34 and rambled all the way to the 15. There he encountered cornerback Rick Frisbie and coughed up the ball. When the third quarter ended, Harvard had the ball and Yale had been held scoreless for the first quarter in 23.

On the first Eli possession of the fourth period, though, Mr. Magic rallied his squad, taking six plays to reach the Harvard five, from where he rolled around his right end for the score. With 10:44 remaining, Yale's Coach Carmen Cozza went for one.

"Bien fait," said the elder sons of Eli.

"We're number one," chanted the younger sons of Eli.

The scoreboard read 29–13. Eight minutes passed before Harvard got another break. At that time Dowling completed a screen pass to Levin on the Yale 32. The fullback took off from there down to the Harvard 14 where he, too, fumbled. The war on the clock was on.

Champi, whose forte was throwing the javelin, conducted a 10-play drive that included a reverse for 17 yards, a sack negated by a holding call, a 17-yard pass to Freeman and—the most unlikely play of all—a Champi fumble recovered in the backfield and advanced 23 yards by a tackle, Fritz Reed. On the following play, Champi hit Freeman for the score.

Harvard went for the two-point conversion. Champi's pass in the end zone to Varney fell incomplete, but Yale was called for interference. On the second try, Crim went over left guard for two points. Yale 29, Harvard 21—42 seconds to play.

Yale, too proud to prepare for the onside kick with nimble-handed backs on the front, sent in its regular kick returning crew. Sure enough, Harvard squibbed the kick and Eli guard Brad Lee was unable to handle the skittering ball. The Crimson's Bill Kelly fell on the ball at the 49.

On the sideline, tackle Steve Zebal was on his knees, praying. On the first play Champi scrambled around his left end for 14 yards to the 35, and an Eli facemask penalty added 15. The javelin-thrower threw two incompletions from the 20 before surprising the

crowd with a draw play to Crim that went to the six. Champi was then dropped for a two-yard loss. Three seconds showed on the clock. Champi took the snap, went into his backfield, dodged the oncoming crowds, scrambled for daylight and found captain Vic Gatto alone in the end zone with a pass. Touchdown. Yale 29, Harvard 27. The field was flooded with fans.

Once the field was cleared, Champi coolly connected with Varney for two points and what Harvardians called a 29–29 triumph.

The Elis hung their heads in defeat, having met the heavy hand of fate and felt its power. The Harvards could not even make it to their lockers for a half-hour for the adoring crowds and the masses that chanted for hours, "Ten thousand men of Harvard . . ."

—N.B.C.

TOP: Yale's Kurt Schmoke (16) puts the blinders on Harvard's Vic Gatto (40) in the 1968 Ivy League match-up. RIGHT: Harvard reserve quarterback Frank Champi throws a pass early in the game. The Crimson's last second tie was considered a victory.

Pro Basketball

THE NIGHT WILT NEVER WILTED

Wilt Chamberlain is the most prolific scorer in
basketball history, and one night in Hershey he singed the cords for 100 points

The big kid grew up and left West Philly. For a while he played ball in Kansas; later he toured the world, playing guard for the Harlem Globetrotters. And now he was in his third year in the NBA and was averaging more than 50 points a game for the Philadelphia Warriors. But people expected that. They expected a lot when your name was Wilt Chamberlain and you were 7 feet, 1 inch tall. But few, if any, really expected Wilt to do what he did to the New York Knickerbockers on March 2, 1962. He scored 100 points. All by himself. Consider this: no *two* players on the same NBA team have ever combined for 100 points in a game.

Like so many of Wilt's other basketball achievements, the 100-point game has gone somewhat unappreciated. Chamberlain was the favorite villain. He was the man fans loved to hate, always the overdog, an ebony Goliath. The fans always expected more from Chamberlain. That night in Hershey, Pennsylvania, he gave them more and they clamored for more still. Even now, there is no plaque in Hershey Sports Arena commemorating Chamberlain's feat. Pictures of the top stars that have played in the arena hang in the press room. Nowhere is there a picture of Chamberlain.

Even before he learned to dip under door jambs

and chandeliers, Wilton Norman Chamberlain caused people to gawk, to treat him differently. The son of a 5 foot 9½ inch mother and a 5 foot 9 inch father, Chamberlain stood 6 feet 3 inches by age 12. By the time he graduated from Overbrook High in West Philadelphia, he had attained the 7 foot 1 inch stature that was to become so familiar to basketball fans. He had also scored 2,252 points, breaking the Philadelphia scoring record set by future Warrior teammate Tom Gola. Then, just a year and a half later, in his first game for the University of Kansas varsity, Chamberlain scored 52 points, a school record that still stands.

Feeling confined by college ball, Wilt dropped out before his senior year. There were no hardship cases in 1958, so Chamberlain toured with the Globetrotters. A year after that he joined the Warriors, who had earned the rights to Chamberlain through prudent maneuvering four years earlier. Warrior owner Eddie Gottlieb coveted the Overbrook star and pushed through a rule that allowed teams to claim high school players in their area and then draft them four years later as territorial picks.

The trumpeted arrival of Chamberlain into the pros was sensational, as he scored 43 points and snared 28 rebounds in his debut against the Knicks. Lowly New York was always an easy game. Twice "the Dipper" blistered the Knicks for 59 points during the 1961–62 season, and a week before the Hershey contest he shredded the Knicks' paper defense with 67 points.

But Chamberlain came to Hershey tired, having spent the night before in New York in the successful (he says) pursuit of a young woman. Perhaps his luck in love was an omen that he would have as little trouble scoring *against* New York as he says he did *in* New York.

It was a day when Wilt scored well in everything. Teammates dragged him to an arcade near the court and bet him he couldn't top 1,800 points shooting targets with a rifle. The bettors had checked with the doorman earlier and learned that 1,800 was the top score, ever. Wilt hit 2,040. A second omen.

Warrior coach Frank McGuire tried to ignite Chamberlain with a clipping from a New York paper in which the Knicks boasted about how they were going to stop Chamberlain. No one stopped Wilt; he finished the

PRECEDING PAGES: *Wilt Chamberlain (13) hangs onto the ball for the 76ers against the Baltimore Bullets' Don Ohl (10) and Bob Ferry in a 1966 game Philadelphia won 114–98.* ABOVE: *Wilt, playing for the Lakers, nudges N.Y. Knick center Jerry Lucas in the 1972 championship final won by L.A. 114–100.*

season averaging 50.4 points a game. Now the Knicks, permanent denizens of the Eastern Division cellar, were going to stop him? If so, they were going to stop him without their regular center because Phil Jordan was injured. The Knicks sent 6 foot 10 inch towhead Darrall Imhoff out to corral Chamberlain. Imhoff had led California to the 1959 NCAA crown and later earned All-America honors, largely for his tough defensive play. A hatchet man, Imhoff was dubbed "Axe" by Laker great Elgin Baylor.

The teams warmed up as 4,124 spectators drifted into the arena, originally built as a home for hockey's Hershey Bears (like Hershey Bars, get it?). It is purported to be the first arena in North America with an all-concrete roof and no support beams obstructing the view. But it wasn't the breakthrough architecture that Imhoff would remember about the arena. "Around the league the baskets in the Hershey Arena were referred

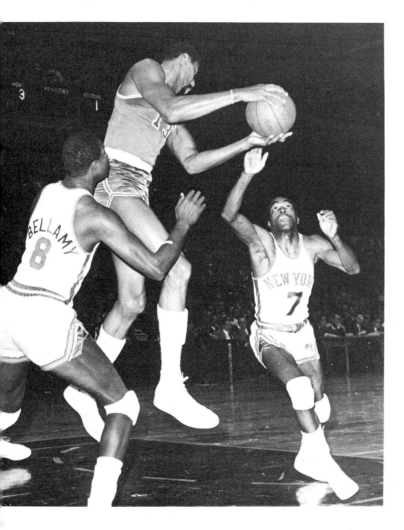

Philadelphia center Wilt Chamberlain soars over the heads of N.Y. Knicks Walt Bellamy (8) and Emmette Bryant (7) in a 1966 game at Madison Square Garden won by the 76ers 113–109. Chamberlain scored 100 points against the Knicks in a 1962 game.

to as sewers," Imhoff recalled later. "They were real soft and sucked up everything."

They certainly took in everything Chamberlain threw their way. He scored 23 points in the first quarter and sent Imhoff to the bench with four fouls. Cleveland Buckner, a rookie who surrendered nearly half a foot to Chamberlain, replaced Imhoff. Though Buckner had no luck stopping Chamberlain, he scored 33 points himself; he experienced the high and low of a mercifully brief career on the same night.

It was tough to fault Buckner for not stopping Chamberlain. A teammate once called Wilt "the most perfect instrument God has ever made to play basketball." He was a rare combination of strength, speed, and stamina—and the Knicks saw it all. He moved his massive form around through the key seemingly uncontested, occasionally springing to cram the ball through the rim. No windmills, no Chocolate Thunder, no two-and-a-half gainers from a piked position. Just right to the hoop and "boom!" He was also sinking his favored fallaway jump shots. And he was hitting his free throws—nine for nine in the first quarter—and that was a surprise, because free throws were his badge of humanity, his Achilles' heel. He changed foul-shooting styles as often as other players changed gym socks. Against the Knicks, though, he clicked, hitting 28 of 32 free throws.

By halftime Wilt had 41 points, and at the end of the third quarter he had 69. He already held the league record with 78 points scored in a triple-overtime contest against the Lakers earlier in the season. He had also set the regulation-game mark with 73 points against the long-defunct Chicago Packers. Those were mere preludes. Chamberlain hit three baskets to start the fourth quarter and break the first record. Two points and several minutes later, the Warriors' talented playmaker, Guy Rodgers, passed to Wilt, who sank a jumper from the foul line for his seventy-ninth point. There were nearly eight minutes left.

The small crowd chanted "Give it to Wilt!" His teammates willingly obliged, passing up open shots to feed Wilt the ball. The Knicks, however, had no interest in accommodating Wilt or the fans. New York fouled Wilt's teammates before the Warriors could work the ball to the pivot. Philadelphia countered by easing up on defense to get the ball back quicker. And they aped the Knicks, fouling them to stop the clock. With 1:19 left, Chamberlain caught a pass from York Larese and dunked. He had 98 points. The Knicks, on their way to a 169–147 defeat, were in no hurry to see Chamberlain

score again and they held the ball at their end of the court. Finally Wilt grabbed a lob pass from teammate Ted Luckenbill and slammed the ball through the rim. Fans stormed the court and hugged Wilt. Eventually, the game ended, and for a night Wilt was a lovable teddy bear rather than a mean ol' grizzly.

The Dipper had sunk 36 field goals on 63 shots and hit 28 foul shots. All three numbers still stand alongside the 100 points as NBA records.

Wilt Chamberlain, playing for San Francisco against the N.Y. Knicks in a 1964 game, takes off to the hoop against Emmette Bryant (7) and Willis Reed (19). Chamberlain had a rare combination of size, speed, strength, and agility. He put these assets together to set several NBA records that still stand.

"It took a lot of effort from me," Wilt told reporters after the game. "But it was just as big an effort for the team. It wouldn't have been close to possible to do this if they didn't want it for me as much as I did."

Rodgers finished with 20 assists. Al Attles, a defensive-minded guard, shot eight for eight from the field and had 17 points. The next morning, a local newspaper account of the game began, "Wilt Chamberlain and Al Attles combined for 117 points last night as . . ."

—Bruce Anderson

GOOD TO THE LAST BOUNCE

Player-Coach Bill Russell leads the Boston Celtics from
a fourth-place finish in the regular season to their eleventh NBA championship in 13 years

Bill Russell seemed as much a part of Boston Garden as the parquet floor or the championship banners that rimmed the top of the arena. But when the floor or the banners grew old, they could be replaced. When Bill Russell grew old, he couldn't be. Born the son of a Louisiana factory worker and his wife on February 12, 1934, Russell was 35 and in his third season as the Celtics' player-coach as they chased the NBA championship. Only two other regulars in the league were as old as 35—one of them Russell's teammate Sam Jones. Their team was no longer the Boston Celtics. It was the aging Boston Celtics. Or the tired Boston Celtics. Never just the Celtics.

Russell, black, 6 feet 9 inches tall, a goatee framing an expressive mouth, was the strangest-looking leprechaun ever to invoke the magic of a shamrock. His Kelly-green band of Celts had won 10 of the last 12 NBA titles. But many Boston fans worried that the magic had evaporated. The Celtics earned the last berth in the Eastern Division playoffs with a precarious fourth-place finish. They had bounced the 76ers and the Knicks out of the playoffs, but trailed the Los Angeles Lakers two games-to-one in the finals and were about to lose another.

The Lakers, ahead 88–87, had the ball out of bounds with 15 seconds left. L.A. forward Elgin Baylor passed the ball into little Johnny Egan. Then Emmette Bryant, a player Boston guru Red Auerbach had rescued from the scrap heap of the expansion Phoenix Suns, stole the ball. Sam Jones missed a jumper but Boston controlled the rebound and called time out. Seven seconds remained.

The Celtics had lost the first two games of the series as Laker Jerry West nullified John Havlicek's 39- and 43-point efforts by scoring 53 points in the opener and 41 in the follow-up. The dynasty was on the brink of disaster. No team had ever won an NBA title after dropping the first two games of the championship series. The Celtics, after winning the third game, did not dare fall behind 3–1, not with two of the last three games scheduled for Los Angeles. With time running short on the Celtic reign, Havlicek looked at his coach—Russell—and said, "There's just enough time for it."

"It" was a last-second play Havlicek and Celtic

Larry Siegfried had learned at Ohio State and Havlicek, the Boston captain, had installed at practice during the playoffs. Russell turned to Jones and said, "O.K., Sam."

Bryant passed inbounds to Havlicek and glided toward the left side of the key, where he was flanked by teammates Bailey Howell and Don Nelson. Jones took a pass from Havlicek and button-hooked around the triple pick, rubbing off West on Howell. The sharp-shooting Jones, near the top of the key, off-balance and perched on the wrong foot, arched a shot with two seconds left. Laker center Wilt Chamberlain poised in front of the basket to collar any rebound. The shot was short; the ball hit the front of the rim, spun back, hit the hinge, bounced up and through the hoop. "It was a lucky shot," Jones said later. Like Lazarus, the Celtics were surprised to find themselves alive. Jones, who had announced that this was his last season, had resuscitated the Celtics with one shot.

It also was another game that had been won by a guard. Fans had expected the series to pivot on the matchup underneath between Russell and Chamberlain. But during most of the early games the two big men neutralized one another. Then Chamberlain, who had led the 76ers to the title two years earlier, dominated game number five in L.A., beating Russell on the boards 31–13 and outscoring the Boston coach 13–2. West scored 39 and Egan 23 as the Lakers won 117–104. With all apologies to Warren Harding, bless his soul, it was a return to normality.

Las Vegas oddsmakers had favored the Lakers 11–5 to win the series. Why the lopsided odds against the defending champs, a team which had beaten the Lakers six times before in the finals? The Celtics had gone 14–16 over the last two months of the season and, though some suspected Boston was resting for the playoffs, most fans believed the Celts were convalescing from the ravages of old age; indeed, the Celtic starting lineup averaged 31 years.

As well, the Lakers had never had the home-court advantage they enjoyed this time. And most importantly, they had never had a center like Wilt Chamberlain to play with West and Baylor. West, however, pulled his left hamstring at the end of the fifth game as Boston rolled to a 99–90 victory back at its friendly

Garden, sending the series to a seventh game in Laker owner Jack Kent Cooke's Fabulous Forum.

Cooke had 5,000 balloons filled with air and placed under the Forum ceiling; they would be released on the adoring mobs that would swarm the court when the Lakers won the final game. But the Celtics took a pin to Cooke's balloons.

Cooke's problems had started much earlier when tension grew and persisted between Chamberlain and coach Butch van Breda Kolff over how Wilt should play. The friction prevented the Lakers from developing any consistency or cohesion. The Celtics, on the other hand, had won 26 of 28 playoff series since Russell had come to Boston after leading the University of San Francisco to successive NCAA titles. In Russell's era Boston had won each of its 10 championships with ex-

Boston star Bill Russell (6) goes up for a hook against the St. Louis Hawks in the 1960 final championship game won by the Celtics.

emplary teamwork, and that now gave the Celtics an edge in the seventh game.

Boston hit eight of its first 10 shots from the field on the way to an early 24–12 advantage. But the gimpy West sparked a Laker rally, and by the end of the first quarter Los Angeles narrowed the gap to 28–25. The difference was still three at the half, Boston on top 59–56.

The Lakers, confident the old men would tire, tied the game 60–60. Then, inexplicably, a team with three of the top seven scorers the league has ever produced—Chamberlain, West, and Baylor—could not find the hoop. The Celtics held L.A. scoreless for five and one half minutes. West, who took but one shot during the drought, finally brought relief with a basket. But the Lakers trailed, 71–62.

A minute later Chamberlain picked up his fifth foul. Wilt had never fouled out of a pro game but that became immaterial now. The Celts opened a 91–76 lead by the end of the third quarter, then Jones, Russell, and Havlicek each picked up his fifth foul early in the fourth quarter. The Lakers crept back, but then Chamberlain wrenched a knee while rebounding and took himself out of the game with 5:19 left and his team behind, 103–94.

Mel Counts, a natural center who had moved to forward during the season, replaced Wilt. The hobbling West scored six points, each unanswered by the Boston offense. Now the score was 103–100 and four minutes remained. Counts sank a jumper and the Lakers prepared to pounce. On the bench, Chamberlain told van Breda Kolff he wanted back in. The coach ignored Wilt.

The Celtics had scored only three points in nearly eight minutes, and they seemed to be in trouble again when Laker Keith Erickson batted the ball away from Havlicek. But Nelson grabbed the loose ball and shot. The ball bounced two or three feet off the back of the rim, then plummeted through the net. A true Celtic bounce.

Los Angeles's shooters suddenly went cold, while the man who still holds nearly every NBA scoring record brooded on the bench. Siegfried and Havlicek then sank three foul shots that sealed the outcome. The Celtics won 108–106, despite an incredible performance by the injured West, who scored 42 points, had 13 rebounds and 12 assists, and was named MVP. All for naught. "It's as if we aren't supposed to win," West said.

For the Celts, however, the ending was all too appropriate: Chamberlain stewing as Russell, that old leprechaun, added a new banner to the Garden ceiling.

—B.A.

CHAMPIONS AT LAST

A hobbled Willis Reed dramatically strides onto the floor and leads the New York Knicks to their first NBA championship

In the fall of 1969, New York City threw a coming-out party for the Mets and Knicks, twin sisters of ineptitude for so long. Those lucky enough to attend discovered that the two were no longer the unsightly, awkward youngsters who had once embarrassed the city. No, the Mets were Amazin' and the Knicks were the toughest ticket in town.

On October 16 the Mets ended their extended run as the clown princes of baseball by beating the Baltimore Orioles four games to one to win the World Series. Two days before the Series finale the Knicks began a season in which they laid claim to the supremacy of the NBA.

In the seven previous years, the Mets had finished tenth and last five times—and ninth twice. They lost badly, but fans still flocked to Shea Stadium because the Mets lost in ways never dreamed possible before—and not duplicated since. But the Mets were greenhorns, Johnny-come-latelies, at losing when viewed alongside the Knickerbockers. In 10 of the 11 seasons from 1955–56 to 1965–66, the Knicks dwelt in the basement of the NBA's Eastern Division. Boy, were they bad. Then, in 1964 the Knicks chose Grambling center Willis Reed in the second round of the draft—and took the first step up the cellar stairs.

A lot of steps were needed, but the Knicks built and climbed. Their terrible records gave them an opportunity to draft Princeton Rhodes scholar Bill Bradley and Michigan's Cazzie Russell, the college players of the year in 1965 and 1966, respectively. They traded for former Chicago White Sox pitcher Dave DeBusschere (who was also basketball's hustling answer to Pete Rose) and veteran guard Dick Barnett. They drafted Dave Stallworth and the stylish Walt Frazier, and signed Mike Riordan out of the bush leagues.

The Knicks were a special blend of scrupulous defense, passing offense, and continuous teamwork. And for the city of New York, the blend started an intense love affair. As the World Series ended, the Knicks opened the season by winning five games, losing one, then winning 18 straight, a league record at the time. As 1969 ended and the new decade beckoned, the Knicks were 33–7 and New York fans became convinced that theirs was the team of the 1970s.

New York finished the season 60–22, and Reed, the Knick captain, received the MVP award. He led the Knicks with 21.7 points and 13.9 rebounds a game despite painful knees that kept him hobbling throughout the season. DeBusschere and Bradley joined Reed in the starting front court and Frazier and Barnett ran the back court. The Minutemen—Russell, Stallworth, and

Willis Reed (19) shoots against the L.A. Lakers' Hairston as Jerry West (44) looks on in a 1970 playoff game.

183

Riordan—provided the Knicks with a strong bench, ready to spark the team—and the fans—at a moment's notice. But the Knicks were vulnerable in one area: they had no competent back-up for Willis Reed at center.

The Knicks began the playoffs by beating Baltimore in the seventh game after nearly blowing a 3-1 advantage. They then met the Milwaukee Bucks, led by rookie center Lew Alcindor (later Kareem Abdul-Jabbar), for the Eastern Division title and a berth in the finals. Alundon needed another year of seasoning—and the addition of Oscar Robertson—before he would win a championship; the Knicks downed the Bucks four games to one and moved into the finals for the first time in 17 years.

The Los Angeles Lakers were waiting for them. After a year spent brooding over their loss to the Celtics in the 1969 finals, the Lakers were eager to play. Los Angeles had earned a playoff berth despite the knee surgery that waylaid Wilt Chamberlain early in the year. But Wilt was back and the center of attention. After the Lakers fell behind Phoenix 3-1 in the first round of the playoffs, they roared into the finals with seven straight wins—an NBA record—over the Suns and the Atlanta Hawks. After wrestling with Alundon and 1969 MVP Wes Unseld, Reed would now have to grapple with Chamberlain, a man with more records than Elvis and purportedly the strongest man ever to play in the NBA.

The rest of the league-leading New York defense would have to stop Elgin Baylor and Jerry West, Mr. Clutch, who had nearly beaten the Celtics on his own the year before.

The Knicks won the opener 124-112 as Reed outscored Wilt 37-17. But West scored 34 points in the second game as the Lakers won 105-103. The series moved to Los Angeles for game number three. The Knicks overcame a 14-point halftime deficit to take the lead 98-97 on a Reed free throw with 50 seconds left. West then hit a jumper but Barnett answered with a basket. Barnett fouled Wilt, who made his second foul shot to tie the game at 100-100. Then DeBusschere apparently iced the win for the Knicks with a basket that fell with three seconds left. But Wilt passed inbounds to West, who took three dribbles and launched a desperation 63-foot shot that slid through the hoop just short of the back of the rim.

Mr. Clutch hit the brake in the overtime, however, missing all five of his shots as the Knicks won 111-108. Reed collected 17 rebounds and 38 points, the last one breaking a 108-108 deadlock. The fourth game was also an overtime affair, but this time, sparked by reserve forward John Tresvant, the Lakers won 121-115. The battle returned to Manhattan.

The Lakers erupted to a 25-15 lead in game five and then the Knicks watched Reed—and their title hopes—crash to the floor with two severely strained muscles in his right thigh.

With Reed out, the Knicks fell behind 53-40 by intermission. In the second half Knick coach Red Holzman chose to use three of his four forwards—Bradley, DeBusschere, Stallworth, and Russell—and no center. New York attacked the Lakers with a pressing, swarming defense that shut off the Lakers, who saw their 13-point lead transformed into a 107-100 defeat. The ill-fated Lakers, losers in seven of the previous 11 finals, had not been able to capitalize on Reed's absence and that failure haunted them. It was a Promethean torture, this repeated building and dashing of title hopes.

Still smarting from the fifth-game loss, the Lakers destroyed the Knicks 135-113, in game number six as Chamberlain—with Reed on the sidelines—scored 45 points and grabbed 27 rebounds. Reed flew back to New York determined to have his leg ready for the seventh game. On May 8, an hour and a half before game time, Reed warmed up on the Garden floor. He returned to the locker room and said he would play. A teammate said it was like having an "arm sewed back on." The Knicks took the floor but Reed stayed behind and received two pain-killing injections. With seven and a half minutes left before tipoff Reed walked down the runway, onto the floor and into the din of nearly 20,000 fans, each one near delirium at the sight of the captain.

The Lakers controlled the opening tip. They missed a shot, New York rebounded, and the action shifted ends. Reed took a pass at the top of the key; Wilt blocked the middle of the key, so Reed shot the open jumper and scored. Reed also sank his next shot. And, though he went scoreless after the second basket, Reed stayed in the game and kept Chamberlain away from the basket. In the first half, he played all but three minutes and held Chamberlain to two field goals.

More than his two baskets and more than his defense, Reed's courageous presence ignited the Knicks. New York built its lead to 61-37 when Reed sat down for some rest. The Knicks finished with a 113-99 victory and their first NBA crown. Frazier scored 36 points, dished out 19 assists, and hauled in seven rebounds. The tenacious DeBusschere had 17 rebounds.

Willis Reed won the game.

—B.A.

Wilt Chamberlain (13), center for the L.A. Lakers, vs. Willis Reed, center for the N.Y. Knicks, in the 1970 Championship Series. Reed, hobbled by a painful knee injury, played in the final game and "The Captain" led the Knicks to the Championship.

College
Basketball

ALL GOOD THINGS MUST COME TO AN END

*U.C.L.A.'s basketball machine takes an 88-game
winning streak to Notre Dame but walks off with a 1-game losing streak*

The streak. It just seemed to roll on and on, effortlessly. "UCLA 118, Stanford 79." "Bruins Do It Again," read the headlines. "UCLA Number 1—What Else Is New?" And so it went, with victory upon victory piling up, from January 1971 through the middle of the 1973–74 season. UCLA wins another—and another. The streak stood at 35, at 47, at 59, at 75. UCLA, the dynasty. UCLA, coached by that professorial basketball genius John Wooden. The Walton Gang, headed by the big redhead himself, Bill. The Team that Couldn't Lose Straight. And the poor opponents. What about the likes of Maryland, Southern Cal, Washington? What choice did they have except to dread the date on their schedule, show up, and try to beat a legend? It was like trying to slay an invisible dragon. The last team to beat the Bruins before the streak began was Notre Dame, a team that was victimized three times during the streak. And on January 19, 1974, a drizzly Saturday in South Bend, it was Notre Dame that stood up to the dragon and knocked it cold.

All the while UCLA had been—ho hum—going undefeated in the fourth season of its streak into history, the Irish had been quietly rolling up an unbeaten season of their own. Always number two in the polls, just an eyelash behind the Bruins, the Irish were coached by the youthful Digger Phelps, in his third season as head coach at just 32. He had come to South Bend after just one season as a head coach at Fordham, and had gradually pumped some vitality back into Irish basketball with his precisely diagrammed system. If John Wooden's preshowdown attitude was one of casual calm, Phelps was deliberate in his attention to detail. He even read a biography of Wooden, hoping to catch some clue, some tiny hint on how to bring the Bruins to their knees.

The Bruins had no such qualms about facing the Irish. To them, it was just one more game en route to their tenth straight NCAA championship. No significance was attached to the fact that it was Notre Dame which had beaten them last, back in the dim memory of 1971. None of the players talked about the streak. "Sure we want to win," Bruin Keith Wilkes said on the day before the game. "But this is like a business. A game just like any other game. We don't sit around talking about

the streak." Nor did the Irish. Keyed up as they were for what would be an historic confrontation in South Bend, Phelps's charges had to dispose of Georgetown first, before heading into the big one on Saturday afternoon. But they were ready for UCLA; Phelps even asked them to practice cutting down the nets, just to be sure there'd be no goof-ups. Phelps himself scouted the Bruins earlier in the week when they played Iowa at Chicago, and returned with elaborate reports and diagrams of UCLA game strategies. The placid Wooden, meanwhile, claimed he hadn't even seen Notre Dame play, and he seemed untroubled by it.

On game day, Notre Dame's athletic center was jammed to the beams with 11,343 spectators who'd been lucky enough to get tickets to this battle of the boards. Just three weeks before, the Irish football team had given credence to the "We're number one!" chant by defeating Alabama in the Sugar Bowl. And anyone who believed in happy endings, Hollywood, and the Gipper, dared to dream, even hope, that the Irish five could duplicate that feat. "We're number one—twice!" And don't think Phelps wasn't recalling that 58-point loss to the Bruins his first year at South Bend, and how nice it would be to avenge that result. The pregame atmosphere of hysteria seen at most big collegiate games was heightened to the point of pure frenzy by the tantalizing possibility of a green-and-gold David—in the form of Gary Brokaw and John Shumate—belting Goliath back onto his own sword.

If the game had been played in Hollywood instead of South Bend, the Irish would have stampeded all over the visitors from the first dribble. Last time Notre Dame beat UCLA, Austin Carr had poured in 46 points. This time there was no Austin Carr. There wasn't even an Austin Carr–like effort. Hollywood would have cringed; the Bruins got on top and, except for four very early, short-lived ties, stayed there. Notre Dame was not playing superior basketball, was not shaking down any thunder on the red head of Bill Walton, playing his first game since suffering a back injury a week earlier.

But wait, Hollywood. Sooner or later, UCLA has to run out of superb passing and minor miracles. With just 3:32 remaining, however, and the Irish on the down side of an 11-point deficit, another UCLA win seemed inevi-

PRECEDING PAGES: *Notre Dame vs. UCLA at South Bend, Indiana, January 19, 1974. Notre Dame's Dwight Clay (15) with the ball on his way to score the final basket that gave Notre Dame the win, 71–70. The UCLA Bruins under coach John Wooden had piled up an 88-game win streak, but the Fighting Irish ended it.*

table. When did these two teams meet again? A week later? Well, maybe Digger's boys would be ready then. But the Irish dug in and hung on, chipping away at the Bruins' lead with calm desperation. And for the first time, the Walton Gang began thrashing about like a panic-stricken swimmer afraid of drowning. UCLA was outscored 12–0 in the last three minutes, fumbling the ball away and missing six consecutive sure-thing shots.

Clearly, the Bruins were grasping for the fraying end of their rope. "Maybe the crowd finally got to them," suggested Notre Dame star Adrian Dantley. "They kept throwing the ball away." Indeed, UCLA tossed the ball too many times to empty space or enemy arms. And with a scant 29 seconds remaining, Notre Dame grabbed the dragon by the tail. The Irish plan to get the ball from Gary Brokaw to sharpshooting center Shumate misfired. Shumate was surrounded by blue-and-gold-clad bodies. Brokaw spun around wildly, saw guard Dwight Clay in a corner, open and waiting. Clay was definitely a clutch man. A year ago he had flicked in a shot that ended Marquette's string of 81 at-home wins. For his cool under just such fire, teammates called him "Iceman." So when Brokaw spied the Iceman, his natural move was to get the ball to Clay. And Clay responded, with a high, clean jump shot that put away UCLA for keeps, reducing the streak to a nice memory. Notre Dame 71, UCLA 70. The roaring disbelief and joy of the partisan crowd masked the sound of UCLA falling from its lofty perch in the weekly polls, a spot it had owned, uncontested, since the end of the 1968 season.

Dantley, Brokaw, Shumate, Clay—all were smothered in hysteria, and Phelps had a chance to see if the Irish had learned anything in practicing the cutting down of nets from rims. Emotion, obviously, had been the key to the abrupt turnabout, but whatever the cause, echoes were indeed waking on the Notre Dame campus in the wake of Clay's last-ditch effort.

Wooden, his responses just that, had no excuses for the outcome. He said the end of the streak meant little, and he reminded anyone who would listen that these two teams would meet again just a week later, and *that* would be a real test.

Notre Dame wasn't looking beyond the confines of its own world at the moment. There was wild celebration in the Irish locker room, alumni toasts in every bar from South Bend to South Carolina, and everywhere, the heady thrill of applying a three-minute arm-twist to a dynasty—and seeing it crumple at last.

—Kathy Blumenstock

TOP: *Adrian Dantley takes down the net as a trophy after the Irish win. ABOVE: Gary Novak of Notre Dame goes up for a jump shot against Keith Wilkes, (52) and Dave Meyers (34) of UCLA in the 1974 game that ended the Bruins' streak at 88 consecutive wins.*

189

CINCINNATI OWNED OHIO AND THE NATION

Underdog Cincinnati upsets mighty Ohio State to win the 1961 NCAA basketball championship

For Cincinnati, the also-ran role was becoming rather tiresome. Both in 1959 and again in 1960 the Bearcats put together strong regular seasons and fully anticipated winning all the marbles for the NCAA title. Both years, the Bearcats' splendid shooting machine Oscar Robertson led the nation in scoring; in 1960 he averaged 33.7 points per game, scoring a total of 1,011, an unheard of number for any collegian. But each time the Bearcats clawed their way up to the semifinals, they met the identical fate: California.

California's disciplined defense threw a net over Cincinnati's more traditional run-and-gun tactics. The Bearcats revolved around just one player, namely the Big O, and when Cal neatly shut down his game, Cincinnati panicked into ball-handling errors. Without Robertson at the usual peak of his precision, the Bearcats were unable to push back the walls of California that effectively blocked them from *their* title.

Robertson graduated in 1960, and Bearcat onlookers wondered what, if anything, Cincinnati had left. As it turned out, the answer was "plenty." After putting in seven seasons as Cincinnati's assistant coach, Ed Jucker took over the top job and immediately rebuilt the Bearcats' brand of basketball. Defense had been the chief ingredient of their downfall in the playoffs, so Jucker junked the up-and-down, shoot-and-score tactics and installed a more complete battle plan. The Bearcats' offense would be a more controlled one, and defensively, they would be tighter and tougher. With no Robertson to serve as centerpiece of team structure, Cincinnati began to work the floor with five men instead of just one main guy. But the sudden switch in styles left the Bearcats shaky in the early part of that season. They went out and lost three of their first eight games, the most notable loss coming at St. Louis as Cincinnati was outdistanced by a whopping 17 points. Jucker's charges adjusted, however, and later reeled off 20 consecutive wins via their new defensive game. It would pay handsomely in their NCAA championship-game showdown against Ohio State.

The Buckeyes, defending NCAA champions, had collected 31 straight wins over two years. They were cool, unlikely to rattle under even the most intense pressure. And they had two of that era's top athletes in Jerry Lucas and John Havlicek. Lucas, a 6 foot 8 inch, 230-pound center, attended OSU on an academic scholarship. He managed to maintain an almost straight-A average, while playing some of the finest all-around basketball in the nation. His thorough knowledge of the game's details helped to lead the Buckeyes to a pair of Big Ten titles and the NCAA crown. Lucas was a rebounder, a scorer in his own right, and a free-throw man.

The 6 foot 5 inch Havlicek served as the reverse side of the coin, playing the kind of defense that frequently halted the opposition cold. Havlicek didn't receive the press recognition that Lucas did, but OSU coach Fred Taylor counted on him as the most dependable of players, one who could and would go out and give a workmanlike performance again and again. The hard-driving Havlicek saw OSU pile up 78 wins against only 6 losses during his career.

En route to meeting Cincinnati, the Buckeyes scrambled past a hungry Louisville team, 56–55 in the first regional tournament, then bounced Kentucky 87–74. The Louisville game threw a scare into Taylor's team, and his drills became longer and more exhausting; the Buckeyes *owned* this title, and weren't about to surrender it on a fluke somewhere along the line.

Cincinnati, meanwhile, rolled easily over Texas Tech in its early-round game, putting together the kind of defensive ballgame that was becoming a trademark.

No one asked, "Where's the Big O?" anymore. Filling his spot this year was a quick sharpshooter named Tom Thacker who fit in anywhere on the floor. And rebounding past every opponent that season were the fast hands of Bob Wiesenhahn and Paul Hogue. Cincinnati had again pointed toward the finals, but the 1961 team was more poised and better balanced. This time, the Bearcats would not be stymied by anybody's defensive strategy; *their* defense was superb, as seen in their semifinal meeting with Utah.

The Utes possessed a fast break that left its opposition breathless, and that's the way they won all year: wear out the enemy, then close in for the easy points while the other side is gasping for air. The Utes' shooting percentage was .494, and their offense was number three nationally. But that was before they faced off against Cincinnati. The Bearcats were familiar with that hard-running style—hadn't they played that game just a year ago?—and were quick to decelerate the Utes' pace, forcing them into costly mistakes and, ultimately, an 82–67 Bearcat victory.

For Cincinnati, this was a step further than they'd ever gotten before, and Jucker's team was flying high. All Cincinnati had to do now was stop Ohio State, and it would have the glorious title that had been snatched away twice before. *All the Bearcats had to do was stop Ohio State,* a team often referred to as "unbeatable," a team that acted as if it did not know the meaning of the word "lose." The Buckeyes never even acknowledged the fact that sometimes they trailed in a game, sometimes at a crucial moment. They just went on and won it anyway. And all Cincinnati had to do was beat them.

OSU's semifinal game wasn't even a test for Lucas and Co. There they were, those big, bad Buckeyes, ready to simply walk in, play some hoops, and walk out with yet another title. If a Louisville-caliber team had

Cincinnati's Tom Thacker (25) grabs a rebound in the NCAA Championship game with Ohio State held in Kansas City, March 25, 1961. Oscar Robinson had graduated from Cincinnati the year before so coach Ed Jucker designed the 1961 team around tough defense and more disciplined offensive patterns.

been their opponent in that semifinal, perhaps the Buckeyes could have at least enjoyed a hard workout. But they drew St. Joseph's, a team with a slow, deliberate offense, and players too short to shut down the towering OSU front and back court. St. Joseph's was the dark horse, the underdog; America loves the underdog, in politics or basketball. But St. Joseph's, though scrappy, didn't perform as well as coach Jack Ramsay had hoped, and OSU won easily, 95–69.

So the stage was set at Kansas City's Municipal Auditorium for the unbeatable Ohio State to slug it out with Cincinnati, a team that had twice tried and failed to get beyond the semifinals. What kind of strategic dynamite could the Bearcats unload on the Buckeyes?

The Bearcat dynamite was simply more of the same poison they'd been dishing out all season: bottle up the opposition and turn it into a defensive battle, a pitcher's duel, as it were. Lucas positioned himself some 15 to 20 feet away from the basket, unable to get much closer. Cincinnati was controlling this one, taking only the most deliberate of shots and making them pay. OSU was clearly frustrated; at the half OSU led only 39–38. For every move OSU made, Cincinnati had a countermove. It was check and checkmate throughout the entire game.

Although Cincinnati had come into the game as the underdog, the matchup proved that the Bearcats were as solid as the heavily favored Buckeyes, and far from outclassed by the unbeatables. The Bearcats held their ground in the second half, blocking and stopping OSU at every turn.

Cincinnati's tough point guard, Carl Bouldin, gave the Bearcats a six point lead mid-way through the period, before OSU took over to lead by five. So closely matched were the two clubs that they were deadlocked 61–61 at the buzzer that ended regulation time. Cincinnati would have to wait till overtime to find out if it could really beat the unbeatable.

And the Bearcats did, coming on with an aggressive, let's-see-who's-best display of defensive tricks. The Buckeyes managed only 4 points in the extra period, and when they woke up, it was over, Cincinnati 70, Ohio State 65. And the NCAA had a new champion.

It was the upset of the year.

—K.B.

LEFT: *Ohio State's Jerry Lucas (11) blocks a shot by Paul Hogue of Cincinnati in the NCAA 1961 Championship game. Ohio State, led by Lucas and Havlicek, was defending NCAA champion, but Cincinnati triumphed 70–65.* RIGHT: *Cincinnati coach Ed Jucker (center) and his staff celebrate the Cincinnati win.*